Critical Thinking for Helping Professionals

Critical Thinking for Helping Professionals

A Skills-Based Workbook
Third edition

EILEEN GAMBRILL
LEONARD GIBBS

OXFORD
UNIVERSITY PRESS
2009

OXFORD
UNIVERSITY PRESS

Oxford University Press, Inc., publishes works that further
Oxford University's objective of excellence
in research, scholarship, and education.

Oxford New York
Auckland Cape Town Dar es Salaam Hong Kong Karachi
Kuala Lumpur Madrid Melbourne Mexico City Nairobi
New Delhi Shanghai Taipei Toronto

With offices in
Argentina Austria Brazil Chile Czech Republic France Greece
Guatemala Hungary Italy Japan Poland Portugal Singapore
South Korea Switzerland Thailand Turkey Ukraine Vietnam

Published by Oxford University Press, Inc.
198 Madison Avenue, New York, New York 10016
www.oup.com

Oxford is a registered trademark of Oxford University Press

ISBN: 978-0-19-533095-3

9 8 7 6 5 4 3 2 1
Printed in the United States of America
on acid-free paper

Preface

This workbook has a single purpose: those who do its exercises will reason more effectively about life-affecting practice and policy decisions. Critical thinking involves the critical appraisal of beliefs, arguments, and claims to arrive at well-reasoned judgments. Critical thinking is essential to helping people because it encourages practitioners to evaluate the soundness of beliefs, arguments, and claims. What helpers believe influences what they do. Thus, it is important to examine beliefs in relation to their accuracy. Will sending a youthful offender to boot camp be more effective in decreasing future offenses than placing him on probation? Will a prescribed drug forestall the progression of confusion among Alzheimer's patients in a nursing home? Will children with learning disorders learn better if mainstreamed into regular classrooms? Professionals make many such judgments and decisions daily. Deciding which actions will help clients is an inescapable part of being a professional. Thinking critically about claims, beliefs, and arguments can help professionals arrive at beliefs and actions that are well reasoned.

Thinking critically is important in all areas of the helping professions, including practice, research, social policy, and administration. Critical thinking skills will help you spot policies and procedures that benefit agencies but not their clients and those that maintain discriminatory patterns of service. These skills and related values and attitudes, such as being open minded and flexible as well as self-critical, will encourage recognition of and respect for cultural differences.

This workbook is designed to learn by doing. It has been revised to make it more interdisciplinary and to include exercises concerning problem-based learning and evidence-based practice. A workbook requires action as well as thinking. It involves readers actively in exercises related to making decisions at the individual, family, group, community, and societal levels and allows for immediate feedback about decisions made. Think as much as you like, you cannot assess the effects of your thinking until you act. For instance, did your thinking result in decisions that benefit clients? Not only may a workbook foster better learning, it makes learning enjoyable. You are more likely to continue learning tasks that are fun. Toward this aim, we have tried to create exercises that are enjoyable as well as instructive. Some of the exercises involve cooperative learning. Here, you will be involved with your peers and/or colleagues in learning adventures designed to hone your critical-thinking skills. The exercises included are designed to be useful in all helping professions curricula. Some have been pretested, others are new. Each exercise includes the following sections: Purpose, Background, Instructions, and Follow-up Question(s).

The workbook exercises illustrate that the knowledge and skills involved in research and practice overlap. Practitioner failure to draw on practice and policy-related research is a problem in all professions. Indeed, this troubling gap was a key reason for the invention of the process of evidence-based practice described in Part 4. Too often, professionals do not take advantage of research in making decisions that affect their clients. Because of this, clients may receive ineffective or harmful "help" (Silverman, 1993). One reason for this lack of integration lies in the structure of some professional education programs. Research courses are typically taught separately from practice and policy courses, encouraging the false impression that research and practice are quite different enterprises. This arrangement hinders understanding of the shared values, attitudes, content knowledge, and performance skills of research, practice, and policy. For example critical discussion, whether with yourself or others, is integral to all. Research and practice are complementary, not competing areas.

Part 1, Critical Thinking, defines critical thinking, discusses why it especially matters in the helping professions, and describes related values, attitudes, knowledge, and performance skills. This part also contains two exercises. The first provides an opportunity to review the criteria you use to make decisions. In Exercise 2, you assess your beliefs about knowledge (what it is and how to get it).

The two exercises in Part 2, Recognizing Propaganda in Human Services Advertising, demonstrate the importance of questioning claims about what helps clients. Presentations of a human-services advertisement and a treatment-program promotion, portray vivid emotional appeals to convince viewers that a method works.

The seven exercises in Part 3, Fallacies and Pitfalls in Professional Decision Making, are designed to help you to identify and remedy common fallacies and pitfalls in reasoning about practice. They rely on vignettes that illustrate situations that arise in everyday practice.

Exercise 5 contains twenty-five vignettes that can be used to assess practice reasoning. The Reasoning-in-Practice Games (Exercises 6–8) involve working with other students to identify practice fallacies. In the Fallacies Film Festival (Exercise 9), students work together to prepare a skit to demonstrate a fallacy. Exercise 10 provides an opportunity to spot fallacies in professional contexts (including your classroom) and Exercise 11 describes group think ploys and provides an opportunity to learn how to spot and avoid them.

Part 4, Evidence-Informed Decision Making, contains seven exercises designed to help you to acquire knowledge and skills in the process of evidence-informed practice including working in teams. Exercise 12, Applying The Steps of EBP, guides you in this process. Exercises 13 and 14, Working in Interdisciplinary Evidence-Based Teams, offer opportunities to apply the steps in a team. Exercise 15, Preparing Critically Appraised Topics (CATs), guides you in applying the process of EBP to specific questions and preparing user-friendly summaries of what you found. Exercise 16 describes how you can involve clients as informed participants. Exercise 17 offers tips and practice opportunities for raising "hard questions" that must be asked if our decisions are informed by the evidentiary status of services. Exercise 18 offers an opportunity to review gaps between an agency's services and what research suggests is most effective.

Part 5, Critically Appraising Different Kinds of Research Reports and Measures, contains seven exercises. Exercise 19 provides guidelines for reviewing the quality of effectiveness studies and describes how to determine a numerical index that quantifies the magnitude of a treatment's effect. Exercise 20 offers guidelines for reviewing the quality of research reviews. Exercise 21, Critically Appraising Self-Report Measures, describes concerns regarding reliability and validity and offers a practice opportunity to appraise a measure. Exercise 22 provides guidelines for estimating risk and making predictions and accurately communicating risk to clients. Exercise 23 provides guidelines for reviewing diagnostic measures. Exercise 24 provides an opportunity to review the clarity of a popular classification model. Lastly, Exercise 25 suggests important concerns regarding research exploring causation.

Part 6, Reviewing Decisions, contains seven exercises applying critical thinking skills to key components of the helping process. Exercise 26 engages students in reviewing the quality of intervention plans used in a case example. Exercise 27 provides an opportunity to think critically about practice-related ethical issues. Exercise 28 provides guidelines for reviewing the quality of arguments. Exercise 29 presents a case example of how practice reasoning can go wrong and some of the reasons why. Exercise 30 applies critical thinking skills to case records and Exercise 31 offers an opportunity to critically appraise service agreements. Exercise 32, Claim Buster involves you in detecting and evaluating claims that may affect clients' lives.

Part 7, Improving Educational and Practice Environments, includes five exercises. Exercise 33 provides a checklist for reviewing the extent to which an educational or work environment demonstrates a culture of thoughtfulness. Exercise 34 includes a rating form for evaluating how much instructors encourage critical thinking in their classrooms. Exercise 35 describes how to set up a journal club and Exercises 36 and 37 offer guidelines for life-long learning.

If working through the exercises contained in the workbook results in better services for clients, all our efforts, both yours and ours, will be worthwhile. We welcome your feedback about each exercise. In the spirit of critical thinking, we welcome negative as well as positive comments, especially those that offer concrete suggestions for improving exercises. We hope that you enjoy and learn from participating in the exercises in this book.

With adoption of this book, instructors will have access to a website including an Instructor's Manual and accompanying audio-visual material. The Instructor's Manual contains descriptions of each exercise in the Workbook including a brief overview, purpose or learning objectives of the exercise, materials and time required, suggestions for using the exercise, and possible answers to Follow-up Questions.

Eileen Gambrill
Leonard Gibbs

Acknowledgments

We owe a great deal to kindred spirits both past and present who cared enough to raise concerns regarding the quality of practice and policy decisions and who have worked to create tools and processes to help practitioners and clients evaluate the quality of decision from both an ethical and evidentiary perspective. All value (or did value) critical evaluation of claims of effectiveness in order to protect clients from ineffective or harmful services. We thank Kathy Finder, Nancy Erickson, Kathryn Colbert (computer consultants), Monica Bares (typing and editorial help), Aaron Harder (video editing), Cyndee Kaiser (cartoons), Connie Kees (videotaping), Donald Naftulin (Dr. Fox lecture), Michael Hakeem (suggestions for some of the counterarguments in Exercise 2), Jim Ziegert, Mary Ann King (vignette for Reasoning-in-Practice Game C), Carol Williams, Brenda Peterson DeSousa, Lisa Roepke, Lisa Furst, Amy Simpson, Jennifer Neyes, Melissa Brown, Jennifer Mortt, Marcia Cigler, Beth Rusch, Carol Weis, Vicki Millard, Kristen Jensen, Mindy Olson, Laurie Buckler, Michelle LeCloux, Jennifer Owen, Tiffany Winrich, Pam McKee, Kelly Meyer, Reggie Bicha, Tara Lehman, Julie Garvey, Richard Lockwood, Kate Kremer, Cory Heckel, Mike Werner, Jill Eslinger (Fallacies Film Festival vignettes), Margie Anderson (permission to use Rogers Hospital material), Macmillan Publishers (permission to use the Professional Thinking Form and Quality of Study Rating Form), Grafton Hull (content areas in suggested uses for our exercises in Five Social Work Curriculum Areas, Exhibit P.I), and Patricia Carey and Cheri Audrain for examples from nursing and medicine, respectively.

Eileen Gambrill extends a special note of thanks to the Hutto-Patterson Chair funders, to the computerized databases provided by the University of California at Berkeley and to Sharon Ikami for her patience, good will, and word processing skills.

Leonard Gibbs acknowledges the influence of a great teacher, Professor Emeritus Michael Hakeem of the University of Wisconsin at Madison, and the encouragement and financial support of the University of Wisconsin at Eau Claire Foundation and the College of Professional Studies, whose support contributed to this work. We both thank Maura Roessner, Senior

Editor, Social Work, Oxford University Press, for her consistent support and good ideas.

Note from Eileen Gambrill

My dear friend and co-author, Emeritus Professor Lenonard Gibbs, died June 13, 2008, following a valliant battle with metatastic prostrate cancer. Epitomizing the essence of critical thinking and evidence-informed decision-making, he took his fight with cancer as an opportunity to help others to make informed decisions by establishing a website, Evidence-based Practice as if Your Life Depended on it (with his wife Betsy McDougall Gibbs). He is deeply missed.

Contents

PART 7   IMPROVING EDUCATIONAL AND PRACTICE ENVIRONMENTS

Detailed Contents

PART 3   FALLACIES AND PITFALLS IN PROFESSIONAL DECISION MAKING: WHAT THEY ARE AND HOW TO AVOID THEM

PART 4   EVIDENCE-INFORMED DECISION MAKING

PART 5   CRITICALLY APPRAISING DIFFERENT KINDS OF RESEARCH

PART 6   REVIEWING DECISIONS

PART 7   IMPROVING EDUCATIONAL AND PRACTICE ENVIRONMENTS

Critical Thinking for Helping Professionals

PART 1

Introduction: The Role of Critical Thinking in the Helping Professions and Its Relationship to Evidence-Informed Practice

Consider the following scenarios. A professor tells you: "some people who have a problem with alcohol can learn to be controlled drinkers; abstinence is not required for all people." Will you believe her simply because she says so? If not, what information will you seek and why? How will you evaluate data that you collect?

Your supervisor says "Refer the client to the Altona Family Service Agency. They know how to help these clients." Would you take her advice? What questions will help you decide?

A case record you are reading states, "Mrs. Lynch abuses her child because she is schizophrenic. She has been diagnosed schizophrenic by two psychiatrists. Thus, there is little that can be done to improve her parenting skills." What questions will you ask? Why?

An advertisement for a residential treatment center for youth claims, "We've been serving youth for over fifty years with success." Does this convince you? If not, what kind of evidence would you seek and why?

You read an article stating that "grassroots community organization will not be effective in alienated neighborhoods." What questions would you raise?

Finally, a social worker tells you that because Mrs. Smith recalls having been abused as a child, insight therapy will be most effective in helping her to overcome her depression and anger. Here too, what questions would you ask?

If you thought carefully about these statements, you engaged in critical thinking. Critical thinking involves the careful examination and evaluation of beliefs and actions. It requires paying attention to the process of reasoning, not just the product.

Paul (1993) lists purpose first as one of nine components of critical thinking (see Box 1.1). (See also Paul & Elder, 2004.) If our purpose is to help clients, then we must carefully consider our beliefs and actions. Critical thinking involves the use of standards such as clarity, accuracy, relevance, and completeness. It requires evaluating evidence, considering alternative views, and being genuinely fair-minded in accurately presenting opposing views. Critical thinkers make a genuine effort to critique fairly all views, preferred and unpreferred using identical rigorous criteria. They value accuracy over "winning" or social approval. Questions that arise when you think critically include the following:

1. What does it mean?
2. Is it true? How good is the evidence?
3. Who said the claim was accurate? What could their motives be? How reliable are these sources? Do they have vested interests in one point of view?
4. Are the facts presented correct?
5. Have any facts been omitted?
6. Have critical tests of this claim been carried out? Were these studies relatively free of bias? What samples were used? How representative were they? What were the results? Have the results been replicated?
7. Are there alternative well-argued views?
8. If correlations are presented, how strong are they?
9. Are weak appeals used, for example, to emotion or special interests?

Specialized knowledge is often required to think effectively in a domain (e.g., see Klein, 1998). Creativity plays a role in critical thinking. For instance, it may be required to discover assumptions, alternative explanations, and biases. Thus, critical thinking is much more than reasoned appraisal of claims and related arguments. Well-reasoned thinking

Box 1.1 Characteristics of Critical Thinking

1. It is purposeful.
2. It is responsive to and guided by intellectual standards (relevance, accuracy, precision, clarity, depth, and breadth).
3. It supports the development of intellectual traits in the thinker of humility, integrity, perseverance, empathy, and self-discipline.
4. The thinker can identify the elements of thought present in thinking about any problem, such that the thinker makes the logical connection between the elements and the problem at hand. The critical thinker will routinely ask the following questions:

   - What is the purpose of my thinking (goal/objective)?
   - What precise question (problem) am I trying to answer?
   - Within what point of view (perspective) am I thinking?
   - What concepts or ideas are central to my thinking?
   - What am I taking for granted, what assumptions am I making?
   - What information am I using (data, facts, observation)?
   - How am I interpreting that information?
   - What conclusions am I coming to?
   - If I accept the conclusions, what are the implications? What would the consequence be if I put my thoughts into action?

   For each element, the thinker must consider standards that shed light on the effectiveness of her thinking.

5. Is it self-assessing and self-improving. The thinker takes steps to assess her thinking, using appropriate intellectual standards. If you are not assessing your thinking, you are not thinking critically.
6. There is an integrity to the whole system. The thinker is able to critically examine her thought as a whole and to take it apart (consider its parts as well). The thinker is committed to be intellectually humble, persevering, courageous, fair, and just. The critical thinker is aware of the variety of ways in which thinking can become distorted, misleading, prejudiced, superficial, unfair, or otherwise defective.
7. It yields a well-reasoned answer. If we know how to check our thinking and are committed to doing so, and we get extensive practice, then we can depend on the results of our thinking being productive.
8. It is responsive to the social and moral imperative to enthusiastically argue from opposing points of view and to seek and identify weakness and limitations in one's own position. Critical thinkers are aware that there are many legitimate points of view, each of which (when deeply thought through), may yield some level of insight.

Source: Paul, R. (1993). *Critical thinking: What Every Person Needs to Survive in a Rapidly Changing World (Revised 3rd. Ed)* (pp. 20–23). Santa Rosa, CA: Foundation for Critical Thinking. www.criticalthinking.org. Reprinted with permission.

is a form of creation and construction. Thinking styles, attitudes, and strategies associated with creativity are

- readiness to explore and to change
- attention to problem finding as well as problem solving
- immersion in a task
- restructuring of understanding
- belief that knowing and understanding are products of one's intellectual process
- withholding of judgment
- emphasis on understanding
- thinking in terms of opposites
- valuing complexity, ambiguity, and uncertainty combined with an interest in finding order
- valuing feedback but not deferring to convention and social pressures
- recognizing multiple perspectives on a topic
- deferring closure in the early stages of a creative task (e.g, see Kaufman & Sternberg, 2006; Runco, 2006).

The Importance of Critical Thinking

Does critical thinking matter? Are clients more likely to avoid harmful services and receive helpful ones if professionals critically appraise practice and policy-related claims? The history of the helping professions demonstrates that caring is not enough to protect people from harmful practices and to maximize the likelihood that they receive helpful services (Silverman, 1998; Szasz, 1994, 2002; Valenstein, 1986). Here are some errors that may occur if we act on inaccurate accounts:

- Overlooking client assets
- Describing behavior unrelated to its context
- Misclassifying clients
- Continuing intervention too long
- Focusing on irrelevant factors
- Selecting ineffective intervention methods
- Increasing client dependency
- Withdrawing intervention too soon
- Not arranging for the generalization and maintenance of positive gains.

Ineffective or harmful methods may be chosen because of faulty reasoning. Time and resources may be wasted. Examples of ineffective intervention and iatrogenic effects (helper-induced harm) include institutionalizing healthy deaf children because they were incorrectly labeled as having emotional problems (Lane, 1991), institutionalizing adolescents for treatment of substance abuse even though there is no evidence that this works (Schwartz, 1989), and medical errors in American hospitals that kill about 100,000 people annually (Kohn, Corrigan, & Donaldson, 2000; Leape & Berwick, 2005). Medication errors are common (Aspden, Wolcott, Bootman, & Cronenwett, 2007). When ineffective methods fail, clients may feel more hopeless than ever about achieving hoped-for outcomes (Jacobson, Foxx, & Mulick, 2005).

What Critical Thinking Offers

You can learn skills that will help you to make sound decisions. Critical thinking can help you and your clients to make *informed* decisions—to select options that, compared with others, are likely to help clients attain outcomes they value and to avoid harming them. It can help interdisciplinary teams to evaluate claims and arguments.

Evaluate the Accuracy of Claims

Professionals (as well as clients) are deluged by claims about the effectiveness of certain methods and the causes of certain behaviors such as antisocial behavior of youth. Are they true? Are claims inflated? Are they accompanied by a clear description of related evidence? People use many different criteria to evaluate claims. We can assess the accuracy of a claim in relation to the accuracy of predictions that have been tested. Or, we can appeal to anecdotal experience or the manner of a speaker's presentation. Methods may be selected based on how entertainingly they are described, not on their effectiveness. Some interventions may be offered because they are easy to administer or because they earn money for the provider. False or questionable claims are often accepted because they are not carefully evaluated.

We begin to think critically about a proposition when we begin to question whether or not it is true. But a critical thinker does not simply want to know that it is true. He also wants to understand what it means and why it is true.

He wants to be able to explain its meaning and its truth to himself and to others in words that both he and they can understand. And he wants, perhaps most of all, to develop the ability and confidence to make a judgment of his own regarding it.

Here it is easy to see how and why deference to authority conflicts with the goals of critical thinking. For we defer to the opinions of experts only when we want to voice an opinion, but are unable or unwilling to risk voicing an opinion of our own. And regardless of whether or not their conclusions are true, arguments from authority do nothing whatsoever either to further our understanding of what their conclusions mean and why they are true, or to develop our ability and confidence to make judgments of our own concerning them (Nottorno, 2000, pp. 132–133).

Evaluate Arguments

Making decisions involves suggesting arguments in favor of pursuing one course of action rather than another; of believing one claim rather than another (see Box 1.2). In an argument, some statements (the premises) support or provide evidence for another statement (the conclusion). When we analyze arguments, we investigate the truth or falsity of a particular claim. A key part of an argument is the claim, conclusion, or

---

Box 1.2 Evaluating Arguments: What Do You Think?

- I think her being abused as a child causes this parent to mistreat her children. That's what she learned as a child. That's all she knew.
- If Constance developed insight into her past relationships with her father, she would understand how she contributes to problems in her own marriage and could then resolve her problems.
- If he could get money to establish a community service agency, the problems in our neighborhood would decrease because we could fund needed programs.
- Cognitive behavioral methods will best serve this client because her negative self-statements cause her substance abuse.
- His authoritarian personality contributes to his lack of success as a community leader; he won't be able to change because that's the way he wants to be.

---

position put forward. A second part comprises the reasons or premises offered to support the claim. A third consists of the reasons given for assuming that the premises are relevant to the conclusion. These are called *warrants*. Here's an example of an argument not supported by its warrant:

- *Premise*: After extensive counseling, Mrs. Elman reported being sexually abused by her father as a child.
- *Conclusion*: Her father sexually abused Mrs. Elman as a child.
- *Warrant*: The (incorrect) assumption that all memories are accurate.

An argument is unsound if (1) there is something wrong with its logical structure, (2) it contains false premises, or (3) it is irrelevant or circular. Can you identify counterarguments to the statements in Box 1.2? Are there "rival hypotheses"? (Huck & Sandler, 1979).

Recognize Informal Fallacies

Knowledge of fallacies and skill in spotting them will help you to avoid dubious claims and unsound arguments. A fallacy is a mistake in thinking. Fallacies result in defective arguments as when the premises do not provide an adequate basis for a conclusion. Fallacies that evade the facts appear to address them but do not. For instance, variants of "begging the question" include alleged certainty and circular reasoning. Vacuous guarantees may be offered, such as assuming that because a condition ought to be, it is the case, without providing support for the position. In the fallacy called "*sweeping generalization*," a rule or assumption that is valid in general is applied to a specific example for which it is not valid. Consider the assertion that parents abused as children abuse their own children. In fact, a large percentage of them do not. Other fallacies distort facts or positions, as in "strawperson arguments," in which an opponent's view is misrepresented, usually to make it easier to attack. Diversions such as trivial points, irrelevant objections, or emotional appeals may be used to direct attention away from the main point of an argument. Some fallacies work by creating confusion, such as feigned lack of understanding and excessive wordiness that obscures arguments. A variety of informal fallacies are discussed in Exercises 6 to 8 (see also www.fallacyfiles.org; Damer, 1995; Engel, 1994; Kahane & Cavender, 1998).

Recognize and Avoid Influence of Propaganda

There is nothing wrong with trying to persuade others to engage in some action. It depends on methods used. The purpose of propaganda is not to inform but to encourage action with the least thought possible (Ellul, 1965). Propaganda stratagems are used to persuade, that is, to convince someone to do or believe a certain thing based on a distorted, incomplete view (see Deyo & Patrick, 2006; Eisenberg & Wells, 2008; Sweeney). Examples include misrepresenting positions, deceptive use of truth (telling only part of the truth), presenting opinion as fact, deliberate omissions, reliance on slogans, and using putdowns. Sources may be hidden (Hochman, Hochman, Bor, et al., 2008). Tufte (2007) uses the term "corruption of evidence" to refer to such ploys. People who use such ploys attempt to persuade not by a clear, transparent reasoned argument, but indirectly, by subtle associations, for example enticing social workers to buy malpractice insurance by alluding to lawsuits or use of vague innuendos. Consider the following gaps between ethical obligations of scholars and researchers and what we often find in the professional literature:

- Inflated claims (e.g., see Rubin & Parrish, 2007)
- Biased estimates of the prevalence of a concern: Propagandistic advocacy in place of careful weighing of evidence (e.g., see Best, 2004)
- Hiding limitations of research (e.g., see Angell, 2005)
- Preparing incomplete unrigorous literature reviews (e.g., see Littell, 2006)
- Ignoring well-argued alternative perspectives and related evidence (e.g., Boyle, 2002)
- Pseudoinquiry: Lack of match between questions addressed and methods used to address them (e.g., Altman, 2002)
- Ad hominem rather than ad rem arguments. See Exercise 7.
- Ignoring unique knowledge of clients and service providers in making decisions about the appropriateness of practices and policies (e.g., see Gibbs & Gambrill (2002) description of misrepresentations of evidence-based practice).

Ellul (1965) argues that propaganda is an integral part of advanced technological societies. It is distributed via communication channels such as television, newspapers, magazines, radio, the Internet, even professional education and publications. It is designed to integrate us into our society as happy (unthinking) consumers.

> **When propaganda becomes controversial and even offends, it poses relatively little danger because the attempt to manipulate has prompted an opposing reaction. Propaganda is most vicious not when it angers but when it ingratiates itself through government programs that fit our desires or world views, through research or religion that supplies pleasing answers, through news that captures our interest, through educational materials that promise utopia, and through pleasurable films, TV, sports, and art.... the chief problem of propaganda is its ability to be simultaneously subtle and seductive—and to grow in a political environment of neutralized speakers and disempowered communities (Sproule, 1994, p. 327, Chapter 8).**

Advertisements describing alleged "therapeutic advances" often rely on propaganda methods, such as implied obviousness or unsupported claims of effectiveness. Thinking critically about claims and arguments will help you to spot propaganda and avoid related influences that may harm clients.

Recognize Pseudoscience, Fraud, Quackery

Critical thinking can help you to spot pseudoscience, fraud, and quackery more readily and thus avoid their influence (e.g., see Bauer, 2004; Bausell, 2007; Dawes, 1994). Pseudoscience refers to material that makes science-like claims but provides no evidence for them (see later discussion). Quackery refers to the promotion and marketing of unproven, often worthless, and perhaps dangerous products and methods by either professionals or others (Porter, 2000; Young, 1992). Fraud refers to the intentional misrepresentation of the effect of certain actions (e.g., taking a medicine to relieve depression) to induce people to part with something of value (e.g., their money). It involves deception and misrepresentation (Miller & Hersen, 1992) (see also Lang, 1998). Corruption and fraud go hand in hand (see reports distributed by Transparency International).

Use Language Thoughtfully

Language is so important in critical thinking that Perkins (1992) uses the phrase "language of thoughtfulness" to highlight its role. Language is important whether you speak, write, or use tools such as graphics (Tufte, 2007). The degree to which a "culture of thoughtfulness" exists is reflected in the language used. For example, if terms are not clarified, confused discussions may result from the assumption of one word, one meaning. Examples of vague terms that may have quite different meanings include abuse, aggression, and addiction. Using a descriptive term as an explanatory one offers an illusion of understanding without providing any real understanding. For instance, a teacher may say that a student is aggressive. When asked to explain how she knows this, she may say he hits other children. If then asked why she thinks he does this, she may say, "Because he is aggressive." This is a pseudoexplanation; it goes round in a circle. Technical terms may be carelessly used, resulting in "bafflegarb," "biobabble," or "psychobabble"—words that sound informative but are of little or no use in understanding concerns or in making sound decisions. Such words are often used to give the illusion of scientific (critical) inquiry, profundity, and credibility, when, in reality, they are propaganda ploys (pseudoscience in the guise of science). People often misuse speculation; they assume that what is true can be discovered by merely thinking about it.

Recognize Affective Influences

Some fallacies could also be classified as social psychological strategies of persuasion; these work through our affective reactions rather than through thoughtful consideration of positions (Cialdini, 2001). For example, because you like to please people you like, you may not question their use of unfounded authority. People often try to persuade others by offering reasons that play on their emotions and appeal to accepted beliefs and values. Social psychological appeals are used by propagandists who wish to encourage action with little thought. Affective influences based on liking (e.g., the "buddy-buddy syndrome") may dilute the quality of decisions made in case conferences (Meehl, 1973). We may be pressured into maintaining a position by being told that if we do not, we are not consistent with our prior beliefs or actions, as if we could not (or should not) change our minds. Other social psychological persuasion strategies include appeals to scarcity—if we don't act now, a valuable opportunity may be lost. Many work through appeals to fear, for example, arguing against intrusion into family life to protect children because this would result in further invasions of privacy (the slippery-slope fallacy). It is a fallacy because the assumed further consequence may be untrue or not inevitable. Learning how to recognize and counter these and other misleading persuasion strategies is valuable when making life-affecting decisions.

Labels such as "personality disorder" may have emotional effects that get in the way of making sound decisions. Consider also labels given to clients at case conferences such as "baby batterer," which may influence judgments in ways that interfere with sound decision making (Dingwall, Eekelaar, & Murray, 1983). We are influenced by our mood changes (Slovic, Finucane, Peters, & MacGregor, 2002). Stress and anxiety created by noisy offices and work overload interfere with the quality of reasoning.

Minimize Cognitive Biases

Critical thinking can help you to avoid cognitive biases that may lead to unsound decisions such as overconfidence and wishful thinking. Other examples include confirmation biases (searching only for data that support a preferred view), assuming that causes are similar to their effects, and underestimating the frequency of coincidences (chance occurrences) (e.g., see Gambrill, 2005; see also Ariely, 2008). You will learn about these biases in this workbook's exercises. Cultivation of attitudes and values associated with critical thinking such as a commitment to accurately understand the views of others and reflect on the soundness of your own reasoning should help you to minimize cognitive biases.

Increase Self-Awareness

Critical thinking and self-awareness go hand in hand. It requires what Zechmeister and Johnson (1992) describe as "reflecting on self" (p. 84). They include detecting self-serving biases (such as overestimating your contributions to group decision making) and recognizing self-deceptions (such as assuming you have helped a client when it is clear that you have not). Self reflection includes recognition of self-handicapping strategies such as not studying for a test so you have a excuse for failure. Nickerson

(1986) suggests that knowledge about oneself is one of three kinds of knowledge central to critical thinking. Critical thinking requires making inferences explicit and examining them. It requires self-criticism. What do I believe? Why do I believe it? Can I make a well reasoned argument for my position? Critical thinking encourages you to critically appraise beliefs, values, claims and arguments (see Box 1.2) whether your own or those of "experts" (Rampton & Stauber, 2002). It encourages you to be aware of uncertainty, vagueness, complexity, and ignorance as well as knowledge and to reflect on your beliefs and actions and their consequences.

Related Knowledge, Skills, and Values

Skills, knowledge, values, and attitudes related to critical thinking are reviewed next.

Related Skills

Skills involved in critical thinking include detecting differences and similarities, critically evaluating arguments and claims and devising tests of claims (see Box 1.3). Identifying patterns of interaction among family members requires skill in "seeing" such patterns. Making accurate inferences about the causes of behavior requires skill in synthesizing data (e.g., see Dishion & Granic, 2004).

Knowledge

Nickerson (1986) suggests that three kinds of knowledge are important in critical thinking. One concerns critical thinking itself. Two others are domain-specific knowledge and self-knowledge.

Domain-Specific Knowledge: To think critically about a subject, you must know something about that subject. For instance, a study of decision making among physicians demonstrated the importance of knowledge of content such as anatomy and biochemistry. The "possession of relevant bodies of information and a sufficiently broad experience with related problems to permit the determination of which information is pertinent, which clinical findings are significant, and how these findings are to be integrated into appropriate hypotheses and conclusions" (Elstein, et al., 1978, p. x) were foundation components related to

Box 1.3 Examples of Critical Thinking Skills

- Clarify problems.
- Identify significant similarities and differences.
- Recognize contradictions and inconsistencies.
- Refine generalizations and avoid oversimplifications.
- Clarify issues, conclusions, or beliefs.
- Analyze or evaluate arguments, interpretations, beliefs, or theories.
- Identify unstated assumptions.
- Clarify and analyze the meaning of words or phrases.
- Use sound criteria for evaluation.
- Clarify values and standards.
- Detect bias.
- Distinguish relevant from irrelevant questions, data, claims, or reasons.
- Evaluate the accuracy of different sources of information.
- Compare analogous situations; transfer insights to new contexts.
- Make well-reasoned inferences and predictions.
- Compare and contrast ideals with actual practice.
- Discover and accurately evaluate the implications and consequences of a proposed action.
- Evaluate one's own reasoning process.
- Raise and pursue significant questions.
- Make interdisciplinary connections.
- Analyze and evaluate actions or policies.
- Evaluate perspectives, interpretations, or theories.

Source: See for example Ennis (1987); Paul (1993).

competence in clinical problem solving. Knowledge is required to evaluate the plausibility of premises related to an argument. (For a recent discussion of knowledge and expertise see Klein, 1998; Lewandowsky, Little, & Kalish, 2007). Consider the following example:

- Depression always has a psychological cause.
- Mr. Draper is depressed.
- Therefore, the cause of Mr. Draper's depression is psychological in origin.

Though the logic of this argument is sound, but the conclusion may be false. The more that is known in an area (the greater the knowledge that can decrease uncertainty about what decision is best), the more important it is to be familiar with this knowledge. Thus, just as domain-specific knowledge is necessary but insufficient for making informed decisions, critical thinking skills cannot replace knowledge of content.

Self-Knowledge: Critical thinking requires evaluating your thinking and learning styles. The term *meta-cognitive* refers to knowledge about your reasoning process (awareness and influence over this process). You ask questions such as How am I doing? Is this true? What does this mean? How do I know this is true? How good is the evidence? Do I really understand this point? What mistakes may I be making? These questions highlight the self-correcting role of critical thinking. Increasingly meta-cognitive levels of thought include the following:

- *Tacit use:* Thinking without thinking about it
- *Aware use:* Thinking and being aware that you are thinking
- *Strategic use:* Thinking is organized using particular "conscious" strategies that enhance effectiveness
- *Reflective use:* "reflecting on our thinking before and after—or even in the middle of—the process, pondering how to proceed and how to improve" (Swartz & Perkins, 1990, p. 52).

Self-knowledge includes familiarity with the strengths and limitations of reasoning processes in general as well as a knowledge of your personal strengths and limitations that influence how you approach learning, problem solving and decision making. Resources include self-criticism such as asking: What are my biases? Is there another way this problem could be structured? as well as tools, for example drawing a diagram of an argument. Three of the basic building blocks of reasoning suggested by Paul in Box 1.1—ideas and concepts drawn on, whatever is taken for granted, and the point of view in which one's thinking is imbedded, concern important background knowledge because it influences how we approach problems. Without this, unrecognized biases can interfere with making sound judgments. A "bucket" theory of learning in which you expect others to "dump in" knowledge with no effort of your own will get in the way of learning. Learning requires thinking about and raising questions about topics discussed. It requires taking chances—do you really understand a concept? It requires a willingness to make mistakes. Indeed, Perkinson (1993) argues that if you are not making mistakes, you are probably not learning.

Related Values, Attitudes, and Dispositions

Critical thinking involves more than the mere possession of related knowledge and skills. It requires using them in everyday situations and acting on the results. That is, it requires motivation to use related knowledge and skills. Predispositions and attitudes related to critical thinking include fair-mindedness (accurate understanding of other views) and open-mindedness (eagerness to critically explore views of others as well as those of your own), a desire to be well informed, a tendency to think before acting, and curiosity (e.g., see Baron, 2000; Brookfield, 1987; Ennis, 1987; Paul, & Elder, 2004; Seech, 1993). These attitudes are related to underlying values regarding human rights and the dignity and intrinsic worth of all human beings (Brookfield, 1987; Nickerson, 1986; Paul, 1993). Popper (1994) argues that they are vital to an open society in which we are free to raise questions and encouraged to do so. Related values, attitudes, and dispositions are illustrated in Boxes 1.4 and 1.5. Walter Sa and his colleagues (2005) found that thinking dispositions (active open-minded thinking) were more influential in predicting decontextualized thinking than cognitive ability. Decontextualed skills refer to operating independently of interfering contexts such as the ability to overcome my-side bias. Many cognitive styles, attitudes, and strategies associated with creativity are also involved in critical thinking, including a readiness to

---

Box 1.4   Values and Attitudes Related to Critical Thinking

- Belief in and respect for human rights and the dignity and intrinsic worth of all human beings.
- Respect for the truth above self-interest.
- Value learning and critical discussion.
- Respect opinions that differ from your own. Value tolerance and open-mindedness in which you seriously consider other points of view; reason from premises with which you disagree without letting the disagreement interfere with reasoning; withhold judgment when the evidence and reasons are insufficient.
- Value being well informed.
- Seek reasons for beliefs and claims.
- Rely on sound evidence.
- Consider the total situation (the context).
- Remain relevant to the main point.
- Seek alternatives.
- Take a position (and change it) when the evidence and reasons are sufficient to do so.
- Seek clarity.
- Deal in an orderly manner with the parts of a complex whole.
- Be sensitive to the feelings, level of knowledge, and degree of sophistication of others.
- Think independently.
- Persevere in seeking clarity and evaluating arguments.

Source: Adapted from Paul, R. (1993). Critical thinking: *What Every Person Needs to Survive in a Rapidly Changing World (Revised 3rd ed.)* (pp. 470–472). Santa Rosa, CA: Foundation for Critical Thinking. www.criticalthinking.org. Reprinted with permission. See also Ennis (1987), Popper (1972).

Box 1.5 Valuable Intellectual Traits

- *Intellectual humility:* Recognize the limits of our own knowledge, including a sensitivity to circumstances in which we are likely to deceive ourselves; sensitivity to bias, prejudice and limitations of our viewpoint. Intellectual humility involves recognizing that we should never claim more than we actually "know." It does not imply spinelessness or submissiveness. It implies a lack of intellectual pretentiousness, boastfulness, or conceit, combined within sight into the logical foundations (or lack of such foundations) of our beliefs.
- *Intellectual courage:* Facing and fairly addressing ideas, beliefs, or viewpoints toward which we have strong negative emotions and to which we have not given a serious hearing. This courage is connected with the recognition that ideas considered dangerous or absurd may be reasonable and that our conclusions and beliefs are sometimes false or misleading. To determine for our self what is accurate, we must not passively and uncritically "accept" what we have "learned." Intellectual courage comes into play here, because inevitably we will come to see some truth in some ideas strongly held by others. We need courage to be true to our own thinking in such circumstances. The penalties for nonconformity can be severe.
- *Intellectual empathy:* Being aware of the need to imaginatively put oneself in the place of others in order to genuinely understand them, which requires awareness of our tendency to identify truth with our immediate perceptions of long-standing thought or belief. This trait includes reconstructing accurately the viewpoints and reasoning of others and reasoning from premises, assumptions, and ideas other than our own. It includes a willingness to remember occasions when we were wrong in the past despite a conviction that we were right.
- *Intellectual integrity:* Honoring the same rigorous standards of evidence to which we hold others; practicing what we advocate and admitting discrepancies and inconsistencies in our own thoughts and actions.
- *Intellectual perseverance:* The pursuit of accuracy despite difficulties, obstacles, and frustrations; adherence to rational principles despite the irrational opposition of others; recognition of the need to struggle with confusion and unsettled questions over time to achieve deeper understanding or insight.
- *Confidence in reason:* Confidence that, in the long run, our higher interests and those of humankind at large will be best served by giving the freest play to reason, by encouraging others to develop their rational faculties; faith that, with proper encouragement and education, people can learn to think for themselves, to form rational views, draw reasonable conclusions, think coherently and logically, persuade each other by reason, and become reasonable persons, despite obstacles to doing so.
- *Fair-mindedness:* Treating all viewpoints alike, without reference to our own feelings or vested interests, or the feelings or vested interests of our friends, community, or nation; this implies adherence to intellectual standards without reference to our own advantage or the advantage of our group.
- *Autonomy:* Motivated to think for yourself.

Source: Adapted from Paul, R. (1993). *Critical thinking: What Every Person Needs to Survive in a Rapidly Changing World (Revised 3rd. Ed)* (pp. 470–472). Santa Rosa, CA: Foundation for Critical Thinking. www.criticalthinking.org. Reprinted with permission.

explore (curiosity) and to change (flexibility), attention to problem finding, and immersion in a task, as discussed earlier.

Critical thinkers question what others take for granted. They ask questions such as: "What does it mean?" "How good is the evidence?" They question values and positions that may be common in a society, group, or their own family. Thus, critical thinking is a radical idea. Raising such questions may make you unpopular. It takes courage to raise questions in settings in which there is "a party line." And you must pick your battles, especially in professional settings in which beliefs may have life-affecting consequences for clients. Skill in raising questions in a diplomatic way are important (see Exercise 17). Critical thinking requires critical discussion and consideration of opposing views. Only by such open dialogue may you discover that you are wrong and that there is a better idea. It involves taking responsibility for claims made and arguments presented. It requires flexibility and a readiness to recognize and welcome the discovery of mistakes in your own thinking. Critical thinking is independent thinking—thinking for yourself.

Critical Thinking: Integral to Evidence-Based (Informed) Practice

The process and philosophy of evidence-based practice (EBP) as described by its originators, is an educational and practice paradigm designed to decrease the gaps between research and practice to maximize opportunities to help clients and avoid harm (Gray, 2001a, 2001b; Sackett, Richardson, Rosenberg, & Haynes, 1997; Sackett, Straus, Richardson, Rosenberg, & Haynes, 2000; Straus, Richardson, Glasziou, & Haynes, 2005). It is assumed that professionals often need information to make important decisions, for example, concerning risk assessment or what services are most likely to help clients attain outcomes they value. Critical thinking skills are integral to EBP (e.g., see Gambrill, 2005; Jenicek & Hitchcock, 2005). EBP as described by its originators involves "the conscientious, explicit and judicious use of current best evidence in making decisions about the care of individual [clients]" (Sackett, et al., 1997, p. 2). It requires "the integration of the best research evidence with our clinical expertise and our [client's] unique values and circumstances" (Straus, et al., 2005, p. 1). It is designed to break down the division between research, practice, and policy, emphasizing the importance of attention to ethical issues including drawing judiciously and conscientiously on practice and policy-related research findings (see Box 1.6).

Box 1.6 An Updated Model for Evidence-Based Decisions

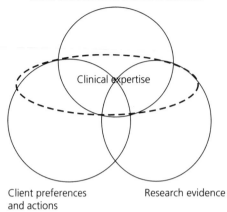

Client characteristics and circumstances

Clinical expertise

Client preferences
and actions

Research evidence

Source: Haynes, R. B., Devereaux, P. J., Guyatt, G. H. (2002). Clinical expertise in the era of evidence-based medicine and patient choice. *ACP Journal Club,* 136, A11. Reprinted with permission.

Best research evidence refers to valid and clinically or policy-relevant research. Clinical expertise refers to use of practice skills, including effective relationship skills, and the past experience of individual helpers to rapidly identify each client's unique circumstances, and characteristics including their expectations and "their individual risks and benefits of potential interventions..."(p. 1). It is drawn on to integrate information from these varied sources (Haynes, Devereaux, & Guyatt, 2002).

> **Without clinical expertise, practice risks becoming tyrannized by external evidence, for even excellent external evidence may be inapplicable to or inappropriate for an individual [client]. Without current best external evidence, practice risks becoming rapidly out of date, to the detriment of [clients] (Sackett, et al., 1997, p. 2).**

Client values refer to "the unique preferences, concerns and expectations each [client] brings to a clinical encounter and which must be integrated into clinical decisions if they are to serve the [client]" (Sackett, Strauss, Richardson, Rosenberg, & Haynes, 2000, p. 1).

Evidence-based practice arose as an alternative to authority-based practice in which decisions are based on criteria such as consensus, anecdotal experience, and tradition (see Box 1.7). It describes a philosophy as well as an evolving process designed to forward effective use of professional

---

Box 1.7 Alternatives to Evidence-Based Practice

Basis for Clinical Decisions	Marker	Measuring Device	Units of Measurement
Evidence	Randomized controlled trial	Meta-analysis	Odds ratio
Eminence	Radiance of white hair	Luminometer	Optic density
Vehemence	Level of stridency	Audiometer	Decibels
Eloquence (or elegance)	Smoothness of tongue or nap of suit	Teflometer	Adhesion score
Providence	Level of religious fervor	Sextant to measure angle of genuflection	International units of piety
Diffidence	Level of gloom	Nihilometer	Sights
Nervousness	Litigation phobia level	Every conceivable test	Bank balance
Confidence	Bravado	Sweat test	No sweat

Source: Issacs, D. & Fitzgerald, D. (1999). Seven alternatives to evidence based medicine. *British Medical Journal*, 319, 1618.

---

judgment in integrating information about each client's unique characteristics, circumstances, preferences, and actions with external research findings. "It is a guide for thinking about how decisions should be made" (Haynes, et al., 2002). Critical thinking knowledge skills, and values are integral to evidence-informed practice and policy.

Although the philosophical roots of EBP are old, its blooming as an evolving process attending to evidentiary, ethical, and application issues in all professional venues (education, practice and policy as well as research) is fairly recent, facilitated by the Internet revolution. Codes of ethics of the American Psychological Association, American Medical Association and National Association of Social Workers as well as other professional organizations, obligate professionals to consider practice-related research findings and inform clients about them. Although the term EBP can be mistaken to mean only that the decisions made are based on evidence of their effectiveness, its use does call attention to the fact that available evidence may not be used or the current state of ignorance in the field may not be shared with clients. It is hoped that professionals who consider related research findings regarding decisions and inform clients about them will provide more effective and ethical care than those who rely on criteria such as anecdotal experience, available resources, or popularity. Some people prefer the term evidence-informed practice (Chalmers, 2004).

Evidence-based practice requires professionals to search for research findings related to important practice and policy decisions and to share what is found (including nothing) with clients. It highlights the uncertainty involved in making decisions and attempts to give both helpers and clients the knowledge and skills they need to handle this uncertainty constructively. Evidence-informed practice is designed to break down the division between research and practice, for example, emphasizing the importance of clinicians' critical appraisals of research and developing a technology to help them to do so; "the leading figures in EBM [evidence-based medicine] . . . emphasized that clinicians had to use their scientific training and their judgment to interpret [guidelines] and individualize care accordingly" (Gray, 2001a, p. 26). Steps in EBP include the following:

Step 1: Converting information needs related to practice and policy decisions into well-structured questions.

Step 2: Tracking down, with maximum efficiency, the best evidence with which to answer them.

Step 3: "Critically appraising that evidence for its validity (closeness to the truth), impact (size of the effect), and applicability (usefulness in our clinical practice)" (Straus, et al., 2005, p. 4).

Step 4: "Integrating the critical appraisal with our clinical expertise and with our [clients'] unique" characteristics and circumstances (e.g., Is a client similar to those studied? Is there access to services needed?).

Step 5: "Evaluating our effectiveness and efficiency in executing steps 1 to 4 and seeking ways to improve them both for next time" (p. 4).

Reasons for the Creation of Evidence-Based Practice

A key reason for the creation of EBP was the discovery of gaps showing that professionals are not acting systematically or promptly on research findings. There were wide variations in practices (Wennberg, 2002).

There was a failure to start services that work and to stop services that did not work or harmed clients (Gray, 2001a, 2001b). Economic concerns were another factor. Inventions in technology were key in the origins of EBP such as the Web revolution that allows quick access to databases. Practitioners who have access to a computer and a modem can now track down research related to decisions they make in real time. Relevant, well-organized databases are rapidly increasing. The development of the systematic review was another key innovation. Meta-analyses and systematic reviews (research syntheses) make it easier to discover evidence related to decisions. The Cochrane and Campbell Databases provide rigorous reviews regarding thousands of questions. Yet another origin was increased recognition of the flawed nature of traditional means of knowledge dissemination such as texts, editorials, and peer review. Gray (2001b) describes peer review as having "feet of clay" (p. 22). Also, there was increased recognition of harming in the name of helping. Gray (2001b) also notes the appeal of EBP both to clinicians and to clients.

The Evidence-Based Practices (EBPs)

The most popular view is defining EBP as considering practice-related research in making decisions including using practice guidelines or requiring practitioners to use empirically based treatments (Norcross, Beutler, & Levant, 2006; Reid, 2002). Rosen and Proctor (2002) state that "we use evidence-based practice here primarily to denote that practitioners will select interventions on the basis of their empirically demonstrated links to the desired outcomes" (p. 743). Making decisions about individual clients is much more complex. There are many other considerations such as the need to consider the unique circumstances and characteristics of each client as suggested by the spirited critiques of practice guidelines and manualized treatments (e.g., Norcross, Beutler, & Levant, 2006). Practice guidelines are but one component of EBP, as can be seen by a review of topics in the book by Sackett et al. (2000), *Evidence-Based Medicine*; they are discussed in one of nine chapters (other chapters focus on diagnosis and screening, prognosis, therapy, harm, teaching methods, and evaluation). The broad view of EBP involves searching for research related to important decision and sharing what is found, including nothing, with clients. It involves a search not only for knowledge but also for ignorance. Such a search is required to involve clients as informed participants. And client values and expectations are vital to consider.

The Propagandistic Approach

Many descriptions of EBP in the literature could be termed business as usual, for example, continuation of unrigorous research reviews regarding practice claims, inflated claims of effectiveness, lack of attention to ethical concerns such as involving clients as informed participants, and neglect of application barriers. A common reaction is relabeling the old as new (as EBP)—using the term evidence-based without the substance, for example, labeling uncritical reviews as evidence-based. (See, for example, Oliver's (2006) critique of Body Mass Index as "evidence-based" (p. 28).

A key choice is thus how to view EBP—whether to draw on the broad philosophy and evolving process of EBP as described by its originators as a way to handle the inevitable uncertainty in making decisions in an informed, honest manner sharing ignorance as well as knowledge, or to use one of the other approaches described (Gambrill, 2006). The choice made has implications not only for clients, practitioners, and administrators, but also for researchers and educators.

Misrepresentation of Evidence-Based Practice

Given the clash with authority-based practices, it is not surprising that EBP is often misrepresented in the professional literature (e.g., see Gibbs & Gambrill, 2002). Also just bad-mouthing a new idea saves time in accurately understanding it. Some people confuse the process and philosophy of EBP as described by their originators with an EBPs approach. Misrepresentations in EBP do not allow readers to make up their own minds about whether the process and philosophy of EBP will benefit clients. Misrepresentations are especially damaging when they appear in flagship journals such as *Social Work* which is circulated to tens of thousands of readers. Consider this distortion of the practice and philosophy of EBP in a guest editorial in the July issue of *Social Work*.

> **EPB serves to validate social work practice by offering empirical data to demonstrate effectiveness. This movement serves to amplify a distinct cultural episteme that decontextualizes and reduces our important and complex work to disintegrate artifacts. For example, local and indigenous knowledge and practice are not acknowledged within the EBP movement and thus are negated (Matsuoka, 2007, p. 198).**

EBP is a way to handle uncertainty in an honest manner, sharing ignorance as well as knowledge so clients can make informed decisions. A search for research related to key decisions is much more likely to reveal that current practices are ineffective or harmful than to "validate practice." Considering each client's unique characteristics and circumstance is a key part of the process of EBP as described in original sources. Such distortions of the process and philosophy of EBP emphasizes the importance of reading original sources. Read Straus et al. (2005) for example. By all means let's criticize new ideas. But let's describe them accurately, rather than attack a strawman.

Why do Evidence-Informed Practice?

Ethical obligations require practitioners to draw on practice and policy-related research findings and to involve clients as informed participants concerning the costs and benefits of recommended services. EBP provides a process and a variety of related tools including decisions aids to help them do so (see O'Connor, et al., 2002). But can inquiry in the social sciences on which evidence-informed practice draws be "scientific"? Can reality be used as a foil against which to test ideas as in the physical sciences? Bauer (2004) argues that the complexity of questions regarding human behavior make it difficult to acquire the kind of knowledge that is available in the physical sciences. However, careful evaluation of practices and policies can help us to discover what practices harm clients and what services help them or are ineffective (e.g., see Chalmers, 2003; Evans, Thornton, & Chalmers, 2006; Jacobson, Foxx, & Mulick, 2005).

How Effective is Evidence-Based Practice?

Exploring the effectiveness of EBP is a complex endeavor. There are many different educational locations, including continuing education as well as degree programs. Second, is the ethical challenge of random assignment of clients. Third is the variety of possible outcome measures. A follow-up of graduates over ten years found that graduates who had experienced a problem-based educational approach at McMaster University medical school in Canada were more up-to-date regarding ways to treat hypertension compared to graduates taught at the medical school in Toronto in a traditional approach (Shin, Haynes, & Johnson, 1993). A before/after case series by Susan Straus and her colleagues (2005) found that a multicomponent intervention designed to teach and support evidence-based medicine, resulted in drawing on higher quality evidence in support of therapies initiated for the primary diagnoses in 483 consecutive patients admitted before and the month after intervention compared to usual practices. Sharon Straus has launched a randomized controlled trial, now in progress.

Helpful Distinctions

Widely Accepted/True

What is *widely accepted* may not be *true* (Dean, 1987). Consider the following exchange:

- *Ms. Simmons (psychiatrist):* I've referred this client to the adolescent stress service because this agency is widely used.
- *Ms. Harris (supervisor):* Do you know anything about how effective this agency is in helping adolescents like your client?
- *Ms. Simmons:* They receive more referrals than any other agency for these kinds of problems. We're lucky if they accept my client.

Many people believe in the influence of astrological signs (their causal role is widely accepted). However, to date, there is no evidence that they have a causal role in influencing behavior, that is, risky predictions based on related beliefs have not survived critical tests. Can you think of other beliefs that are widely accepted but not true?

A Feeling That Something Is True Versus Whether it Is True

Another helpful distinction is between a "feeling" that something is true and whether it is true. Not making this distinction helps to account for the widespread belief in many questionable causes of behavior such as astrological influences, crystals, spirit guides, and so on (e.g., see Dawes, 2001; Shermer, 1997). People often use their "feeling" that something is true as a criterion to accept or reject possible causes. However, a "feeling" that something is true may not (and often does not) correspond to what is true.

Reasoning/Rationalizing

Reasoning involves reviewing both the evidence against and in favor of a position. *Rationalizing* is a selective search for evidence in support of a belief or action. This selective search may occur automatically (without our awareness) or deliberately. When we rationalize, we focus on building a case rather than weighing evidence for and against an argument. This is not to say that there is no interest in persuading others about the soundness of our arguments. The differences lies in the means used. (See later discussion of persuasion and propaganda.) When we rationalize we engage in defensive thinking. Notturno (2000) suggests that defensive thinkers are not inspired by the search for truth.

> **They are inspired by a need to vindicate themselves from error, to show that they themselves are not to blame for their beliefs. Their concern for justification, however, often leads them to focus upon evidence that supports their beliefs, and to disregard evidence that presents problems.**
>
> **Political thinking, on the other hand, is motivated by a need to be accepted, or to get ahead. To think politically is to forget about what you think is true and to voice opinions that you think are likely to win approval from your friend ... (Notturno, 2000, p. 130).**

Justifiable/Falsifiable

Many people focus on gathering support for (justifying) claims, theories, and arguments. Let's say you see 3000 swans and they are all white. Does this mean that *all* swans are white? Can you generalize from the particular (seeing 3000 swans, all of which are white) to the general ("All swans are white."): Karl Popper (and others) argue that we cannot discover what is true by induction (generalizing from the particular to the general) because we may later discover exceptions (some swans that are not white). In fact, black swans are found in some parts of the world. Popper argues that falsification (attempts to falsify, to discover the errors in our beliefs via critical tests of claims) is the only sound way to develop knowledge (Popper, 1972, 1994). We subject our beliefs to critical tests to discover errors, and learn from these errors to make more informed guesses in the future.

Truth and Credibility

Karl Popper defines truthful statements as those that correspond with the facts. Credible statements are those that are possible to believe. Dennis Phillips (1992) points out that just about anything may be credible. This does not mean that it is true. Simply because it is possible to believe something does not mean that it is true. Although scientists seek true answers to problems (statements that correspond to the facts), this does not mean that there is certain knowledge. Rather, certain beliefs (theories) have (so far) survived critical tests or have not yet been exposed to them. An error "consists essentially of our regarding as true a theory that is not true" (Popper, 1992, p. 4). People can avoid error or discover it by doing all they can to discover and eliminate falsehoods (p. 4).

Personal and Objective Knowledge

Personal knowledge refers to what you as an individual believe you "know." Objective knowledge refers to assumptions that have survived critical tests or evaluation. It is public. It is criticizable by others. We typically overestimate what "we know"—that is, our self-assessments of our "knowledge" and skills are usually inflated (Dunning, Heath, & Suls, 2004) (see also next distinction).

Knowing and the Illusion of Knowing

There is a difference between accurately understanding content and the illusion of knowing—"a belief that comprehension has been attained when in fact, comprehension has failed" (Zechmeister & Johnson, 1992, p. 151). Research shows that we often think we "know" something when we do not. The illusion of knowing is encouraged by mindless reading habits, for example, failing to read material carefully and failing to monitor one's comprehension by asking questions such as "Do I understand this? What is this person claiming? What are his reasons?," and so on. There is a failure to take remedial action such as rereading. There is a failure to detect contradictions and unsupported claims. (See discussion of uncritical documentation in Exercise 6.) Redundant information may be collected creating a false sense of accuracy (Hall, Ariss, & Todorov, 2007). The illusion of knowing gets in the way of taking remedial steps because you think "you know" when you do not. There is a failure of comprehension without the realization that this has occurred. Zechmeister and Johnson (1992) suggest that the illusion of knowing may be encouraged by a feeling of familiarity concerning claims made. Claims may appeal to "grand narratives" in a society—generally accepted ideas about "What is a family," what is a social problem, or what causes a certain problem, such as depression. These authors suggest that the illusion of knowing in which information is treated mindlessly is encouraged by thinking in terms of absolutes (e.g., "proven," "well established") rather than thinking conditionally (e.g., "This may be ..." "This could be ...").

What to Think and How to Think

Critics of the educational system argue that students are too often told what to think and do not learn how to think. Thinking critically about any subject requires us to examine our reasoning process. This is quite different from memorizing a list of alleged facts. Examining the accuracy of "facts" requires thinking critically about them.

Intuitive and Analytic Thinking

Intuition ("gut reaction") is a quick judgment. It comes quickly into a person's consciousness. The person doesn't know why they have this feeling. Yet, this is strong enough to make an individual act on it. What a gut instinct is not is a calculation (Gigerenzer, 2007). A judgment is made based on your first feeling. These quick judgments are based on heuristics (simple rules-of-thumb) such as the recognition heuristic. That is, "If one of two alternatives is recognized, infer that it has the higher value on the criterion" (p. 24). This heuristic is ecologically rational if the cues recognized have a probability >.5 (Gigerenzer, 2008, p. 24). Another heuristic suggested by Gigerenzer is "imitate the successful." "Look for the most successful person and imitate his or her behavior" (p. 24). We make what Gigerenzer calls a "fast and frugal decision." It is rapid (fast) and relies only on key cues (it is frugal). We ignore irrelevant data, we do not engage in calculation such as balancing pros and cons. Gigerenzer (2008) suggests that we select a heuristic based on reinforcement learning. He notes that logic may not be of help in a variety of situations and that it is correspondence with ecology that matters. "Rationality is defined by correspondence [to a certain environment] rather than coherence" (p. 25). Related research shows that such judgments are often superior to calculating pros and cons. *But* not always. When "our gut reaction" is based on vital cues, it serves us well. When it is not (when in Hogarth's term, it is not "informed intuition"), it is best to use a more analytic approach to making decisions. Jonathan Baron defines intuition as "an unanalyzed and unjustified belief" (1994, p. 26) and notes that beliefs based on intuition may be either sound or unsound. Kahneman (2003) encourages us to use our analytic skills to make best use of intuition.

Intuitions (inferences) may refer to looking back in time (interpreting experience) or forward in time (predictions). For example, a psychiatrist may "diagnose" a client by gaining information about her past or she may predict that a client will act in a certain manner in the future. The view that intuition involves responsiveness to information that although not consciously represented, yields productive insights, is compatible with the research regarding expertise (Klein, 1998). No longer remembering where we learned something encourages attributing solutions to "intuition." When a professional is asked what made her think a particular method would be effective in increasing motivation of a client to address his concerns, his answer may be, my "intuition." When asked to elaborate, he may offer sound reasons reflecting related evidence. That is, his "hunch" was an informed one.

Intuition will not be a sound guide for making decisions when misleading cues are focused on, such as different prices (e.g., see Waber, Shiv, Carmon, & Ariely, 2008). Research comparing clinical and actuarial judgment consistently shows the superior accuracy of the latter (e.g., Grove & Meehl, 1996; Quinsey, Harris, Rice, & Cormier, 1998). Actuarial judgments are based on empirical relationships between variables and an outcome, such as future abuse. Attributing judgments to "intuition" decreases opportunities to teach others. One has "it" but doesn't know how or why "it" works. If you ask your supervisor "How did you know to do that at that time," and he says, "My intuition," this will not help you to learn what to do. And, intuition cannot show which method is most effective in helping clients; a different kind of evidence is required for this—one that provides critical comparisons controlling for biases.

Propaganda/Bias/Point of View

Propaganda refers to encouraging beliefs and action with the least thought possible (Ellul, 1965; see also Best, 2004; Brody, 2007; Combs & Nimmo, 1993; Tavris, 1994). Propagandists play on our emotions (see Exercise 3).

Bias refers to an emotional leaning to one side. Biased people who try to persuade others may or may not be aware that they are doing so. They may appeal to our fears to gain uncritical, emotional acceptance of a position. Common propaganda tactics include appealing to our emotions, presenting only one side of an argument, hiding counterarguments to preferred views, and attacking the motives of critics to deflect criticism, for example assuming that anyone who doubts the effectiveness of services for battered women must be trying to undermine efforts to help women.

People with a point of view are aware of their interests, but they describe their sources, state their views clearly, and avoid propaganda tactics (MacLean, 1981). Their statements and questions encourage rather than discourage critical appraisal. They clarify their statements when asked to do so.

Reasoning/Truth

Reasoning does not necessarily yield the *truth*. "People who are considered by many of their peers to be reasonable people often do take, and are able to defend quite convincingly, diametrically opposing positions on controversial matters" (Nickerson, 1986, p. 12). However, effective reasoners are more likely to critically examine their views than ineffective reasoners. Also the accuracy of a conclusion does not necessarily indicate that the reasoning used to reach it was sound. For example, errors in the opposite direction may have cancelled each other out. Lack of evidence for a claim does not mean that it is incorrect. Similarly, surviving critical tests does not mean that a claim is true. Further tests may show that it is false; Popper (1994) argues that we must value truth, the search for truth, the approximation to truth through the critical elimination of error, and clarity in order to overcome the influence of other values (e.g., trying to appear profound by using obscure words or jargon, p. 70). This tentative view of the nature of knowledge (critical rationalism) is very different from a justification approach to knowledge.

Reasoning/Persuasion

Both reasoning and social psychological persuasion strategies, such as appeals to scarcity (e.g., this offer is only available for one day), are used to encourage people to act or think in a certain way. We all try to persuade people to believe or act in a certain way. The question is, How do we do so? *Reasoning* involves a *critical evaluation of claims*. The major intent of propagandistic persuasion is not to inform or arrive at a sound decision, but to encourage action with little thought. "The genius of most successful propaganda is to know what the audience wants and how far it will go" (Johnson, 2006, p. A23). Persuasive appeals include propaganda ploys such as appeals to fear, special interests and scarcity (Brock & Green, 2005; Cialdini, 2001; Pratkanis & Aronson, 2001). (See earlier discussion of propaganda.)

Consistency, Corroboration, and Proof

Assigning proper weight to different kinds of evidence is a key part of what it means to be reasonable. People often use consistency or agreement among different sources of data, to support their beliefs. For example, they may say that Mrs. X is depressed currently because she has a prior history of depression. However, saying that A (a history of "depression") is consistent with B (alleged current "depression") is to say only that it is possible to believe B given A. Two or more assertions thus may be consistent with each other but yield little or no insight into the soundness of an argument.

Proof implies certainty about a claim as in the statement, "The effectiveness of case management services to the frail elderly has been proven in this study." Since future tests may show a claim to be incorrect, even one that is strongly corroborated, no assertion can ever be proven (Popper, 1972). If nothing can ever be proven, we can at least construct theories that are falsifiable: theories that generate specific hypotheses that can be critically tested. Psychoanalytic theory is often criticized on the grounds that contradictory hypotheses can be drawn from the theory. As Popper (1959) points out, irrefutability is not a virtue of a theory but a vice. The "Great Randi" has offered one million dollars to anyone who can demonstrate parapsychology effects (such as psychic predictions) via a controlled test. So far, no one has won the prize.

Beliefs, Preference, and Facts

Beliefs are assumptions about what is true or false. They may be testable (e.g., support groups help the bereaved) or untestable (God exists). They may be held as convictions (unquestioned assumptions) or as guesses about what is true or false, which we seek to critically test. Popper (1979) suggests that *facts* refer to well-tested data, intersubjectively evaluated. These can be contrasted with "factoids"—claims with no related evidence, claims that although there is no evidence to support them, may be believed because they are repeated so often. What is viewed as "a fact" may differ in different cultures. In a scientific approach it is assumed that the accuracy of an assertion is related to the uniqueness and accuracy of related critical appraisals. Facts can be checked (e.g., shown that they are not true); beliefs may not be testable. *Preferences* reflect values. It does not make sense to consider preferences as true or false, because people differ in their preferences, as in the statement, "I prefer insight-oriented treatment." This is quite different than the assertion: "Play therapy can help children overcome anxiety." Here, evidence can be gathered to find out if it is accurate. Other examples of preferences and beliefs follow. The first one is a preference. The last two are beliefs.

- I like to collect payment for each session at the end of the session.
- Insight therapy is more effective than cognitive-behavioral treatment of depression.
- My pet Rotweiler helps people with their problems (quote from a psychologist on morning talk show, 4/6/88).

We can ask people what their preferences are and some ways of exploring this are more accurate than others.

Science and Scientific Criteria

Science is a way of thinking about and investigating the accuracy of assumptions about the world. It is a process Popper (1972) suggests that it is a process for solving problems in which we learn from our mistakes. Both critical thinking and scientific reasoning provide a way of thinking about and testing assumptions that is of special value to those in the helping professions, such as social workers. Both rely on shared standards that encourage us to challenge assumptions, consider opposing points of view, be clear, and check for errors. Science rejects a reliance on authority, for example, pronouncements by officials or professors, as a route to knowledge. Authority and science are clashing views of how knowledge can be gained. The history of science and medicine shows that the results of experimental research involving systematic investigation often frees us from false beliefs that harm rather than help and decrease our susceptibility to fraudulent claims.

There are many ways to do science and many philosophies of science. Discovering what is true and what is false often requires ingenious experiments and the invention of new technologies such as the microscope and the long range telescope. Consider the creative experiment developed by a 12-year-old to test the effectiveness of therapeutic touch (Rosa, Rosa, Sarner, & Barrett, 1998). The terms *science* and *scientific* are sometimes used to refer to any systematic effort-including case studies, correlational studies, and naturalistic studies-to acquire information about a subject. All methods are vulnerable to error, which must be considered when evaluating the data they generate. Nonexperimental approaches include natural observation (the study of animal behavior in real-life settings), and correlational methods that use statistical analysis to investigate the degree to which events are associated. These methods are of value in suggesting promising experiments as well as when events of interest cannot be experimentally altered or if doing so would destroy what is under investigation. Where does magic fit in? Magic has been defined by anthropologists As an intervention designed to reduce anxiety at times of uncertainty (p. 364); for example, doing a rain dance. Frazer (1925) suggested that there is a much closer relationship between magic and science, than between science and religion. For example, in both magic and science there is an interest in predicting the environment.

The view of science presented here, critical rationalism, is one in which the theory-laden nature of observation is assumed (i.e., our assumptions influence what we observe) and rational criticism is viewed as the essence of science (Phillips, 1992; Popper, 1972). "There is no pure, disinterested, theory-free observation" (Popper, 1994, p. 8). Concepts are assumed to have meaning and value even though they are unobservable. By testing our guesses, we eliminate false theories and may learn a bit more about our problems; corrective feedback from the physical world allows us to test our guesses about what is true or false. For example, the cause of ulcers was found to be *Helicobacter pylori*, not stress (Marshall & Warren, 1984; Van der Weyden, Armstrong, & Gregory, 2005). Stress may exacerbate the results, but is not the cause. It is assumed that nothing is ever "proven" (Miller, 1994; Popper, 1972). Science is conservative in insisting that a new theory account for previous findings. It is revolutionary in calling for the overthrow of previous theories shown to be false, but this does not mean that the new theory has been "established" as true. Although the purpose of science is to seek true answers to problems (statements that correspond to facts), this does not mean that we can have certain knowledge. Rather, we may say that certain beliefs (theories) have (so far) survived critical tests or have not yet been exposed to them. And, some theories have been found to be false.

Criticism Is the Essence of Science

The essence of science is creative, bold guessing, and rigorous testing in a way that offers accurate information about whether a guess (conjecture or theory) is accurate (Asimov, 1989). The interplay between theories and their testing is central to science. Scientists are often wrong and find out that they are wrong by testing their predictions. Popper argues that "The growth of knowledge, and especially of scientific knowledge, consists of learning from our mistakes" (1994, p. 93). The scientific tradition is "a tradition of criticism" (Popper, 1994, p. 42). Popper considers the critical method to be one of the great Greek inventions. *"I hold that orthodoxy is the death of knowledge, since the growth of knowledge depends entirely on the existence of disagreement"* (Popper, 1994, p. 34). For example, an assumption that verbal instructions can help people to decrease their smoking could be tested by randomly assigning smokers to an experimental group (receiving such instructions) and a control group (not receiving instructions) and observing their behavior to see what happens. There is a comparison. Let's say that you think you will learn some specific skills in a class you are taking. You could assess your skills before and after the class and see if skills have increased. Testing your belief will offer more information than simply thinking about it. What if you find that your skills have increased? Does this show that the class was responsible for your new skills? It does not. There was no comparison (e.g., with students who did not take the class). There are other possible causes, or rival hypotheses. For example, maybe you learned these skills in some other context.

Scientists make their own observations. Observation is often structured to increase the likelihood that results will yield information sought. Observations are always "theory laden"—this is a basic assumption of science as we know it today. Some claims are testable but untested. If tested, they may be found to be true, false, or uncertain (Bunge, 2003). Consider the question, "How many teeth are in a horse's mouth?" You could speculate about this, or you could open a horse's mouth and look inside. If an agency for the homeless claims that it succeeds in finding homes for applicants within 10 days, you could accept this claim at face value or systematically gather data to see whether this claim is true. A theory should describe what cannot occur as well as what can occur. If you can make contradictory predictions based on a theory, it cannot be tested. Testing may involve examining the past as in Darwin's theory of evolution. Some theories are not testable (falsifiable). There is no way to test them to find out if they are correct. Psychoanalytic theory is often criticized on the grounds that contradictory hypotheses can be drawn from the theory. As Karl Popper points out, irrefutability is not a virtue of a theory, but a vice. Theories can be tested only if specific predictions are made about what can happen and also about what cannot happen.

Popper maintains that attempts to falsify, to discover the errors in our beliefs by means of critical discussion and testing is the only sound way to develop knowledge (Popper, 1992, 1994). (For critiques of Popper's views, see, e.g., Schilpp, 1974.) Explanations that are untestable are problematic. "A scientific theory...must specify not only what is and what can happen, but...what cannot be, what cannot happen, according to its logic as well" (Monte, 1975, p. 93). Can you make accurate predictions based on a belief? Popper emphasizes falsifiability as more critical than confirmation because the latter is easier to obtain. Confirmations of a theory can readily be found if one looks for them. Popper uses the criterion of falsifiability to demark what is or could be scientific knowledge from what is not or could not be. For example, there is no way to refute the claim that "there is a God," but there is a way to refute the claim that "assertive community outreach services for the severely mentally ill reduces substance abuse." We could, for example, randomly distribute clients to a group providing such services and compare those outcomes with those of clients receiving no services or other services. Although we can justify the selection of a theory by its having survived more risky tests concerning a wider variety of hypotheses, compared with other theories that have not been tested or that have been falsified, we can never accurately claim that this theory is "the truth." Further tests may show otherwise.

> **My view of the method of science is very simply that it systematizes the pre-scientific method of learning from our mistakes. It does so by the device called *critical discussion*.**

My whole view of scientific method may be summed up by saying that it consists of these four steps:

1. We select some *problem* – perhaps by stumbling over it.
2. We try to *solve* it by proposing a *theory* as a tentative solution.
3. Through the *critical discussion of our theories* our knowledge grows by the elimination of some of our errors, and in this way we learn to understand our problems, and our theories, and the need for new solutions.
4. The critical discussion of even our best theories always reveals new problems.

Or to put these four steps into four words: *problems – theories – criticisms – new problems.*

Of these four all-important categories the one which is most characteristic of *science* is that of error-elimination through *criticism.* For what we vaguely call the *objectivity of science* and the *rationality of science* are merely aspects of the *critical discussion* of scientific theories (Popper, 1994, pp. 158–159).

Some Tests Are More Rigorous Than Others

Some tests are more rigorous than others and so offer more information about what may be true or false. Many "hierarchies" of evidence have been suggested. Compared with anecdotal reports, experimental tests are more severe tests of claims. Unlike anecdotal reports, they are carefully designed to rule out alternative hypotheses such as the effects of maturation, history or testing (Campbell & Stanley, 1963) and so provide more opportunities to discover that a theory is not correct. Making accurate predictions (e.g., about what service methods will help a client) is more difficult than offering after-the-fact accounts that may sound plausible (even profound) but provide no service guidelines. Every research method is limited in the kinds of questions it can address successfully. The question raised will suggest the research method required to explore it. Thus, if our purpose is to communicate the emotional complexity of a certain kind of experience (e.g., the death of an infant), then qualitative methods are needed (e.g., detailed case examples, thematic analyses of journal entries, open- ended interviews at different times).

A Search for Patterns and Regularities

It is assumed that the universe has some degree of order and consistency. This does not mean that unexplained phenomena or chance variations do not occur or are not considered. For example, chance variations contribute to evolutionary changes (Lewontin, 1991, 1994; Strohman, 2003). Uncertainty is assumed. Since a future test may show an assumption to be incorrect, even one that is strongly corroborated (has survived many critical tests), no assertion can ever be "proved." This does not mean that all beliefs are equally sound; some have survived more rigorous tests than have others (Asimov, 1989). In the physical sciences, there is a consensus about many of the phenomenon that need to be explained and some degree of consensus about explanations as Bauer notes. This consensus does not mean that a theory is accurate, for example, a popular theory may be overthrown by one that accounts for more events and make more accurate predictions. There are scores of different theories in the social sciences. They cannot all be correct. Paradoxically, in the social sciences theories are often claimed to be true with excessive confidence, ignoring the fact that they cannot all be accurate.

Parsimony

An explanation is parsimonious if all or most of its components are necessary to explain most of its related phenomena. Unnecessarily complex explanations may get in the way of detecting relationships between behaviors and related events. Consider the following two accounts:

1. Mrs. Lancer punishes her child because of her own unresolved superego issues related to early childhood trauma. This creates a negative disposition to dislike her oldest child.
2. Mrs. Lancer hits her child because this temporarily removes his annoying behaviors (he stops yelling) and because she does not have positive parenting skills (e.g., she does not know how to identify and reinforce desired behaviors).

The second account suggests specific behaviors that could be altered. It is not clear that concepts such as "unresolved superego issues" and "negative disposition" yield specific guidelines for altering complaints.

Scientists Strive for Objectivity

Popper (1992) argues that "the so-called objectivity of science lies in the objectivity of the critical method; that is, above all, in the fact that no theory is exempt from criticism, and further, in the fact that the logical instrument of criticism – the logical contradiction – is objective" (p. 67). (Two different proposed theories for an event cannot both be true.)

> It most important to see that a critical discussion always deals with more than one theory at a time. For in trying to assess the merits or demerits even of one theory, it always must try to judge whether the theory in question is an *advance*: whether it explains things which we have been unable to explain so far – that is to say, with the help of older theories (Popper, 1994, p. 160).

"What we call scientific objectivity is nothing else than the fact that no scientific theory is accepted as dogma, and that all theories are tentative and are open all the time to severe criticism – to a rational, critical discussion aiming at the elimination of errors" (Popper, 1994, p. 160). Basic to objectivity is the critical discussion of theories (eliminating errors through criticism). Objectivity implies that the results of science are independent of any one scientist so that different people exploring the same problem will reach the same conclusions. It is assumed that perception is theory-laden (influenced by our expectations). This assumption has been accepted in science for some time (Phillips, 2005).

A Skeptical Attitude

Scientists are skeptics. They question what others view as fact or "common sense." They ask for arguments and evidence (e.g., see Caroll, 2003). They do not have sacred cows.

> Science... is a way of thinking.... [It) invites us to let the facts in, even when they don't conform to our preconceptions. It counsels us to consider hypotheses in our heads and see which ones best match the facts. It urges on us a fine balance between no-holds-bared openness to new ideas, however heretical, and the most rigorous skeptical scrutiny of everything – new ideas and established wisdom (Sagan, 1990, p. 265).

Scientists and skeptics seek criticism of their views and change their beliefs when they have good reason to do so. Skeptics are more interested in arriving at accurate answers than in not ruffling the feathers of supervisors or administrators. They value critical discussion because it can reveal flaws in their own thinking which should enable better guesses about what is true, and these in turn can be tested. Knowledge is viewed as tentative. Scientists question what others view as facts or "common sense." They ask: "What does this mean? How good is the evidence?" Skepticism does not imply cynicism (being negative about everything). Scientists change their beliefs if additional evidence demands it. If they do not, they appeal to science as a religion—as a matter of authority and faith—rather than as a way to critically test theories. For example, can a theory lead to guidelines for resolving a problem? Openness to criticism is a hallmark of scientific thinking. Karl Popper considers it the mark of rationality.

Other Characteristics

Science deals with specific problems that can be solved (that can be answered with the available methods of empirical inquiry). For example, is intensive in-home care for parents of abused children more effective than the usual social work services? Is the use of medication to decrease depression in elderly people more (or less) effective than cognitive-behavioral methods? Examples of unsolvable questions are: "Is there a God?"; "Do we have a soul?" Saying that science deals with problems that can be solved does not mean, however, that other kinds of questions are unimportant or that a problem will remain unsolvable. New methods may be developed that yield answers to questions previously unapproachable in a systematic way. Science is collective. Scientists communicate with one another, and the results of one study inform the efforts of other scientists.

Misunderstandings and Misrepresentations of Science

Misunderstandings about science may result in ignoring this problem-solving method and the knowledge it has generated to help us enhance the quality of our lives. Misconceptions include the following:

- There is an absence of controversy.
- Theories are quickly abandoned if anomalies are found.
- Intuitive thinking has no role.

- There is no censorship and blocking of innovative ideas.
- It is assumed that science knows, or will soon know, all the answers.
- Objectivity is assumed.
- Chance occurrences are not considered.
- Scientific knowledge is equivalent to scientific thinking.
- The accumulation of facts is the primary goal.
- Linear thinking is required.
- Passion and caring have no role.
- There is one kind of scientific method.
- Unobservable events are not considered.

Surveys show that many people do not understand the basic characteristics of science (National Science Foundation, 2006). Misunderstandings and misrepresentations of science are so common that D. C. Phillips, a philosopher of science, entitled one of his books *The Social Scientist's Bestiary: A Guide to Fabled Threats to and Defenses of Naturalistic Social Science* (2005). Even some academics confuse logical positivism (discarded by scientists long ago) and science as we know it today. Logical positivism emphasizes direct observation by the senses. It is assumed that observation can be theory free. It is justification focused, assuming that greater verification yields closer approximations to the truth. This approach to knowledge was discarded decades ago because of the induction problem (see earlier discussion), the theory-laden nature of observation, and the utility of unobservable constructs. Misrepresentations of science are encouraged by those who view science as a religion—as offering certain truths. Science is often misrepresented as a collection of facts or as referring only to controlled experimental studies. People often confuse values external to science (e.g., what should be) with values internal to science (e.g., critical testing) (Phillips, 1987). Many people confuse science with pseudoscience and scientism (see Glossary). Some people protest that science is misused. Saying that a method is bad because it has been or may be (or has been) misused is not a cogent argument; anything can be misused. Some people believe that critical reflection is incompatible with passionate caring. Reading the writings of any number of scientists, including Loren Eiseley, Carl Sagan, Karl Popper, and Albert Einstein, should quickly put this false belief to rest. Consider a quote from Karl Popper:

> **I assert that the scientific way of life involves a burning interest in objective scientific theories – in the theories**

in themselves, and in the problem of their truth, or their nearness to truth. And this interest is a *critical* interest, an *argumentative* interest (1994, p. 56).

Far from reinforcing myths about reality, as some claim, science is likely to question them. All sorts of questions that people may not want raised may be raised such as: "Does this residential center really help residents? Would another method be more effective? Is osteoporosis a disease? Should I get tested for cancer? (Welch, 2004). Should I take Paxil for my social discomfort? How accurate is this diagnosis?" Many scientific discoveries, such as Charles Darwin's theory of evolution, clashed with (and still does) some religious views of the world. Consider the church's reactions to the discovery that the earth was not the center of the universe. Only after 350 years did the Catholic church agree that Galileo was correct in stating that the earth revolves around the sun. Objections to teaching evolutionary theory remain common (see *reports* published by the National Center for Science Education). Discovery of accurate answers is usually preceded by false starts and disappointing turns. This history of uncertainty is typically hidden because of page limits enforced by journal editors. The "messiness" of inquiry is hidden by the organized format of texts and journals.

> The differences between formal scientific texts and the activities required to produce them are well known in science studies: scientists tinker in the privacy of the laboratory until they are ready to 'go public' with neatly packaged results; their published work systematically elides the contingencies of actual research; and at times, they even stage spectacular public demonstrations, displaying results dramatically and visually in a carefully arranged theater of proof (Hilgartner, 2000, p. 19).

Dispute and controversy is the norm rather than the exception in science (e.g., see Hellman, 2001). Consider differences of opinion in the study of nutrition and health:

> Some researchers argued that in the area of nutrition, epidemiology should be regarded primarily as a source of hypotheses rather than a means of testing them. In their view, experimental studies in laboratory animals – or, better yet, clinical trials in humans – were needed to resolve the scientific

issues. Other researchers placed much more confidence in epidemiology, arguing that its critics displayed an unscientific bias against a valid research method. Still another axis of debate concerned the standards of proof that should apply when incomplete evidence bears on public health. In particular, the question of whether public health agencies should aim dietary recommendations intended to reduce chronic disease at the general public was controversial, with some health professionals arguing that physicians should assess risks and offer advice on an individual basis. Disputes also broke out about what types of nutrition information should appear on food labels, and about whether fast food restaurants should be required to disclose the nutritional content of their burgers, shakes, and fries (Hilgartner, 2000, p. 31).

Bell and Linn (2002) note that "when textbooks attempt to synthesize historical accounts of discovery, they often omit controversy and personality. These accounts may overemphasize and give an incorrect illusion of a logical progression of uncomplex discovery when indeed the history is quite different: "serendipitous, personality-filled, conjectural, and controversial..." (p. 324). "Scientific journal articles often erase controversy from the record, leaving the disputes and discussions behind the closed doors of the scientific laboratory" (p. 324). Great clashes have, do, and will occur in science. New ideas and related empirical evidence often show that currently accepted theories are not correct, however as Kuhn (1970) argued, old paradigms may continue to be uncritically accepted until sufficient contradictions (anomalies) force recognition of the new theory. Kuhn emphasized "conversion" and persuasion and argued that most investigators work within accepted (and often wrong) paradigms. They do "normal science."

> ...the 'normal' scientist, as Kuhn describes him, is a person one ought to be sorry for...The 'normal' scientist, in my view, has been taught badly. I believe, and so do many others, that all teaching on the University level (and if possible below) should be training and encouragement in critical thinking. The 'normal' scientist, as described by Kuhn, has been badly taught. He has been taught in a dogmatic spirit: he is a victim of indoctrination. He has learned a technique which can be applied without asking for the reason why...As a consequence,

he has become what may be called an applied scientist, in contradistinction to what I should call a pure scientist. He is, as Kuhn puts it, content to solve 'puzzles' (quoted in Notturno, 2000, p. 237; Popper, 1970). Normal science and its dangers (pp. 52–53).

As "big science" becomes more common (research institutes jockeying for limited research funds and collaboration between industry and universities) resistance to new ideas becomes more likely. Political correctness (censorship of certain topics and the castigation of those who raise good questions) is not confined to cultural diversity. For example, Bauer (2007) asks how likely it is that scientists who question the causal relationship between HIV/AIDS will be selected to review grant applications. As he suggests, only competent people are selected and questioning the HIV/AIDS connection is assumed to render one incompetent.

Science and Pseudoscience

The term *pseudoscience* refers to material that makes science-like claims but provides no evidence for them. Pseudoscience is characterized by a casual approach to evidence (Bauer, 2002, 2004) (weak evidence is accepted as readily as strong evidence). Hallmarks of pseudoscience include the following (Bunge, 1984; Gray, 1991):

- Uses the trappings of science without the substance
- Relies on anecdotal evidence
- Is not self-correcting
- Is not skeptical
- Equates an open mind with an uncritical one
- Ignores or explains away falsifying data
- Relies on vague language
- Produces beliefs and faith but not knowledge
- Is often not testable
- Does not require repeatability
- Indifferent to facts
- Often contradicts itself
- Creates mystery where none exists by omitting information

- Relies on the wisdom of the ancients, the older the idea, the better
- Appeals to false authority (or authority w/out evidence), emotion, sentiment, or distrust of established fact
- Argues from alleged exceptions, errors, anomalies, and strange events

A critical attitude, which Karl Popper (1972, 1992) defines as a willingness and commitment to open up favored views to severe scrutiny, is basic to science, distinguishing it from pseudoscience. Indicators of pseudoscience include irrefutable hypotheses and a continuing reluctance to revise beliefs even when confronted with relevant criticism. It makes excessive (untested) claims of contributions to knowledge. Results of a study may be referred to in many different sources until they achieve the status of a law without any additional data being gathered. Richard Gelles calls this the "Woozle Effect" (1982, p. 13). Pseudoscience is a billion-dollar industry. Products include self-help books, "subliminal" tapes, and call-in advice from "authentic psychics" who have no evidence that they accomplish what they promise. Pseudoscience can be found in all fields (e.g., see Lilienfeld, Lynn, & Lohr, 2003; Moncrieff, 2008; Ortiz de Montellano, 1991; and Sarnoff, 2001). Pseudoscientists make use of the trappings of science without the substance (see Bauer, 2004). The terms *science* and *scientific* are often used to increase the credibility of a view or approach, even though no evidence is provided to support it. The term *science* has been applied to many activities that in reality have nothing to do with science. Examples are "scientific charity" and "scientific philanthropy." Prosletizers of many sorts cast their advice as based on science. They use the ideology and "trappings" of science to pull the wool over our eyes in suggesting critical tests of claims that do not exist. The misuse of appeals to science to sell products or encourage certain beliefs is a form of propaganda. Classification of clients into psychiatric categories lends an aura of scientific credibility (Boyle, 2002; Houts, 2002; Kutchins & Kirk, 1997).

Historians of science differ regarding how to demark the difference between pseudoscience and science. Some such as Bauer (2001) argue that the demarcation is fuzzy as revealed by what scientists actually do, for example, fail to reject a favored theory in the face of negative results (e.g., perhaps a test was flawed) and the prevalence of pseudoscience within science (e.g., belief in N rays and cold fusion). He contrasts Natural Science, Social Science, and Anomalistics. He suggests that anomalistics share some of the characteristics that all interdisciplinary search for knowledge has as well as searches for knowledge in fields that do not yet belong to any recognized discipline (p. 15).

Quackery

Quack reasoning reflects pseudoscience. A quack:

1. Promises quick, dramatic, miraculous cures
2. Describes problems and outcomes in vague terms
3. Uses anecdotes and testimonials to support claims
4. Does not incorporate new ideas or evidence; relies on dogma
5. Objects to testing claims
6. Forwards methods and theories that are not consistent with empirical data
7. Influences by a charismatic promoter
8. Claims that effects cannot be tested by usually accepted methods of investigation such as clinical trials
9. Mixes bona fide and bogus evidence to support a favored conclusion (see example, Herbert, 1983; Jarvis, 1987; Porter, 2000)
10. Attacks those who raise questions about claims

Millions of dollars are spent by consumers on worthless products. Millions of dollars are spent on use of magnetic devices to treat pain with no evidence that this is effective (e.g., Winemiller, Robert, Edward, & Scott Harmsen, 2003). Fads are often advanced on the basis of quackery (Jacobson, et al., 2005). Fraud takes advantage of pseudoscience and quackery. Fraud is so extensive in some areas that special organizations have been formed and newsletters are written to help consumers evaluate claims (e.g., *Health Letter* published by Public Citizens Health Research Group) (see also Transparency International website). For every claim that has survived critical tests, there are thousands of bogus claims in advertisements, newscasts, films, TV, newspapers, and professional sources, whose lures are difficult to resist.

Dangers of Scientific Illiteracy Including the History of Science

An accurate understanding of science can help us to distinguish among helpful, trivializing, and bogus uses—between science and pseudoscience. Bogus uses, as seen in pseudoscience, quackery, and fraud may create and maintain views that leave unchanged or decrease the quality of our lives. If we do not understand what science is and are not informed about the history of science, we will fall into the following errors:

1. Assume science can discover final answers and so make inflated claims of knowledge.
2. Assume that there is no way to discover what may be true and what may be false because scientists make errors and have biases and so make inflated claims about what is not possible to discover.
3. Assume that those who question accepted views, for example about mental illness, or the HIV/AIDS connection, or ductal carcinoma in situ (DCIS) are crackpots when indeed they raise well-argued questions (e.g., see Bauer, 2007; Boyle, 2002; Lang, 1998; Welch, 2004).

The history of science highlights that what was thought to be true, such as the cause of ulcers, was often found to be false. It also shows that new ideas are censored and that those proposing them have great difficulty getting a hearing for their views in scientific journals and in the media. Thus, there is science as open criticism, and science as propaganda—for example, censorship of competing well-argued views. Confusing these may have harmful results for clients. Indeed history shows that prestigious journals often rejected the work of scientists who overturned prevailing beliefs about the cause of illnesses (e.g., ulcers), and the effectiveness of a treatment or the harm of a treatment. This should raise a red flag whenever someone gets hot under the collar when asked a question about their views and responds with an ad homimum attack ("He is a crackpot"), rather than addressing the question (arguing ad rem). Bauer (2007) suggests that when we feel a rise of temperature when asked a question, it is a sign that we may be unsure of our grounds because we do not get hot under the collar when someone raises a question about a belief that we can easily support, for example, that the earth is not flat or that the earth revolves around the sun. Think about it.

Antiscience

Antiscience refers to rejection of scientific methods as valid. For example, some people believe that there is no such thing as "privileged knowledge," that some knowledge is more sound than others. Typically, such views are not related to real-life problems such as building safe airplanes and to a candid appraisal of the results of different ways of solving a problem. That is, they are not problem focused, allowing a critical appraisal of competing views. Antiscience is common in academic settings (Gross & Levitt, 1994; Patai & Koertge, 2003) as well as in popular culture (e.g., John Burnham, *How Superstition Won and Science Lost*, 1987). Many people confuse science, scientism, and pseudoscience, resulting in an antiscience stance (see Glossary).

Relativism

Relativists argue that all methods are equally valid in testing claims (e.g., anecdotal reports and experimental studies). Postmodernism is a current form of relativism. It is assumed that knowledge and morality are inherently bounded by or rooted in culture (Gellner, 1992, p. 68). "Knowledge or morality outside of culture is, it claims, a chimera." "...meanings are incommensurate, meanings are culturally constructed, and so all cultures are equal..." (p. 73). Gellner (1992) argues that in the void created, some voices predominate, throwing us back on authority, not a criterion that will protect our rights and allow professionals to be faithful to their code of ethics. If there is no means by which to tell what is accurate and what is not, if all methods are equally effective, the vacuum is filled by an "elite" who are powerful enough to say what is and what is not (Gellner, 1992). He argues that the sole focus on cognitive meaning in postmodernism ignores political and economic influences and "denies or obscures tremendous differences in cognition and technical power" (pp. 71–72). Gellner emphasizes that there are real constraints in society that are obscured within this recent form of relativism (postmodernism) and suggests that such cognitive nihilism constitutes a "travesty of the real role of serious knowledge in our lives" (p. 95). He argues that this view undervalues coercive and economic constraints in society and overvalues conceptual ones. "If we live in a world of meanings, and meanings exhaust the world, where is there any room for coercion through the whip, gun, or hunger?" (p. 63).

Gellner (1992) suggests that postmodernism is an affectation "Those who propound it or defend it against its critics, continue, whenever facing any serous issue in which their real interests are engaged, to act on the non-relativistic assumption that one particular vision is cognitively much more effective than others" (p. 70). Consider for example, the different criteria social workers want their physicians to rely on when confronted with a serious medical problem compared to criteria they say they rely on to select service method offered to clients. They rely on criteria such as intuition, testimonials, and experience with a few cases when making decisions about their clients but want their physicians to rely on the results of controlled experimental studies and demonstrated track record of success based on data collected systematically and regularly when making decisions about a serous medical problem of their own (Gambrill & Gibbs, 2002).

The Costs and Benefits of Critical Thinking and Evidence-Informed Practice and Policy

The benefits of critical thinking and evidence-informed practice and policy include discovering better alternatives, enhancing the accuracy of decisions, and making ethical decisions in which the interests of all involved parties are considered. You will be more likely to discard irrelevant, misleading, and incomplete accounts that may result in harm to clients and to avoid questionable alternatives. You will be more likely to

1. Ask questions with a high payoff.
2. Select valid assessment methods.
3. Accurately describe hoped-for outcomes.
4. Make accurate inferences regarding the causes of client concerns.
5. Choose relevant outcomes to focus on.
6. Select intervention methods that are likely to be successful.
7. Make accurate predictions.
8. Make well-informed decisions at case conferences.
9. Choose effective policies.
10. Distinguish between possible and impossible goals.
11. Enhance and maintain your self-learning skills.

Because you will

1. Recognize and avoid influence by weak appeals.
2. Recognize and avoid influences of propaganda.
3. Identify pseudoscience and quackery.
4. Use tests effectively.
5. Use language effectively.

6. Minimize cognitive biases.
7. Identify personal and environmental obstacles to making informed decisions.
8. Select valid measures of progress.

The process of EBP and related tools such as decision aids and systematic reviews make it easier to critically appraise practice and policy-related claims about what may help clients.

Costs include "ruffling others' feathers," forgoing the comfortable feeling of "certainty," and the time and effort required to consider opposing views (Gambrill, 2005). Critical thinkers often encounter a hostile environment in which careful appraisal of assumptions is viewed as a threat to favored beliefs. Others may turn a seemingly deaf ear to questions such as, What evidence is there that we actually help our clients? Could there be another explanation? It is not in the interests of many groups (e.g., advertisers, politicians, professional organizations) to reveal the lack of evidence for claims made and policies recommended. Personal barriers include lack of education in related knowledge, skills, and attitudes; misunderstandings of scientific reasoning; and misunderstanding about how we learn. Many costs of not thinking critically about practice and policy-related claims and arguments are hidden. By not looking carefully you are not as likely to discover the consequences of inaccurate beliefs or ignored or suppressed knowledge, including harming done in the guise of helping. Curiosity is likely to languish if vague, oversimplified accounts are accepted that obscure the complexity of issues, giving an illusion of understanding but offering no guidelines for helping clients. Unwanted sources of control may continue to be influential if they remain hidden, and clients are less likely to receive effective services.

Decisions about whether or not to think carefully about a topic or problem will be influenced by your history. Has thinking paid off in the past? Some people believe that good intentions protect us from harming others. History shows that they do not. (See, e.g., a history of medicine or psychiatry.) Appeals to good intentions may be combined with extreme relativism—the belief that all methods are equally good because there is no way of discovering what works best. If you believe that little can be done to help a client, you probably won't spend time thinking about how to do so. If you believe you are helpless, you will act helpless. The stark realities that confront professionals and assumptions that nothing can change may result in not thinking carefully and so overlooking opportunities that do exist. However, this starkness is itself a compelling reason to take advantage of critical thinking skills and the related philosophy, process and tools of evidence-informed practice.

Summary

Critical thinking and its reflection in the philosophy and evolving process of evidence-informed practice will help you and your clients to make informed decisions. It will help you to honor ethical obligations to clients to draw on practice and policy-related research and to involve clients as informed participants. It will help you to chose wisely among options—to select those that, compared to others, are most likely to help clients attain outcomes they value. The purpose of social work practice is to help clients achieve outcomes they value, whether clients be individuals, families, organizations, or communities. Helping entails avoiding harming clients. Keeping an eye on your basic purpose—to help clients and avoid harming them is key to EBP and critical thinking. Related knowledge, skills, and values can help you to evaluate the accuracy of claims and arguments, use language effectively, and avoid cognitive biases that interfere with sound decision making.

As a critical thinker, you will spot propaganda pitches, pseudoscience, and quackery more readily. This in turn should help you to offer more effective services to your clients. Both critical thinking and evidence-informed practice involve a careful appraisal of claims, a fairminded consideration of alternative views, and a willingness to change your mind in light of evidence that refutes a cherished position. Both encourage you and your clients to ask "What does this mean? How good is the evidence?" Differences and disagreements are viewed as opportunities to learn—to correct mistaken beliefs. Both value testing as well as guessing. Critical thinking, and its reflection in evidence-informed practice and policy, is especially important in helping professions such as social work where clients confront real-life problems. Related knowledge, skills, and attitudes can help you to avoid misleading directions due to relying on questionable criteria such as appeals to popularity or manner of presentation. It will not necessarily increase your popularity, especially among "true believers," those who accept claims based on faith and authority.

Purpose

Professionals have to make decisions about how to address certain problems. This exercise provides an opportunity for you to review the criteria you use to make decisions.

Background

People in the helping professions often become so involved in the process of helping that they forget to step back and examine the basis for their decisions. This exercise encourages you to examine the criteria you use to make decisions.

Instructions

1. Please answer the questions on the form that follows.
2. Review your answers using the guidelines provided. To get the most out of the exercise, complete the questionnaire before you read the discussion questions.

Your Name _____ Date _____

Course _____ Instructor's Name _____

SITUATION I

Think back to a client (individual, family, group, agency, or community) with whom you have worked. Place a checkmark next to each criterion <u>you used to make your practice decisions.</u> If you have not yet worked with a client, think of the criteria you would probably rely on.

CRITERIA

_____ 1. Your intuition (gut feeling) about what will be effective

_____ 2. What you have heard from other professionals in informal exchanges

_____ 3. Your experience with a few cases

_____ 4. Your demonstrated track record of success based on data you have gathered systematically and regularly

_____ 5. What fits your personal style

_____ 6. What was usually offered at your agency

_____ 7. Self-reports of other clients about what was helpful

_____ 8. Results of controlled experimental studies (data that show that a method is helpful)*

_____ 9. What you are most familiar with

_____ 10. What you know by critically reading professional literature

_____

*Controlled experimental studies involve the random assignment of people to a group receiving a treatment method and one not receiving the treatment.

SITUATION 2

Imagine that you have a potentially serious medical problem, and you seek help from a physician to examine treatment options. Place a check mark next to each criterion <u>you would like your physician to rely on</u> when he or she makes recommendations about your treatment.

CRITERIA

_____ 1. The physician's intuition (gut feeling) that a method will work

_____ 2. What he or she has heard from other physicians in informal exchanges

_____ 3. The physician's experience with a few cases

_____ 4. The physician's demonstrated track record of success based on data he or she has gathered systematically and regularly

_____ 5. What fits his or her personal style

_____ 6. What is usually offered at the clinic

_____ 7. Self-reports of patients about what was helpful

_____ 8. Results of controlled experimental studies (data that show that a method is helpful)

_____ 9. What the physician is most familiar with

_____ 10. What the physician has learned by critically reading professional literature

SITUATION 3

Think back to a client (individual, family, group, agency, or community) with whom you have worked. Place a checkmark next to each criterion <u>you would like to use ideally</u> to make practice decisions. If you have not yet worked with a client, think of the criteria you would ideally like to rely on.

CRITERIA

_____ 1. Your intuition (gut feeling) about what will be effective

_____ 2. What you have heard from other professionals in informal exchanges

_____ 3. Your experience with a few cases

_____ 4. Your demonstrated track record of success based on data you have gathered systematically and regularly

_____ 5. What fits your personal style

_____ 6. What was usually offered at your agency

_____ 7. Self-reports of other clients about what was helpful

_____ 8. Results of controlled experimental studies (data that show that a method is helpful

_____ 9. What you are most familiar with

_____ 10. What you know by critically reading professional literature

SCORES   *Your instructor will provide scoring instructions.*
Situation 1 (Your Actual Criteria):
Situation 2 (Physician's Criteria):
Situation 3 (Your Ideal Criteria):

DISCUSSION

If you scored five to ten points, you are basing your decisions on criteria likely to result in a well-reasoned judgment (results from controlled experimental studies, systematically collected data, and critical reading). If you scored below two in any of the situations, you are willing to base decisions on criteria that may result in selecting ineffective or harmful methods.

When making decisions, professionals often use different criteria in different situations. For instance, they may think more carefully in situations in which the potential consequences of their choices matter more to them personally (e.g., a health matter). Research on critical thinking shows that lack of generalization is a key problem; that is, people may use critical thinking skills in some situations but not in others.

FOLLOW-UP QUESTIONS

Do your choices differ in these situations? If so, how? Why do you think they differ? If you scored below two on Situation 1 and two or more on Situation 2, you may not believe that what's good for the goose is good for the gander. Your approach may be "science for you and art for them." If you scored below 2 in Situations 2 and 3, you may be prone to disregard sound evidence generally.

_____

_____

_____

When is intuition (your "gut reaction") a sound guide to making decisions about what practices or policies to recommend? When is it not? (See for example Gigerenzer, 2007, 2008; Hogarth, 2001; Kahneman, 2003).

_____

_____

_____

EXERCISE 2   REVIEWING YOUR BELIEFS ABOUT KNOWLEDGE

Purpose

This exercise provides an opportunity to review your beliefs about knowledge (what it is and how it can be obtained).

Background

All professionals make decisions. These decisions reflect their underlying beliefs about what can be known and how it can be known. These beliefs influence how they evaluate claims concerning how best to help clients. Many exercises in this workbook concern criteria for evaluating claims. Beliefs about knowledge that can get in the way of critically evaluating claims are described in this exercise.

Instructions

1. Please answer the questions by circling the response that most accurately reflects your view (A = Agree; D = Disagree; N = No opinion). Write a brief explanation below each statement to explain why you circled the response you did.
2. Compare your replies with those provided by your instructor.

Your Name _____ Date _____

Course _____ Instructor's Name _____

A = Agree   **D** = Disagree   **N** = No Opinion

1.   Since we can't know anything for sure, we really don't know anything.   **A   D   N**

2.   Since our beliefs influence what we see, we can't gather accurate knowledge about our world.   **A   D   N**

3.   There are things we just can't know.   **A   D   N**

Note: Items 3–8 are based on W. Gray (1991), Thinking critically about new age ideas. Belmont, Calif.: Wadsworth.

4.   It's good not to be too skeptical because anything is possible.   **A   D   N**

5.   We can't be certain of anything.   **A   D   N**

6.   Everything is relative. All ways of "knowing" are equally true.   **A   D   N**

7.   Scientists/researchers don't know everything.   **A   D   N**

8.   Some things can't be demonstrated scientifically.   **A   D   N**

9.   Trying to measure client outcome dehumanizes clients,
        reducing them to the status of a laboratory rat.   **A   D   N**

10. Scientific reasoning and data are of no value in planning social policy and social action.

        A   D   N

11. Science is a way of thinking developed by white, male, Western Europeans. It doesn't apply to other people and cultures.

        A   D   N

SCORE _____ Your instructor will provide scoring instructions.

FOLLOW-UP QUESTIONS

1. Imagine a practitioner who agrees with your instructor's suggested answers and reasons and another who does not. Which one would do the least harm to clients? Why?

_____

_____

_____

_____

2. Which one would most likely help clients? Why?

_____

_____

_____

_____

PART 2
Recognizing Propaganda in Human-Services Advertising: The Importance of Questioning Claims

Both rhetoric and propaganda are used to persuade and influence others. These differ in vital ways as shown in Box 2.1. *Propaganda can be defined as encouraging actions and beliefs with the least thought possible* (Ellul, 1965). Jowett and O'Donnell (2006) define propaganda as "deliberate and systematic efforts to influence perceptions, alter thoughts, and influence behavior to achieve aims valued by propagandists."

> …Propaganda is most vicious not when it angers but when it ingratiates itself through government programs that fit our desires or world views, through research or religion that supplies pleasing answers, through news that captures our interest, through educational materials that promise utopia, and through pleasurable films, TV, sports, and art.…the chief problem of propaganda is its ability to be simultaneously subtle and seductive—and to grow in a political environment of neutralized speakers and disempowered communities (Sproule, 1994, p. 327).

Propaganda is one-sided. Slick emotional appeals can block critical thinking and related evidence-informed decisions about any subject. Many advertisements that encourage practitioners to use a particular method

Box 2.1   Rhetoric and Propaganda: What's the Difference

Rhetoric	Issues Relevant to Democratic Process	Propaganda
Participant in decision making; person worthy of equal respect	1. Other (Audience)	Target or recipient; instrument of propagandist's will
Significant and informed	2. Nature of Choice	Limited because not fully informed
Thinking, reasoned	3. Desired Response	Reactionary; thinking response is short-circuited
Effective and ethical appeals Reason is primary, supported with both logic and imagination to appeal to emotions	4. Appropriate Means Use of reason Use of emotion Use of imagination	Most effective appeals Emotional appeals designed imaginatively to produce the quickest action
Socially constructed; constituted and reconstituted in open debate	5. Determining Contingent "Truth"	Determined by primary goal; determined by propagandist; often irrelevant or glossed
Coparticipant in decision making; seeks to engage others; post-Copernican; often less powerful	6. Self (Communicator)	More important than others; above, greater; pre-Copernican; often more powerful

Source: Bennett, B. S. & O'Rourke, S. P. (2006). A prolegomenon to the future study of rhetoric and propaganda: Critical foundations. In G. S. Jowett & V. O'Donnell (Eds.), *Readings in propaganda and persuasion: New and classic essays* (pp. 51–71). Thousand Oaks: Sage.

fit this definition. Some medical educators are so concerned about the influence of pitches by pharmaceutical companies on medical students that courses are included designed to help students avoid these influences (Wilkes & Hoffman, 2001; Wofford & Ohl, 2005). Content analysis of television direct-to-consumer advertising shows that these provide little information of an educational nature and oversell the benefits of drugs in ways that conflict with the promotion of health (Frosch, Krueger, Hornik, Cronbolm, and Barg, (2007). Stange (2007) argues that DTC ads manipulate the patient's agenda and take time away from the clinician's concerns regarding the patient, among other negative consequences. Advertisements may fail to reveal risk and promote false claims regarding benefits (Eisenberg & Wells, 2008) and create needless worry (Hadler, 2008). An engaging and polished presentation by a charismatic speaker may lure us into believing that someone is deeply learned in a subject when indeed they are not as illustrated by Naftulin, Ware, and Donnelly (1973) over a quarter of a century ago. Their study showed that even experienced educators "can be seduced into feeling satisfied that they had learned despite irrelevant, conflicting, and meaningless content conveyed by the lecturer" (p. 630). The authors concluded that "student satisfaction with learning may represent little more than the illusion of having learned" (p. 630). Many professional conferences present ideal conditions for the Dr. Fox Effect: The audience is exposed only once to a speech, the audience expects to be entertained, and the audience will not be evaluated on mastery of content in the speech. Student evaluations of their teachers may be based more on their style or charisma than on how accurately they present course content (see e.g., Ambady, & Rosenthal, 1993; Williams & Ceci, 1997).

Anyone who tries to persuade via propaganda rather than rhetoric to get you to adopt a method may encourage decisions that harm rather than help clients (see Boxes 2.1 and 2.2). Learning how to avoid beliefs and actions encouraged by propaganda ploys, such as emotional appeals, is a vital step in learning to think critically. In your role as practitioner, you face a situation analogous to that of Odysseus, a character in Greek mythology, who had to guide his ship past the treacherous sirens' song. He was forewarned that the sirens song was so seductive that anyone who heard it would be lured to a reef, where the ship would strike and all would drown. Odysseus put wax in his crew's ears so they couldn't hear the sirens' song, but he had them chain him to the mast so that he would hear it but not take over the helm and steer the ship toward the sirens and the reef. As a practitioner, you must steer a course toward effective methods while avoiding the sirens' call of propaganda pitches that could lead you to choose harmful or ineffective methods. Here is an example of reliance on reasoned judgments: An instructor searches for research regarding the effectiveness of psychological debriefing as a way to decrease post-traumatic stress disorder. He consults the Cochrane database and locates a systematic review of randomized controlled trials (Rose, Bisson, & Wessely, 2004). This review indicates that this intervention is not effective. Indeed, there is some evidence that it is harmful. The instructor shares the results of this review with her students.

Box 2.2   Ten Tips for the Pharmaceutical Industry: How to Present Your Product in the Best Light

- Think up a plausible physiological mechanism why the drug works and become slick at presenting it. Preferably, find a surrogate end point that is heavily influenced by the drug, though it may not be strictly valid.

- When designing clinical trials, select a patient population, clinical features, and trial length that reflect the maximum possible response to the drug.

- If possible, compare your product only with placebos. If you must compare it with a competitor, make sure the latter is given at subtherapeutic dose.

- Include the results of pilot studies in the figures for definitive studies ("Russian doll publication"), so it looks like more patients have been randomized than is actually the case.

- Omit mention of any trial that had a fatality or serious adverse drug reaction in the treatment group. If possible, don't publish such studies.

- Get your graphics department to maximize the visual impact of your message. It helps not to label the axes of graphs or say whether scales are linear or logarithmic. Make sure you do not show individual patient data or confidence intervals.

- Become master of the hanging comparative ("better" but better than what?).

- Invert the standard hierarchy of evidence so that anecdote takes precedence over randomized trials and meta-analyses.

- Name at least three local opinion leaders who use the drug and offer "starter packs" for the doctor to try.

- Present a "cost-effectiveness" analysis that shows that your product, even though more expensive than its competitor, "actually works out cheaper."

Source: Greenhalgh, T. (2006). *How to read a paper: The basics of evidence-based medicine* (3rd. ed.) (p. 91). Malden, MA: Blackwell.

And, we must remember that good intentions do not ensure good results. Many books have documented the harmful effects from efforts intended to help clients (e.g., Breggin, 1991; Jacobson, Foxx, & Mulick, 2005; Ofshe & Watters, 1994; Scull, 2005; Sharpe & Faden, 1998; Valenstein, 1986; Welch, 2004). In all professions, sincere efforts to help can result in harm as shown by avoidable errors or lapses related to the tens of thousands of adverse events in hospitals (see for example Kohn, Corrigan, & Donaldson, 2000). Medication prescribed to alter abnormal brain states assumed to be related to "mental illness" may create such states (Moncrieff, & Cohen, 2006). Medication errors harm 1.5 million people a year and consume billions of dollars annually (Aspden, Wolcott, Bootman, & Cronenwett, 2007 [*Preventing Medication Errors*]). Approximately 10,000 babies were blinded as a result of giving oxygen at birth, resulting in Retrolental fibroplasias (Silverman, 1980). No one cared enough to critically test whether this treatment did more harm than good. Follow-up studies of a program designed to decrease delinquency found that it increased related behaviors (Mc Cord, 2003).

Consider also efforts to help mentally impaired aged living in the community (Blenkner, Bloom, & Nielsen, 1971). Intensive social casework was offered to a sample of the aged in the Cleveland area. Four experienced social workers with master's degrees were hired and instructed to "Do or get others to do, whatever is necessary to meet the needs of the situation" (p. 489). Intensive services included "financial assistance, medical evaluation, psychiatric consultation, legal consultation, fiduciary and guardianship services, home aide and other home help services, nursing consultation and evaluation, and placement in a protective setting" (p. 489). During a year of intensive helping, the four caseworkers conducted 2421 personal casework interviews with 76 aged persons and their helpers (an average of 31.8 interviews per participant). At the end of the demonstration year, the death rate for clients in the intensive treatment group was 25%; the death rate in the control group was 18%. How could this be? It turned out that the social workers in the treated group had relocated 34% of their clients to nursing homes, while only 20% of clients in the control group were relocated. The researchers concluded that relocation stressed their aged clients. Had Blenkner and her colleagues relied purely on their emotions and impressions, deciding not to record and analyze data about the death rate, they would never have known they were doing harm (for critiques of this study and replies to them, see Berger & Piliavin, 1976; Fischer & Hudson, 1976). These examples illustrate that the best of intentions, the sincerest wishes to do good, the most well-meaning of purposes do not ensure good results. To avoid being taken in, watch for the following:

1. Always keep in mind the central questions: What conclusion does the material/person want me to accept? What kind of evidence is presented in support of that argument? How good is the evidence? Is all related evidence presented, or is some hidden such as clinical trials of a drug showing harm?
2. Be aware of emotional appeals such as a strikingly attractive person, background music to set a mood, or a pleasant or shocking setting in which the argument is presented.

3. Keep in mind that editors can alter material to support favored views. For example, they may juxtapose events to suggest a causal relationship and include only material that supports a given mood or conclusion.

4. Beware of the style of presentation, including the presenter's apparent sincerity, which suggests a valid belief that the treatment method works; the fluid ease of a well-prepared presentation, which supports confidence in the conclusion; the presenter's attempts to appear similar to the audience; and the use of anecdotes and humor that entertain but do not inform.

5. Beware of the effect of the presenter's status on the audience; degrees and titles (e.g., professor, MD, MSW, RN), affiliations with organizations familiar to the audience, favorable introduction by someone familiar to us.

6. Keep in mind the following hierarchy, from most to least informative regarding claims of effectiveness. (Other kinds of questions may require other research methods.)

   • A systematic review or meta-analysis of well-designed randomized controlled experiments in which subjects are randomly assigned to different treatments or to a treatment and a control group (see Cochrane and Campbell Libraries)
   • Replicated randomized controlled trials (RCTs)
   • A single well-designed RCT
   • Multiple experimental single-case designs
   • Pre-, post-group designs that do not involve random assignment
   • A number of single-subject designs that involve repeated measures over baseline and intervention
   • Experience with a client where clearly defined outcomes have been measured before and after intervention
   • Anecdotal reports from a client
   • Opinions of experts

About the Exercises

Learning to think critically requires practice. Consequently, the exercises in Part 2 use examples to demonstrate emotional and other misleading appeals in human-service advertisements, professional conferences, and the media. You will view these examples, then respond to the corresponding exercise in the Workbook. Exercise 3 demonstrates the characteristics of human-service advertisements. You will watch a presentation and evaluate what you have seen on a form. In Exercise 4, you will view and think about a widely aired television special about the Juvenile Awareness Program at Rahway Prison in New Jersey. We recommend that you carefully follow your instructor's suggestions for completing exercises. Some instructors may want you to see this section only *after* you have reacted to videotaped material. Others may want you to read about each exercise *before* you see the videotapes.

Purpose

1. To demonstrate what health and human-services advertisements look like.
2. To increase your skills in recognizing weak appeals.

Background

Most people are somewhat skeptical about advertisements that appear on the Internet, in newspapers, and on television. Such advertisements use various emotional appeals and arguments to encourage you to buy all kinds of things: Buy this product and a lush growth of hair will sprout thickly like a rug on your head. If you're over 60, take these pills, and you'll leap around like a kid again. Dab a bit of this scent behind your years, and attractive people will smile at you and want to spend time with you. Buy this washing machine and your maintenance worries are over. Rank (1982, p. 147) has identified five features of advertising:

- *Attention Getting*: physically (visual images, lighting, sound) and emotionally (words and images with strong emotional associations).
- *Confidence Building*: establishing trust by stating that you should believe the expert because he or she is sincere and has good intentions.
- *Desire Stimulating*: The pleasure to be gained, the pain to be avoided, the problem solved. This is the main selling point as to why one should buy the idea or product.
- *Urgency Stressing*: the encouragement to act now to avoid problems later-to act before it is too late. Advertising that utilizes this approach is often called the "hard" sell; that which does not is a "soft" sell. Urgency stressing is common but not universal to all advertising.
- *Response Seeking*: Trying to learn if the advertisement worked, if the product was bought, if the customer acted in some way desired by the advertiser.

Advertising works—that is why billions of dollars are spent on advertisements. It is one thing for people to spend a few dollars on products that they may not need or that will not deliver what they promise, quite another for professionals to make decisions based on propagandistic appeals. If we fall for propaganda, clients may be harmed rather than helped. Human-services advertisements are prepared by organizations or individuals offering a service or treatment and distributed through brochures, videotapes, films, CDs, audiotapes, the Internet, videodiscs to encourage professionals and/or potential clients to use a service without presenting any evidence that the service is effective in achieving the outcomes promised (e.g., an evaluation study, an experimental study, or a reference to studies evaluating the service), or presenting survey data to support generalizations made about clients' responses. Emotions, rather than data, are appealed to. Advertisements present only the positives. They do not refer to counterevidence, and they tend to ignore or oversimplify complex issues. Advertisers set out in a deliberate way to influence the actions of service providers (e.g., refer clients to a given treatment; pay for a certain kind of training or buy an assessment tool such as an anatomically correct doll). Profit is a key motive in human service advertisements. Although a concern for profit is not incompatible with truthful accounts, advertising generally avoids giving data and arguments pro and con. Most advertisements do not present any evidence regarding the effectiveness of the advertised products (such evidence may or may not be available), but instead appeal to our emotions. So too do researchers often forward inflated claims (see, e.g., Rubin & Parrish, 2007). Terms such as "well-established"and "empirically validated" convey a certainty that cannot be had.

Human service advertisements that rely on emotional appeals tend to have the following features:

1. They involve persons of status, who may sincerely believe in a program and argue that the method works but do not describe critical tests of claims.
2. The presentation is well rehearsed and smooth, relying on style, not evidence, to support its claims.
3. The presentation relies heavily on visual and auditory images to lull the audience into not asking questions about whether the method works.

4. The presentation presents only one side of an argument, never referring to evidence that the program is ineffective or might do harm.
5. The presentation often relies on common fallacies, for example, testimonials (statements by those who claim to have been helped by the method) and case examples (descriptions of individual cases that supposedly represent the client population that has benefited from the treatment). You will learn more about fallacies later in this workbook.

In your area, there are probably various groups of practitioners, hospitals, and organizations that advertise their programs. They may create websites with promotional material and send out promotional CDs. Professional journals contain full-page advertisements. Promotional television programs advertise weight loss, study skills, smoking cessation, and other types of programs. Often, professional conferences include presentations that meet the criteria for an advertisement: A charismatic, well-known person describes a treatment method, presents it in an entertaining way, and does not raise the issue of effectiveness. Your instructor may use promotional material from Rogers Memorial Hospital, in Oconomow, Wisconsin, or direct you to other sources of human service advertisements.

Instructions

1. Watch the presentation.
2. Answer the questions on the Human-Services Advertisement Spotting Form.

Practice Exercise 3   Human-Services Advertisement Spotting Form

Your Name _____ Date _____

Course _____ Instructor's Name _____

Please answer the following questions by circling your responses. The presentation...

1.	Argued that some form of treatment or intervention works.	YES NO
2.	Gave data or measures of outcome (i.e., figures based on an evaluation study involving relevant outcome measures and random assignment of clients to different groups to determine if the program works).	YES NO
3.	Presented testimonials as evidence (testimonials are statements by those who claim to have been helped by a program).	YES NO
4.	Appealed to your emotions (e.g., sympathy, fear, anger) as a persuasive tactic. Such appeals may include music or strikingly attractive or unattractive people and/or locations.	YES NO
5.	Presented case examples as evidence (e.g., a professional describes or Shows in detail what went on in the treatment and how the client responded.	YES NO
6.	Mentioned the possibility of harmful (iatrogenic) effects of the treatment.	YES NO
7.	Presented evidence for and against the use of the program.	YES NO

8. Was presented by a speaker whose presentation and manner was well rehearsed, smooth, polished, and attractive.   YES   NO

9. Was presented by a well-known person or a person of high status, implying that the claim of treatment effectiveness is true because this high-status person says it is.   YES   NO

10. Encouraged you to think carefully about the effectiveness of the method before referring clients to it.   YES   NO

Score: *Your instructor will provide scoring instructions.* Score: _____

1. Which human-service advertisement features does the promotional material demonstrate?

_____

_____

EXERCISE 4 DOES SCARING YOUTH HELP THEM "GO STRAIGHT"?: APPLYING PRINCIPLES OF REASONING, DECISION MAKING, AND EVALUATION

Purpose

To be learned as you do the exercise.

Background

The Juvenile Awareness Program at Rahway Prison in New Jersey has served as a model for many similar programs. The program is run by Lifers, who are inmates serving a life sentence. The program is intended to prevent delinquency.

Instructions

1. View and take notes on the example.
2. Following this, read the situation that follows, then record your answers to the three questions about the material in "Scared Straight." You may use one of the pieces of paper that accompany this exercise for your notes; the other is for your answer to three questions below. Please write clearly.

Your Name _____ Date _____

Course _____ Instructor's Name _____

SITUATION

Assume that you have taken a job as a probation-parole officer working with juvenile clients who are adjudicated by a local juvenile court. Your supervisor has asked you to view this material and to suggest whether juveniles served by your agency, should participate in a program like the one in "Scared Straight."

1.   What is the one central conclusion that the makers of "Scared Straight" would have you draw regarding the Juvenile Awareness Program? (List the *one* major conclusion below.)

_____

_____

_____

_____

_____

2.   Would you, based purely on what you have seen, recommend   YES   NO
     that your agency try such a program with its clients? (Circle one.)

3.   Please explain your answer to Question 2.

_____

_____

_____

_____

_____

_____

_____

_____

_____

_____

_____

_____

_____

_____

_____

SCORE _____. Your instructor will provide scoring instructions.

FOLLOW-UP QUESTIONS

1. What is the dominant form of evidence in the "Scared Straight" material?

    _____

    _____

    _____

2. Why did you respond as you did to the emotional argument in the "Scared Straight" material?

    _____

    _____

    _____

3. Do you think the Juvenile Awareness Program might produce harmful effects on juveniles?

    _____

    _____

    _____

4. Is this measure a valid test of critical thinking? (e.g., see Gibbs, Gambrill, Blakemore, Begun, Keniston, Peden, et al., 1995) Please explain your answers.

    _____

    _____

    _____

    _____

    _____

    _____

    _____

    _____

PART 3
Fallacies and Pitfalls in Professional Decision Making: What They Are and How to Avoid Them

How you think about practice and policy decisions affects the quality of services clients receive. Let's say you attend a conference to learn about a new method for helping clients, and the presenter says that you should adopt the method because it is new. Would that be sufficient grounds to use the method? What if the presenter described in detail a few clients who had been helped by the method, and had a few clients describe their successful experiences with it? Would you use the method? Or, let's say that when staff who manage a refuge for battered women test residents' self-esteem before and after residents participate in a support group, they find that the women score higher after taking part in the support group. Can we assume that the support group caused an increase in residents' self-esteem? What if staff in an interdisciplinary team decides that a child requires special education services? The group's leader encourages the group to arrive at a unanimous decision. Can we assume that because none of the participants raised objections that all major evidence and relevant arguments regarding placement have been heard?

Each of these situations represents a potential for error in reasoning about practice. In the first, the presenter encourages acceptance of

Fallacy Spotting in Professional Contexts (Exercise 10) asks you to select an example of fallacious reasoning, quote its source, and explain the fallacy. Exercise 11 describes indicators of group think and offers practice opportunities in detecting and avoiding them.

We hope that these exercises will help you to use sound reasoning on the job. All the exercises try to bridge the gap between critical thinking and practice by involving you in *doing* something. Although we encourage you to have fun with the exercises, we also ask you to remember that the kinds of decisions involved in the vignettes are serious business such as deciding whether a neurosurgeon should refer a client with glioblastoma (fast-acting brain tumor) to a trial of GLI-238 (a form of gene therapy); whether sexually abused siblings should be placed for adoption in the same home or in homes distant from each other; whether a speech therapist working with a child with cerebral palsy who cannot speak should use a particular augmentative procedure (computer, signing, picture pointing) to help the child; and so on.

Purpose

1. To test your skill in identifying common practice fallacies
2. To help you to identify fallacies in reasoning about practice

Background

The Professional Thinking Form evaluates your skill in spotting fallacies that cloud thinking in the helping professions. Each of its twenty-five vignettes describes an example of thinking in practice. Some involve a fallacy; others do not. Vignettes include examples of practice decisions related to individuals, families, groups, and communities in various areas including health, mental health, child welfare, chemical dependency, and research.

Instructions

Each situation describes something that you may encounter in practice.

1. Consider each situation from the standpoint of critical, analytical, scientific thinking.
2. In the space provided, write brief responses, as follows:

    a. If an item is objectionable from a critical standpoint, then write a statement that describes what is wrong with it. Items may or may not contain an error in thinking.
    b. If you cannot make up your mind on one, then mark it with a question mark (?), but leave none blank.
    c. If you are satisfied with the item as it stands, then mark it "OK."

   Please write your main point(s) as concisely as possible. The form takes about thirty minutes to complete.

Practice Exercise 5   The Professional Thinking Form*
By Leonard Gibbs and Joan Werner

Your Name _____ Date _____

Course _____ Instructor's Name _____

SITUATIONS FROM PRACTICE

1. "Did you attend the workshop on strategic family therapy? Marian Steinberg is an excellent
    speaker, and her presentation was so convincing! She treated everyone in the audience like
    colleagues. She got the whole audience involved in a family sculpture, and she is such a
    warm person. I must use her methods with my clients."

_____

_____

_____

_____

_____

_____

2. "Have you heard of thrombolytics [clot-dissolving medications] being given immediately
    after cerebrovascular accident [stroke]? It's a new treatment that seems to minimize the
    amount of damage done by the stroke, if the medication is given soon enough. The treatment
    has just been tried, with promising results. You ought to try it with your patients."

_____

_____

* Revised by Leonard Gibbs and Joan Stehle-Werner (School of Nursing, University of Wisconsin-Eau Claire) and
adapted from L. Gibbs (1991), *Scientific Reasoning for Social Workers* (New York: Macmillan), pp. 54–59, 274–278.

8. "Dr. Trevor H. Noland has degrees from Harvard, MIT, and Stanford. He has held the prestigious Helms Chair of Human Service Studies for ten years. He has been director of psychiatry departments in three universities and has served as a consultant to the National Institute of Mental Health. His stature supports the truth of his ideas in his book on psychotherapy."

9. "I think that we need to exercise caution when we make judgments that our efforts are truly helping clients. Other possible reasons may account for change. Perhaps people just mature. They may get help from some other source. Maybe they get better simply because they expect to get better."

10. At a professional conference, a colleague leans over to you and whispers in your ear, "I don't understand how anyone could accept an opinion from Ms. Washington. Just look at her. Her hair is unkempt. How can we accept an idea from someone who looks like a fugitive from a mental hospital?"

_____

_____

_____

_____

_____

_____

11. A director of an evaluation-research consulting firm was overheard saying, "We conduct studies for agencies to determine how effective their programs are. We never agree to do an evaluation unless we are sure we can produce positive results."

_____

_____

_____

_____

_____

_____

12. Here is a statement made by an agency supervisor to a colleague: "Michelle is one of the most difficult staff members to deal with. I asked her to decide between supporting either nutritional or health-care programs to meet the needs of the elderly here in Dane County. She responded that she needed some time to get evidence to study the matter. She said that there may be other alternatives for our resources. As I see it, there are only two ways to go on this issue."

_____

_____

_____

_____

_____

_____

_____

13. At a professional conference, Dr. McDonald asked a family who had participated in "Strategic Family Therapy" to tell the audience how the method worked for them. The husband said to the audience, "Frankly, I didn't think we had a prayer of saving our marriage. When my wife and I made our first appointment with Dr. McDonald, I thought we would go through the motions of seeing a counselor, and we would get a divorce. But as Dr. McDonald requested, my wife and I brought our 13-year-old, David, and our 11-year-old, Emily, with us to counseling. All of us have been surprised, to say the least, by Dr. McDonald's approach. Instead of engaging in a lot of deep, dark discussions, we do exercises as a family. Last time we were requested to go on a treasure hunt with me as a leader for the hunt. Dr. McDonald's exercises have been fun to do. His exercises teach us about our family system. The methods have really helped us, and I highly recommend them to you."

_____

_____

_____

_____

_____

14. Shortly after the city planners announced their intent to build a vocational training facility, they were deluged with phone calls and letters from angry citizens protesting the plan. Planners were surprised that the whole community opposed the plan so strongly.

_____

_____

_____

_____

15. "Most likely this client is depressed."

16. Joe Armejo is a typical war veteran, like most of the clients we see at the Veterans Administration. At seventeen, he entered the marines, went through his basic training, and then "all hell broke loose," as he tells it: "One day I was home on leave riding around with my girl; the next, I was headed for Iraq." Joe served in Iraq sixteen months, often in combat, with a small unit. Among those in his unit, he lost two close buddies, one whose family he still contacts. After being discharged, Joe drifted from job to job, seemed unable to form a lasting relationship with a woman, and descended into an alcohol addiction that was so deep, "I just reached up and pulled the whole world down on my head." Joe occasionally encountered counselors, but he never opened up to them-not until he joined an Iraq War veterans' group. After six months of weekly visits, Joe began to turn his life around. He got and held a job, and he has been dating the same woman for a while now. His dramatic change is typical of men who join such groups.

17. An interviewer asks the following question: "Will you be able to drive yourself to the hospital weekly and eat without dentures until January 1st?"

_____

_____

_____

_____

_____

_____

18. An interviewer asks a female victim of domestic abuse the following question: "You don't want to stay in a home with a violent wife-beater, do you?"

_____

_____

_____

_____

_____

_____

19. "Electroconvulsive (shock) therapy is the most effective treatment for psychotic depression."

_____

_____

_____

_____

_____

_____

20. "One way of describing 'progress' in clients seeking independence from their families is to assess their gradual increase in independence from their families."

_____

_____

_____

_____

_____

_____

21. "The effectiveness of our program in family therapy is well documented. Before families enter treatment, we have them fill out a Family Adjustment Rating Scale, which has a Cronbach's alpha reliability of .98 and is validly associated with indices of sexual adjustment and marital communication. After treatment, we have family members fill out the Scale again. Statistically significant improvement in these scores after family therapy proves that our program is effective."

_____

_____

_____

_____

_____

22. A psychologist remarks to a client, "It is extremely difficult to work with people who have adolescent adjustment reactions. Adolescents have not had sufficient experience to reality test. This is why those who work with adolescents use existential and reality-oriented approaches."

_____

_____

_____

_____

23. Don Jaszewski, a teacher at Parkview Elementary School, administered the Rosenberg Self-Concept Scale to all 100 students in the schools fifth grade. For the ten students who scored lowest on the test, Don designed a special program to raise their self-esteem. All ten participated in a weekly rap session, read materials designed to foster self-acceptance and self-assurance, and saw Don individually at frequent intervals during the academic year. When Don again administered the Rosenberg Self-Concept Scale at the end of the program, he was pleased to note the participants' statistically significant improvement from their pretreatment scores. In fact, Don noted that seven of the ten students in his program scored almost average this time. Because of this evidence, Don urged the school administration to offer his program in the future.

24. Mr. Rasmussen, director of the Regional Alcoholic Rehabilitation Clinic, is proud of his treatment facility's success rate. The clinic draws clients who are usually leading citizens in the area and whose insurance companies are willing to pay premium prices for such treatment. Mr. Rasmussen points out proudly that 75% of those who complete this treatment, according to a valid and reliable survey done by an unbiased consulting group, abstain completely from alcohol during the six months following treatment. In contrast, the same consulting firm reports that alcoholics who complete treatment at a local halfway house for unemployed men have a 30% abstinence rate for the six months after their treatment. Mr. Rasmussen says, "The difference between 75% and 30% cannot be ignored. It is obvious that our clinic's multidisciplinary team and intensive case-by-case treatment are producing better results than those at the halfway house."

_____

_____

_____

_____

_____

_____

25. With help from a noted researcher, the Cree County Social Service Department has developed a screening test for families to identify potential child abusers. Experience with this test in the Cree County School District has shown that, among confirmed abusers who took the test, the result was positive (indicating abuse) for 95% of couples who abused their child within the previous year (sensitivity). Also, among nonabusers the test results were negative (indicating no abuse) for 95% (specificity). Cree County records show that abuse occurs in 3 of 100 families (prevalence rate of 3%) in the Cree County School District. County Social Service Department workers note that the Donohue family tested positive (indicating abuse). They conclude that the Donohue family has a 95% chance that they will abuse their child.

Do you agree with the County Social Service Department's estimate? If not, what is the probability that the Donohue family will abuse their child?

_____

_____

_____

_____

_____

_____

SCORE   Your instructor will provide scoring instructions.

_____

FOLLOW-UP QUESTION

Do any of the Professional Thinking Form's situations reflect real situations particularly well? Which one(s)?

_____

_____

_____

_____

_____

_____

_____

The Reasoning-in-Practice Games

Purpose

1. To have some fun
2. To learn how to identify common fallacies or pitfalls related to making practice and policy decisions
3. To learn how to avoid common fallacies and what countermeasures can be taken
4. To foster more effective interdisciplinary teams by teaching principles of sound reasoning

Background

A fallacy is an error in reasoning. Many fallacies are so common they have their own names; some have been recognized for so long (thousands of years) that they have Latin names. For example, ad hominem refers to attacking a person rather than critically examining their argument. Much has been written about fallacies by those who teach critical thinking (Browne & Keeley, 2006; Chaffee, 2006; Damer, 1995; Gambrill, 2005; Engel, 1994; Halpern, 2003; Paul & Elder, 2004; Thouless, 1974; Tindale, 2007; Walton, 1995). This workbook focuses on how to spot fallacies that occur in practice-related situations. Fallacies about practice are called practitioners' fallacies, or pitfalls in reasoning about practice. Merely knowing about fallacies or pitfalls may not help you to avoid them. We have developed Reasoning-in-Practice Games to engage you actively in spotting, defining, and countering fallacies. The fallacies in Game A (Common Practice Fallacies) are grouped together because they are possibly the most universal and deceptive. Many involve selective attention or partiality in using evidence (e.g., case example, testimonial, focusing only on successes). Those in Game B (Group and Interpersonal Dynamics) describe fallacies that often occur in task groups, committees, and agency politics. Additional sources of error are illustrated in Game C (Cognitive Biases in Practice), which draw on research about judgments and decision making in psychology and other helping professions. Many others could be added to those described in these games such as the ecological fallacy (assuming what is true for a group is true for an individual), and biases created by encouraging emotional reasoning (e.g., creating anger or empathy). Sources of bias on clinical decisions include gender, ethnicity, racial, and social class biases (see Garb, 1998; Lambert, 2004). Questions such as "How good is the evidence?" are key tools in avoiding the influence of fallacies and biases described in Part 3.

General Instructions for Games A, B, and C

Please read these general instructions before doing Exercises 6 to 8.

1. Read the Definitions section for the game you want to play. Study the definitions for about one hour. By doing this, you will get the most from the game. Imagine how the fallacy and its countermeasures might apply to your clients and to your work with fellow professionals. Most vignettes depict just one fallacy. We hope that your active participation, the realistic vignettes, and the immediate feedback will help you learn critical-thinking skills and transfer them to your work. These vivid examples may help you to recall the principles involved when you encounter similar situations.

This game works best with four to six participants in a group. We recommend that as many persons as possible get a chance to read aloud and act out parts in starred (*) vignettes. The vignettes can be made into individual cards by copying the workbook pages onto card stock and then cutting them apart.

2. Pick a moderator from the class to serve as referee, time keeper, and answer reader. (Your instructor may elect to be moderator). Prior to the game, the moderator makes sure that all groups agree on some small reward(s) (actual or symbolic) to be awarded to the most successful group. Possible incentives include help with a task. For example the low scorers give the high scorers ten minutes of help with a simple task they agree on. The high scorers give the low scorers five minutes of help with a task they agree on, for example reviewing fallacy definitions.

    During the game, the moderator needs (1) a watch or timer that counts seconds, (2) access to the game's answer key in the Instructor's Manual, and (3) a pencil and paper to record and periodically announce group points as the game progresses. The moderator also reminds participants to shield their answers so that others cannot see them.

    If the class contains eighteen students, the moderator can divide the class into thirds, starting at any point, by counting off "one, two, three." When all have counted off, different groups can go to different parts of the room, far enough away so that within-group discussions are not overheard by members of other groups. If the class contains more students, the moderator can divide the class into groups (about four to six in a group) so that Group A can compete against Group B; Group C can compete against Group D, and so on. More than one game going on concurrently in the same room can get noisy. If the noise gets too distracting, competing groups can conduct their games in other classrooms (if available) or, even in the hallway.

3. Each group picks a leader. Participants should sit in a circle facing each other, but far enough away from other groups so as not to be heard during group conversations.

4. When participants are ready, either read or act out the first vignette. Starred (*) items are acted out, unstarred items are read. Groups can take turns reading or acting out the vignettes. Ham it up if you like, but stick to the text.

5. After the vignette has been read or acted out, the moderator gives all participants at most *two minutes* to write down the fallacy number that best describes the vignette. Each participant should place his or her game card face down so others cannot see it. Participants *do not discuss the item's content at this time*, but they can read the item to themselves and review the fallacy definitions.

6. As soon as all the member of a group have finished selecting a fallacy, they display their choice to others in their group.

7. After the two minutes are up, each leader tells the moderator whether their group is unanimous or has a disagreement. The moderator then consults Box 3.1 to determine which group gets what points. The moderator gives points for unanimity only if the group's choice agrees with the answer key located in the Answers to Exercises section of the Instructors' Manual.

8. If both team have some disagreement, each group talks privately to arrive at a choice. Each group's leader should try to ensure that all members of his or her group get a chance to express an opinion. After a maximum of *three minutes* of discussion, the leader takes a vote, notes the majority choice, and places the card face down on the table,

where it remains until the leader of the group signals that his or her group has also made its choice. Then the leaders show the moderator their choices.

9.   If the leaders mark the correct fallacy, all groups receive five points. If one group gets the correct answer, but the others do not, the former receives ten points. If all groups are wrong, they receive no points, and the moderator e-mails the authors, telling us that we have written a vague vignette and definition.

10.   This process continues until all the vignettes are finished, until the class runs out of time, or until one group gets 100 points and become Reasoners in Practice. The instructor may also decide that whoever has the most points at some predetermined time limit is the winner.

11.   At the end of each game, all groups may be rewarded for participating, but the winning group should get the greater reward.

These procedures and rules are only suggested. If your group can agree on changes that make the game more fun, go for it! Please e-mail to first author describing changes that can improve the game.

Playing the Game by Yourself

You could work through each vignette and keep a score of your "hits" (correct fallacy spotting) and your "misses." See where your total score places you on the Reasoning-in-Practice Ladder when you finish the game. You could also prepare a response to each item and compare your responses with suggestions provided by your instructor.

Purpose

To learn how to spot and avoid fallacies common across the helping professions

Background

The fallacies in this game stalk unwary practitioners in all helping professions. Watch for them creeping into thinking during interdisciplinary case conferences when participants assume that a client's improvement following treatment was caused by the treatment (after this), that what may be true of one person or many is true for all (case example), or that unclear descriptions of hoped-for client outcomes offer sufficient evidence to judge client improvement (vagueness).

Instructions

1. Please follow earlier Instructions for Games A, B, and C. Act out starred (*) vignettes and read others aloud.
2. Read the description of each fallacy.

Definitions, Examples, and Countermeasures

1. Relying on Case Examples: This refers to drawing conclusions about many people from only one or a few unrepresentative individuals. A generalization is made about the effectiveness of a method, or about what is typically true of clients based on one or just a few people. This is a hasty generalization and reflects the Law of Small Numbers: the belief that because a person has intimate knowledge of one or a few cases, he or she knows what is generally true about clients. This fallacy is also referred to as the fallacy of experience (Skrabanek & Mc Cormick, 1998, pp. 56–58). Experience with a few cases may be highly misleading (see discussion of the law of small numbers in Exercise 8). We can easily become immersed in the details of a case, forgetting that it is just one instance. A case example is worth little as evidence. Case examples often portray individuals so vividly that their emotional appeal distracts from seeking evidence about what helps clients or is generally true of clients. Case examples also encourage oversimplification of what may be complex problems. They are notoriously open to intentional and unintentional biases, including confirmation biases in which we seek examples that support our favored assumption and overlook contradictory evidence. If we search long enough for it, we can find a case that will support almost any conclusion. This is not to say that case material cannot be valuable. For example, it can be used to demonstrate practice skills. A videotape of an interview with an adolescent mother may demonstrate important practice competencies such as high-quality empathic reactions. An instructor may model a family therapy technique. Such use of case material is a valuable part of professional education. The problem arises when we generalize to all clients from case examples.

Example: A 2-year-old boy with behavior problems, placed in a foster home was to be removed and placed elsewhere because the mother with whom the child had a strong attachment, could not manage his behavior. Day treatment was arranged to allow the boy to stay in his foster home. This treatment made it easier for the foster family to provide a good environment for the child and handle visits from his biological mother, to whom the boy will probably return. Because of this case, I believe that day treatment helps troubled foster children.

Countermeasures: To make accurate generalizations about a population, collect a representative sample from this population. For example, to judge whether client change is related to a particular intervention, search for a systematic review of well-designed experimental studies. You may find a high-quality review in the Cochrane or Campbell Libraries.

2. Relying on Testimonials: Claims that a method is effective are often based on one's own experience. Testimonials are often given in professional conferences, in professional publications, or on film or videotape. Clients may report how much participating in a particular treatment benefited them. To qualify as a testimonial, a person must (1) assert that a given method was helpful, (2) offer his or her own experience as evidence that the method works, and (3) describe the experience, not to demonstrate how the treatment method is applied, but to argue that the method is effective. Testimonials do not provide evidence that a treatment is effective. Though people who give testimonials may generally be sincere, their sincerity does not assure accuracy. Those who give a testimonial may feel pressure to please the person who requested their testimonial. Promoters often choose people to give testimonials because of their personal attractiveness, charismatic qualities, and other features that play on an audience's emotions. Those who give testimonials may not have been trained to make the systematic and objective observations they would need to determine if change truly has occurred or to compare this treatment to another or no treatment at all, as in an experimental study.

> *Example:*
> **After taking so many other medicines without being helped, you can imagine how happy and surprised I felt when I discovered that Natex was doing me a lot of good. Natex seemed to go right to the root of my trouble, helped my appetite and put an end to the indigestion, gas and shortness of breath. (Local lady took Natex year ago—had good health ever since, 1935, May 27, p. 7).**

This woman's testimonial appeared on the same page of a newspaper as her obituary!

Countermeasures: Conduct a controlled study to evaluate the effects of the treatment or consult literature that describes such studies. Both case examples and testimonials involve partiality in the use of evidence—looking at just part of the picture. They rely on selected instances, which often give a biased view.

3. Vagueness: Descriptions of client concerns and related causes, hoped-for outcomes and progress measures may be vague. Specific problem-related behaviors, thoughts, or feelings may not be clearly described. Examples of vague terms include aggression, antisocial, poor parenting skills, poor communicator. The Barnum effect in which we assume ambiguous words apply to us and indicate the accuracy of advice for example from astrologers, take advantage of vague words and phrases. Common terms for vague accounts include bafflegab, bureaucratese, and gobbledygook (Kahane & Cavender, 1998, p. 135). Vague description of hoped-for outcomes and progress indicators make it impossible to clearly determine if progress has been made. Vague terms foster fuzzy thinking, and obscure the results of efforts to help clients. Examples of vague terms that describe outcomes include *improved, better, coming along nicely, somewhat better, functioning at a higher level,* and *substantially improved.* If the client "improved" without our defining how, how would we know if this were the case? Examples of clear outcomes include initiating three conversations a day (a conversation is defined as more than a greeting and at least one minute long), or a client with a weight problem losing ten pounds within a given six-week interval, or a client with hypertension maintaining a blood pressure of 140/80, or below, on all six monthly meetings at the clinic.

Example: "Our community prevention programs have been effective. After six weeks of meetings, residents seemed to feel more in charge of their health."

Countermeasures: Clearly describe presenting concerns, related hoped-for outcomes, and progress measures. Descriptions of outcomes should be so clearly stated that all involved parties can readily agree on when they have been attained. The descriptions should answer the questions Who? What"? Where? When? and How often?

4. *Assuming Hardheaded Therefore Hardhearted:* This refers to the mistaken belief that one cannot be both a warm, empathic, caring person and an analytical, scientific, rational thinker. There are two important dimensions to the helping process: (1) a caring, empathic attitude; (2) skill in offering effective methods. As Meehl (1973) argued, it is precisely because clinicians do care (are softhearted) that they should rely on the best evidence available (be hardheaded) when making judgments. Softheartedness is a necessary, but not a sufficient condition in the helping process. Assuming that one has to be either caring or rational misses the point: A person can be both. Paul Meehl (1973) documented in 1954 that, in spite of the fact that statistical prediction (statistical tables based on experience with many clients) consistently outpredicted judgments made by senior clinicians, helpers still relied on their gut-level feelings when making important predictions. Over 100 studies now support Meehl's conclusions about the superiority of statistical prediction over gut-level (intuitive) feelings (Grove & Meehl, 1996). Meehl (1973) speculated that clinicians often ignore better statistical evidence because they believe that they would be less feeling and caring about clients if they based their judgments on statistical evidence. (See also Houts, 1998.)

Example:
Today it seems more apparent that the research stance and the posture of the therapist are quite the opposite of each other.

The researcher must keep distant from his data, be objective, and not intrude on or influence what he is studying. He must also explore and explain all the complex variables of every issue, since he is a seeker after truth [why wouldn't a therapist want to know the truth too?]. The therapist's stance is quite different. He must be personally involved and human, not distant and objective (Haley, 1980, p. 17).

Countermeasures: Be hardheaded (analytical, scientific, data-driven) because you are softhearted (really do care about what helps people) (see Box 6.1).

5. ***Confirmation Bias****:* This refers to the tendency to look only for data that supports initial beliefs and to ignore disconfirming evidence (Nickerson, 1998). We attend only to events consistent with a preferred practice theory. This may occur with or without our awareness. We "cherry pick" (Tufte, 2007). An administrator may infer that a method is effective by focusing only on successes—only on instances where improvement followed use of a method. Failures, instances of spontaneous recovery, and persons not treated who got worse are ignored. When we examine an association to infer cause, we often rely on evidence that confirms our hypothesis, that is, those who were in treatment and improved (see Cell A in Box 6.2) and ignore counterevidence (Nickerson, 1998). We may be so committed to support a particular view that counterarguments are ignored or not reported and evidence against views are deliberately suppressed. This kind of biased thinking may result in decisions that harm rather than help clients. "In matters controversial, my perception's rather fine. I always see both points of view: the one that's wrong and mine."

Example: I sought information related to my belief that the client was depressed and found many instances of depressed feelings and related indicators. For other examples of confirmation biases, see professional advertisements, presentations at professional conferences by those seeking to sell a method of intervention (particularly if they want you to pay for related training), and literature reviews by instructors who present only one point of view about an issue.

Countermeasures: Question your initial assumptions. Search for data that do *not* support your preferred view. Keep in mind that your initial assumption may be wrong. All four cells must be examined to get an accurate picture of whether an intervention works. In addition

Box 6.1   Four Practitioner Types

Type I Softhearted/ Hardheaded (Ideal)	Concerned about effects of methods, persists when asking questions, asks specific questions, devises tests to measure effectiveness, bases conclusions on facts properly evaluated, tries to answer questions objectively, identifies key elements in arguments before reacting to them, not easily led in sheep-like fashion, critically appraises claims.	**Type II** Hardhearted/ Hardheaded
Reflects feelings of others accurately, a good listener, more comfortable dealing with people than with things, senses when others need help, concerned about social injustice, resolves to help others, often puts concerns of others ahead of own, others come to talk to him/her about problems.	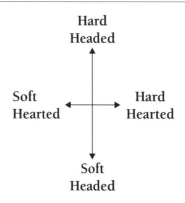	More comfortable dealing with things than with people, believes that those in trouble must get themselves out, puts own concerns ahead of others, unconcerned about social justice, jumps in to tell of own problems when others talk of their problems, lacks empathy.
Type III Softhearted/ Softheaded (Dangerous Combination)	Rarely questions effects of methods, easily discouraged or distracted when approaching a problem, gullible and swayed by emotional appeals, asks vague questions, thinks "one opinion is as good as another," reacts to arguments without identifying elements in the arguments, jumps to conclusions, follows the crowd, believes in magic.	**Type IV** Hardhearted/ Softheaded

Source: Gibbs, L. E. (1991), *Scientific Reasoning for Social Workers*, (p. 36). New York, NY: Macmillan.

to considering successes, look for failures, persons not treated who got better, and those not treated who got worse. Don't trust your memory. Keep a systematic record of successes, failures, those not treated and improved, and those not treated and not improved. The latter two groups might be estimated by reading literature about what generally happens to untreated persons. Look fearlessly at *all* the evidence, not just data that

Client Outcome

		Improved	Not Improved	
Client Participated in Treatment	Yes	Cell A Successes N = 75	Cell B Failures N = 35	Proportion Successful $= \dfrac{A}{A + B} \times 100$
	NO	Cell C Spontaneous Recovery N = 75	Cell D Untreated, Unimproved N = 60	Proportion in Spontaneous Recovery $= \dfrac{C}{C + D} \times 100$

Source: Gibbs, L. E. (1991). *Scientific Reasoning for Social Workers*, (p. 70). New York, NY: Macmillan.

support a hypothesis (i.e., cases where the treatment worked). How else can an accurate judgment be made? Be skeptical of anyone who presents just one side of anything. The world's not that simple. Seek and present alternative views and data in your own work. How else can you arrive at approximations to the truth? The more you are committed to a particular view, the more vigorously you should seek counterevidence.

6. Relying on Newness/Tradition Fallacy: This fallacy occurs if (1) an assertion is made about how to help clients or what is true of clients; (2) the assertion is said to be true because it has been held to be true or practiced for a long time (tradition), because the idea or practice has just been developed (newness), and (3) no studies or data are given to support the claim. The practice of bleeding (applying leeches, cutting into a vein with a scalpel) as a treatment for infection was practiced for hundreds of years, in spite of the fact that there was no evidence that it worked (see Box 6.3). Conversely, the mere fact that a treatment method has just been developed does not insure its effectiveness. All treatments were new at some time, including ones that promised great effectiveness but were later found to be ineffective or even harmful. For example, the sex hormone diethylstilbestrol (DES) was enthusiastically adopted in the 1940s and early 1950s to treat various problems with pregnancy even though there had been no careful evaluation using randomized control trials. Tragically, DES was found to produce cancer in the daughters of women who had been treated with DES (Apfel & Fisher, 1984; Berendes & Lee, 1993; Dutton, 1988). Many popular treatments such as use of "magnetic"

Box 6.3 Death of General George Washington

The death of this illustrious man, by an abrupt and violent distemper, will long occupy the attention of his fellow citizens. No public event could have occurred, adapted so strongly to awaken the sensitivity and excite the reflections of Americans. No apology will therefore be needful for relating the circumstances of this great event. The particulars of his disease and death being stated by the physicians who attended him, their narrative deserves to be considered as authentic. The following account was drawn up by doctors Craik and Dick.

"Some time in the night of Friday, the 13th of December, having been exposed to a rain on the preceding day, General Washington was attacked with an inflammatory affection of the upper part of the wind pipe, called, in technical language, *Cynanche Trachealis*. The disease commenced with a violent ague, accompanied with some pain in the upper and fore part of the throat, a sense of stricture in the same part, a cough, and a difficult, rather than a painful, deglutition, which were soon succeeded by fever and a quick and laborious respiration. The necessity of blood-letting suggesting itself to the General, he procured a bleeder in the neighbourhood, who took from his arm, in the night, twelve or fourteen ounces of blood. He could not be prevailed on by the family, to send for the attending physician till the following morning, who arrived at Mount Vernon at about eleven o'clock on Saturday. Discovering the case to be highly alarming, and foreseeing the fatal tendency of the disease, two consulting physicians were immediately sent for, who arrived, one at half after three, and the other at four o'clock in the afternoon: in the mean time were employed two copious bleedings, a blister was applied to the part affected, two moderate does of calomel were given, and an injection was administered, which operated on the lower intestines, but all without any perceptible advantage, the respiration becoming still more difficult and painful. On the arrival of the first of the consulting physicians, it was agreed, as there were yet no signs of accumulation in the bronchial vessels of the lungs, to try the effect of another bleeding, when about thirty-two ounces of blood were drawn, without the least apparent alleviation of the disease. Vapors of vinegar and water were frequently inhaled, ten grains of calomel were given, succeeded by repeated doses of emetic tartar, amounting in all to five or six grains, with no other effect than a copious discharge form the bowels. The power of life seemed now manifestly yielding to the force of the disorder; blisters were applied to the extremities, together with a cataplasm of bran and vinegar to the throat. Speaking, which had been painful from the beginning, now became almost impracticable: respiration grew more and more contracted and imperfect, till half after eleven on Saturday night, when, retaining the full possession of his intellects, he expired without a struggle!"

Source: Death of General George Washington. (1799). *The Monthly Magazine and American Review*, 1(6), 475–477.

devices to cure ailments are popular even though there is no evidence that they are effective (Pittler, Brown, & Edwards, 2007; Winemiller, Robert, Edward, Scott Harmsen, 2000).

Example of Appeal to Tradition: A nursing home social workers says,

We have always classified our residents according to their level of nursing care on the four floors of Rest Haven. No matter

what reasons you might give for changing this practice, I doubt that the administration would change a practice that has been in place for many years.

Example of Appeal to Newness: "This method of family therapy is described in a new book by Dr. Gerbels. It's the latest method. We should use it here."

Countermeasures: Point out that being new or old does not make an idea or practice valid. Ask to see evidence and data to judge the effects of methods.

7. Appeal to Unfounded Authority (Ad Verecundium): Here, there is an attempt to trick someone into accepting a claim by focusing on, for example, the "status" of an individual as an expert. The purpose is to block efforts to critically appraise the claim. We are often reluctant to question the conclusions of a person with high status or who is viewed as an "expert" (Engel, 1994, pp. 208–210). There are many forms of this fallacy including appeal to tradition and appeal to expert opinion as in "Experts agree that cognitive behavioral methods are best." Appealing to expert opinion is often accompanied by a convincing manner of presentation or charismatic presence. An author or presenter may appeal to his or her experience with no description of what this entails. Other sources of authority include legal, religious, and administrative (Walton, 1997). Context is vital in reviewing related dialogue, for example, is critical appraisal of a claim of key interest? Authority may refer to cognitive authority "which is always subject to critical questioning and institutional or administrative authority which often tends to be more coercive and absolutistic in nature" (Walton, 1997, p. 250). Illicit shifts in dialogue may occur in which there is an "unlicensed shift from one type of 'authority' to another portraying an argument as something it is not" (p. 251).

Example: A master of ceremonies introduces a speaker to a professional audience: "Dr. MacMillan is one of the most renowned experts on therapeutic touch in the world. He has published three books on therapeutic touch and he now holds a prestigious William B. Day Lectureship at the University of Pennsylvania. His reputation supports what he'll tell us about the effectiveness of his approach."

Accepting *Uncritical Documentation* is an example of appeal to questionable authority. This refers to the mistaken belief that if an idea has been described in the literature (book, journal, article, newspaper) or if a reference is given following a claim, the claim must be true. To be classified as uncritical documentation, literature must be cited, but no information is given about the method by which the cited author arrived at a particular conclusion (e.g., research method used, reliability and validity of measures used, sample size) as in "This test is reliable and valid" (Trickster, 2008). Unless the writer describes key content in Trickster (2008) we have no way of knowing if this reference provides any evidence for the claim. Even the most preposterous ideas have advocates. For example, see the *National Inquirer* to find that Elvis still lives and that a woman revived her gerbil after it had been frozen stiff in her freezer for six months.

Countermeasures: Ask to see the authority's evidence and evaluate that. How good is the evidence? Here again we se the vital role of questions. For example, to discover whether a cited reference provides evidence for a claim you will have to find out more information; you may have to read that reference yourself. Is the alleged expert in a position to know certain information? Other questions suggested by Walton (1997) include How credible is E (the expert) as an expert source? Is E an expert in related fields of concern? Is E personally reliable as a source? Is the assertion made based on evidence?

8. *Oversimplifications*: This refers to overlooking important information. This could involve how an outcome is viewed (e.g., focusing on surrogate indicators and omitting outcomes vital to clients such as quality of life, mortality), how causes are viewed (e.g., "It's in the brain," "It's in the genes"), or selection of intervention methods (e.g., use of manualized treatment that ignores unique client characteristics. Oversimplifications that result in poor decisions may arise at many points in decision making including structuring concerns, selecting interventions and evaluating progress. Simply labeling a behavior and believing that you then understand what it is and what causes it is a common fallacy—*the fallacy of labeling*. Treating multidimensional phenomena as unidimensional and viewing changing events as static are examples of oversimplifications. "Overinterpretation" may occur in which we consider data suggestive of new alternatives that do not support a preferred view as consistent with this preferred view.

Example: "It is clear that social anxiety is a mental disorder. It is a brain disease. We should place the client on Paxil." It is not at all clear that social anxiety is a mental disorder. Indeed this view was promoted by a public relations agency hired by the pharmaceutical company which produces Paxil (Moynihan & Cassels, 2005). (See also the study of fear over the centuries, Naphy & Roberts, 1997.)

Countermeasures: Ask questions regarding other potentially important factors. For example, if a client is anxious in social situations find out whether he or she has requisite social skills and whether he uses these in appropriate situations. Become historically informed (e.g., see Gowland, 2006). Critically appraise claims common in a profession (e.g., see Horwitz & Wakefield, 2007; Moncrieff, 2008). Oversimplifications are important to spot because they may get in the way of helping clients and avoiding harm. (For a discussion of complexities, see Haynes, 1992.)

9. *Confusing Correlation with Causation: Assuming Associations Reflect a Causal Relationship*: Tindale (2007) identifies three kinds of problematic causal reasoning: (1) assuming a causal relation based on a correlation or mere temporal order (post hoc reasoning); (2) confusing causal elements involved (misidentified causes); and (3) predicting a negative causal outcome for a proposal or action, perhaps on the basis of an expected causal chain (slippery slope reasoning) (pp. 173–174). It may be assumed that statistical association reflects causal relationships. Just because two events are associated does not mean that one causes the other. A third variable may cause both. Pellagra, a disease characterized by sores, vomiting, diarrhea, and lethargy was thought to be related to poor sanitation. It is caused by inadequate diet. It is often assumed that alcohol causes violence since violence and drinking often occur together (e.g ., alcohol acts as a disinhibitor). There is little evidence to claim that alcohol is "of primary importance in explaining family violence" (Gelles & Cavanaugh, 2005).

Example: "We studied the correlation between a number of risk factors and depression and found that having parents who are depressed is a risk factor. Depression in parents causes depression in their children."

Countermeasures: Keep in mind that correlations, for example as found in descriptive studies exploring relationships among variables, cannot be assumed to reflect causal relationships. (See also discussion of oversimplification in this exercise.) Here again questions provide a pathway for avoiding errors such as "Does X *always* occur together with Y?" "Does X (the presumed cause) occur before Y (the presumed effect)?" "Does the presumed effect occur without the presumed cause?"

10. Post Hoc *Ergo Propter Hoc* (*After This Therefore Because of This*): This refers to the mistaken belief that if event A precedes event B in time, then A caused B. It occurs because of a confounding of correlation with causation (see item 9). Practitioners often use temporal order as a causal cue. As Medawar notes, "If a person (a) feels poorly or is sick, (b) receives treatment to make him better, and (c) gets better, then no power of reasoning known to medical science can convince him that it may not have been the treatment that restored his health" (1967, pp. 14–15). If A causes B, it is true that A must precede B, but there may be many other events preceding B that could be the cause. A's preceding B is a *necessary* but not a *sufficient* (always enough) condition to infer cause. Let's consider an example: Robins migrate north to Wisconsin each year. Shortly after the robins arrive, the flowers start to bloom; therefore, robins cause flowers to bloom.

This fallacy occurs in practice when (1) a problem exists, (2) the practitioner takes action to remove the complaint (event A), and (3) the complaint disappears (event B). The practitioner then assumes that his or her action caused the complaint to disappear. The practitioner takes credit for effective action when, in fact, some other event may have caused the change.

Example: "Mr. James just started our support group for the recently bereaved and a few meetings later seemed to be much less depressed. That support group must work."

Countermeasures: Think of other possible causes for improvement, or deterioration, before taking responsibility for it. For example, you may think that your client acquired a new social skill as a result of your program, but your client may have learned it from interactions with friends or family. You may believe that cognitive behavioral therapy helped a depressed client, but the client may have improved because she saw a psychiatrist who prescribed an antidepressant. A break in hot weather, rather than your community crisis team's efforts to head off violence, may have been responsible for a decrease in street violence. There are cyclical problems that get worse, improve, and again get worse. A large percentage of medical problems clear up by themselves (Skrabanek & McCormick, 1998). A well-designed study can help rule out these and other explanations of client change.

11. *Nonfallacy Items: Items That Do Not Contain Fallacies*: In these items, a fallacy is named and avoided (e.g., "You are attacking me personally, not examining my argument; that's an ad hominem appeal"), or the helper applies sound reasoning and evidence (e.g., cites and critiques a study, uses a valid outcome measure to judge client change).

Use Box 6.4 to review the names of the fallacies.

Box 6.4 Fallacies in Game A

1. Case examples
2. Testimonials
3. Vagueness (vague descriptions of problems, outcomes, and/or progress measures)
4. Assuming softhearted, therefore, softheaded
5. Confirmation biases
6. Reliance on newness/tradition
7. Appeals to unfounded authority including uncritical documentation
8. Oversimplifications
9. Confusing correlation with causation
10. After This—post hoc *ergo propter hoc*
11. Nonfallacy item

Practice Exercise 6 Vignettes for Game A: Common Practice Fallacies

Your Name _____ Date _____

Course _____ Instructor's Name _____

REMINDERS

Act out the starred (*) items (3, 9, 13). Take turns reading the others out loud. Remember that some items do not contain fallacies. In these items, a fallacy is named and avoided (e.g., "You are attacking me personally, not examining my argument; that's an ad hominem appeal"), or the helper applies sound reasoning and evidence (e.g., cites and critiques a study, applies a valid outcome measure to judge change). Use Box 6.4 to review the names of the fallacies.

1. *Client speaking to potential clients*: I participated in six weekly encounter-group meetings conducted by Sally Rogers, my nurse, and the group helped. My scores on the Living With Cancer Inventory have increased. I recommend that you attend the group too.

2. *One counselor speaking to another*: I think that Tom's chemical dependency problem and codependency have definitely worsened in the past six months.

3. Two administrators speaking with each other:

   First administrator: In what proportion of hard-to-place adoption cases did the child remain in the placement home at least two years?

   Second administrator: We have had fifty successful placements in the past two years.

   First administrator: How many did we try to place? I'm trying to get some idea of our success rate.

   Second administrator: We don't have information about that.

4. *Politician critical of welfare benefits and welfare fraud among recipients of Aid-for-Dependent-Children*: One "welfare queen" illustrates the extent of the problem. She used twelve fictitious names, forged several birth certificates, claimed fifty nonexistent children as dependents, received Aid for Families with Dependent Children (AFDC) for ten years, and defrauded the state of Michigan out of $40,000. She drove an expensive car, took vacations in Mexico, and lived in an expensive house.

5. *Psychologist*: Our agency offers communication enrichment workshops for couples having some rough spots in their relationships. Four to five couples participated as a group in ten weekly two-hour sessions. Each participant completed the Inventory of Family Feelings (IFF) during the first and last meetings. These scores show marked improvement. Our workshops enhance positive feelings.

6. *A supervisor arguing against critical thinking.* There are two kinds of helpers: those who have people skills and who can interact warmly with clients, and those who lack this natural gift but try to make up for it by consulting studies, measures, surveys, and other such trash.

7. *Author in a professional journal:* This literature review summarizes six articles. Our library assistants were instructed to find articles that support the effectiveness of family-based treatment. All six articles support the effectiveness of family-based treatment for adolescent runaways and related problems.

8. *Psychiatrist:* My client, Mr. Harrison, had a Beck Depression Inventory (BDI) score that placed him in the severe range when I saw him at intake. I worked with him using cognitive behavioral methods for six weeks. In the seventh week, his score was in the normal range. My methods worked with Mr. Harrison. His BDI scores were lower after treatment.

*9. *An intern speaking to another intern:*

   First intern: Mrs. A was very anxious in our first interview. She was so nervous that I ended the interview early and gave her a prescription for Paxil.

   Second intern: I think you did the right thing since social anxiety is a brain disorder.

10. *Situation:* A county board meeting:

   Jenny: My staff and I have conducted a survey of Hmong families here in Davis County to determine their service needs. We obtained a list of families from county census records and records kept by the Hmong Mutual Assistance Organization (HMAO). Fifty-seven Hmong families live in the county, a total of 253 persons. With the help of an HMAO interpreter, we asked two head persons from each family about their needs. You have the interview guide before you that we used in the survey. In that interview, we asked them to rank their needs from most important to least important. As a result, their most pressing need is

   Board member (speaking softly to his neighbor): Jenny seems to have done her home work, but I don't agree with her assessment of the situation. Remember Dr. Morrison, who spoke for an hour to us about the needs of Hmong communities? I place much more confidence in his conclusions. Dr. Morrison is more widely know on this topic.

11. *Two nurses discussing the effectiveness of therapeutic touch in decreasing pain.*

   First nurse: I looked up research regarding therapeutic touch and found some well-designed experimental studies that do not support the effectiveness of this method in reducing pain.

   Second nurse: Thanks for taking the time to take a close look at the evidentiary status of this method that we have been using. Let's see if we can locate methods to reduce pain that have been critically tested and have been found to reduce pain.

12. *Senior practitioner speaking to a student:* If you try to measure your client's progress, you will destroy your rapport with the client. Clients know when they are being treated like a guinea pig and resent it. You will be better off if you rely on your intuition and attend to how you react toward your client. As I see it, you're either an intuitive type or an automaton.

13. *Dean, School of Arts and Sciences speaking to Chair, Department of Social Work:*

   Dean: How did the social-work majors who graduated last June fare in the job market during their first six months after graduation?

Department Chair: We've been pretty successful. Thirty are employed in social work, and one is in graduate school.

14. *Speech therapist speaking to a teacher*: Have you heard about facilitated communication? It has just been developed as a way to communicate with autistic children. A facilitator can help the child type messages out on a computer keyboard that communicates the child's thoughts. These thoughts would remain locked in the child without this new technology and its skillful use.

15. *An advertisement, including pictures of Bill in The American Journal of Psychiatry*: **Name**: Bill. **Occupation**: Unemployed administrative assistant. **Age**: 48. **Height**: 5' 10" **Weight**: 170 lb. **History**: Patient complains of fatigue, inability to concentrate, and feelings of worthlessness since staff cuts at the corporation where he worked for 21 years resulted in the loss of his job. He has failed to begin a company-sponsored program and to look for a new job. **Initial Treatment**: After 2 months of antidepressant treatment, patient complained of sexual dysfunction (erectile failure and decreased libido), which had not been a problem prior to antidepressant treatment. . . .

 Recommendation: Discontinue current antidepressant and switch to a new-generation, nonserotonergic antidepressant. Start Wellbutrin to relieve depression and minimize risk of sexual dysfunction. **Outcome After 4 Weeks of Therapy With Wellbutrin**: Patient reports feeling more energetic. Sexual performance is normal. He has enrolled in job retraining program . . ., **Wellbutrin (BUPROPION HCL) relieves depression with few life-style disruptions** (WELLBUTRIN, 1992, A33–35).

16. *An administrator in a group home for developmentally disabled adults*: According to a study I read about functional-communication training, this treatment reduced severe aggressive and self-injurious behaviors in self-injuring adults. Let's try this method with Mark and Olie.

17. *Director of a refuge home for battered women*: The women who attend our program for physically and emotionally abused women report on their levels of self-esteem. Generally, their self-esteem improves.

18. *One psychologist to another*: I read a study that explored the correlation between parenting styles in early childhood and later antisocial behavior. The correlations showed that parenting style is a major cause of later delinquency.

19. *Child-welfare worker to students in class*: Open adoption is one of the newest advances in adoptions. In open adoption, the biological parents are allowed to stay in touch with the adoptive parents, and in many cases, the biological parents contribute to rearing the child. Your agency should try this increasingly popular option.

20. *Client treated by a chiropractor*: Mrs. Sisneros was experiencing lower-back pain. She saw her chiropractor, felt better afterward, and concluded that the chiropractor helped her back.

FOLLOW-UP QUESTION

Do any of this game's vignettes reflect real situations particularly well?
Which one(s)?

_____

_____

_____

_____

_____

_____

_____

Purpose

To learn how to identify and avoid fallacies that often occur in case conferences, staff meetings, interdisciplinary teams, and conferences

Background

Professionals participate in a wide variety of groups including multidisciplinary teams, case conferences, task groups, seminars, and workshops where decisions are made that affect the lives of clients. Many groups include both professionals and laypersons such as self-help and support groups (e.g., renal dialysis support groups). Groupwork is a common part of practice including, for example, community advocacy groups, group cognitive-behavioral therapy, and task-centered work with clients. Community-action groups include neighborhood block organizations, conflict-resolution, and other grass-roots groups. Advantages of groups include multiple points of view and approaches to problems and a variety of skills and knowledge among members. On the other hand, without sound leadership and knowledge and skills regarding group process and practice fallacies, unwise decisions may be made. The fallacies described in this exercise can occur without awareness and stall or sidetrack effective group decision making.

Instructions

1. Before playing Game B, review the instructions located before Exercise 6.
2. Read the descriptions of each fallacy given in Exercise 7 including the definition, example, and suggested countermeasures. This will help you to become familiar with the fallacies discussed in Exercise 8, and how to avoid them (see Box 7.1).
3. Read each vignette aloud when playing the game. This will make the situations more real. Starred (*) items require volunteers to take turns acting out the example while others follow along in the script or watch the actors.

Box 7.1   Fallacies in Game B

1. Ad hominem (At the Person)
2. Begging the question
3. Diversion (red herring)
4. Stereotyping
5. Manner or style
6. Groupthink
7. Bandwagon (popularity)
8. Either-or (false dilemma)
9. Strawperson argument
10. Slippery-slope
11. Nonfallacy item

Definitions, Examples and Countermeasures

1. Ad Hominem (At the Person): Attacking (or praising) the person, or feeling attacked (or praised) as a person, rather than examining the substance of an argument. Arguing ad hominem is the reverse of arguing ad rem (at the argument). The ad hominem fallacy may arise when someone lacks supporting evidence but nonetheless wants his or her point of view to prevail. It is a variety of the *genetic fallacy* (devaluing an argument because of its source, for example, see www.fallacyfiles or skepdic.com). Instead of addressing the substance of another person's argument, he or she may seek to discredit you by calling you a name or by attacking your character or motives. Or, he may try to "seduce" you by offering irrelevant praise of you and/or some characteristic you have.

Example: Joel Fischer (1973) published a review of studies about the effectiveness of social casework. He concluded that casework was ineffective and might even be harmful. One opponent accused Fisher of being "in a bag" (Crumb, 1973, p. 124).

Countermeasures: Address the issue. Argue ad rem. Examine the argument and evidence related to claims. Guidelines for evaluating different kinds of research related to different kinds of questions are offered in later Exercises.

2. *Begging the Question:* We assume as a premise some form of the point at issue. As Engel (1994) notes, "We can't prove something by simply assuming that it is true or by appealing to something that is equally questionable" (p. 52). "A statement that is questionable as a conclusion is equally questionable as a premise" (p. 53). Different words are often used, making those, seemingly obvious, ploys difficult to spot. This is a remarkably common ploy and one that often goes undetected, especially when pronounced with an air of confidence (see also Walton, 1991).

   Example: Manualized treatments are best because they provide detailed instructions which improve effectiveness. Notice that the reason given restates (but in different words) the conclusion.

   Countermeasure: First be on the lookout for such assertions. Second ask the proclaimer to give her argument for her conclusion. Here again raising questions such as "how good is the evidence?" are key in avoiding such "slight of hand" (Browne & Keeley, 2006, p. 96) (see also Walton, 1991).

3. *Diversion (Red Herring):* Here, there is an attempt to sidetrack people from an argument. *Red herring* originally referred to a fugitive's use of dead fish scent to throw tacking dogs off the trail. Sometimes unethical adversaries create a diversion because they know their argument is too weak to stand up to careful scrutiny; they sidetrack the group's attention to a different topic (they drag a red herring across the trail of the discussion). Creating emotional reactions such as angering your opponent creates a diversion (Walton, 1992a). More commonly, the diversion just happens as attention wanders, gets piqued by a new interest, or is side-tracked by humor.

   Example: Discussion during a case conference:

   Paul: Edna, my 87-seven-year-old client, lives alone. She has looked frail lately, and I'm worried that she is not eating a balanced diet. Her health seems generally good, no major weaknesses or injuries, just dietary problems. What do you think of her as a candidate for the Meals-on-Wheels Program?

   Craig: I saw a Meals-on-Wheels meal recently. The fish looked pulpy.

   John: Speaking of fish, did you know that the Walleyed Pike were biting last Sunday on Halfmoon Lake?

   Countermeasures: Gently bring the discussion back to the point at issue (e.g., We were talking about....)

4. *Stereotyping*: "A stereotype is an oversimplified generalization about a class of individuals, one based on a presumption that every member of the class has some set of properties that is (probably erroneously) identified with the class" (Moore & Parker, 1986, p. 160). Stereotypes can influence decisions (e.g. see Gray-Little, & Kaplan, 2000; Schneider, 2004). They can bias judgments, including notions about what to expect from persons from low socioeconomic backgrounds (Williams, 1995). Stereotyping clients is particularly pernicious because it can lead to erroneous judgments and decisions about how to help individual clients.

>   *Example:*

>   *Income maintenance worker:* I think that Mrs. Owens is probably a typical low- income client. She lacks the coping skills she needs to be an effective parent.

>   *Countermeasures:* Judge individuals and their ideas from a careful assessment of their behavior and thinking not from some preconceived notion about what to expect from them because of their membership in some group or class of individuals. Racism, sexism, classism, and ageism are based on stereotypes that can lead to inappropriately negative or positive attitudes and behaviors toward individuals.

5. *Manner or Style:* This refers to believing an argument because of the apparent sincerity, speaking voice, attractiveness, stage presence, likeability, or other stylistic traits of an argument's presenter. The reverse of this argument, not believing an argument because you find the speaker's style or appearance offensive or distracting, can also be a problem. This fallacy captures many gullible victims in this age of the Internet, television, videotape, film, and videodisc. Williams and Ceci (1997) found that simply using a more enthusiastic tone of voice increased student ratings of effectiveness. (See also Ambady & Rosenthal, 1993.) Beware of advertisements for treatment facilities, as well as slick descriptions and portrayals of intervention methods that focus on how pleasant and clean the facilities' grounds are or how enthusiastically attractive clients may advocate for the program. Slick propagandistic portrayals are often used in place of data about attained outcomes (e.g., What percentage of clients benefit in what ways? How do we know? Do any clients get worse?).

Example:

> *First student*: Take Ames's class. You'll love it. She has a quick sense of humor that will leave you laughing. She rivals some stand-up comics who I have seen on TV for her sense of humor.
>
> *Second student*: I was wondering what I'd learn in Ames's class.
>
> *First student*: Forget that. You'll see what I mean.

Countermeasures: Base your judgments and decisions on the evidence presented, not on the speaker's style or lack of it. Even if the idea comes form an "oddball," only the idea's utility and soundness matter.

6. *Groupthink:* Here, concurrence-seeking [seeking agreement] becomes so dominant in a cohesive group that it tends to override realistic appraisal of alternative courses an action" (p. 43). Janis (1971, November). Group members (e.g., of interdisciplinary teams, task groups, service-coordination groups, staff meetings) may avoid sharing useful opinions or data with the group because they fear they might be "put down," hurt the feelings of other group members, or cause disunity. Indicators of groupthink include stereotyping or characterizing the leaders of opposing groups as evil or incompetent, exerting direct pressure on group members to stay in line and fostering an [incorrect] belief that group members are unanimous in their opinion (Janis, 1982). (See also Exercise 11.) Such behaviors may interfere with sound decision making by hindering discussion of alternative views and important facts pertinent to making a sound decision. Unless a culture of inquiry is encouraged, groups may stifle dissenting opinions. Efforts to test a number of assumptions concerning "groupthink" (conformity to group values and ethics have met with equivocal results) (Turner & Pratkanis, 1998). (See also Baron, 2005.)

Example: A student is in a seminar on psychology. The instructor is well known as an expert in his area. The instructor makes a claim that the student knows is wrong, but she does not bring it up because she is afraid she would be criticized.

Countermeasures: Janis (1982) suggests three ways to counter groupthink: (1) assign the role of critical evaluator to some of the group's members, (2) indicate at the beginning of a discussion that the leader will be impartial to the group's decision, and (3) for important decisions, set up independent committees to gather evidence and deliberate independently of the other groups, with each committee led by a different person (pp. 262–265). You can decrease vulnerability to groupthink by considering arguments both pro and con regarding issues to be discussed prior to meetings; being aware of the indicators of groupthink, keeping in mind harms to clients of groupthink such as making decisions that harm rather than help clients (e.g., see Nemeth & Goncalo, 2005).

7. *Bandwagon (Popularity):* In this fallacy, "there is an attempt to persuade us that a claim is true or an action is right because it is popular—because many, most, or all people believe it or do it, because the crowd is going in that direction—we have . . . the bandwagon appeal" (Freeman, 1993, p. 56, see also Walton, 1999). Examples include the belief that if many people accept a particular conclusion about clients or many people use a particular treatment method, then the conclusion must be true or the treatment must be effective. The bandwagon appeal implies that by the sheer weight of number of people, the point in question cannot be wrong.

    Example: Two social workers speaking over lunch in a cafeteria of an alcohol and other drug-abuse (AODA) treatment facility:

    First social worker: A lot of the AODA treatment facilities in our area seem to be adopting the matching hypothesis. More and more facilities try to systematically match clients with treatment.

    Second social worker: I agree. I think we should too.

    Countermeasures: Critically evaluate popular notions. Examine the evidence before you join the herd. For example, see if there is a systematic review related to the question.

8. *Either-Or (False Dilemma):* This refers to stating or implying that there are only two alternatives when indeed there may be more than two. Either-or reasoning prematurely limits options for problem solving. Other options may be available.

    Example: "The way I see it, you're either for us, or you're against us. Which is it?'

    Countermeasures: Identity alternative views of what might be done. Ask each group member to write down independently a list of possible courses of action. Assure group members that whatever they write will be read anonymously and discussed seriously (see also discussion of group think).

9. *Strawperson Argument :* This fallacy refers to misrepresenting a person's argument and then attacking the misrepresentation. This

is often used as a diversion in order to block critical appraisal of a claim.

Example: Here is an example from the first author's experience at a faculty meeting.

Professor A: We think we should offer two courses on diversity to our students.

Professor Strawman: How can we possibly pay for five to 10 new courses?

Countermeasures: Accurately represent your position. Carefully listen to another person's position; restate that position in your own words as accurately as you can; request feedback as to whether you have restated the position accurately, then react.

10. ***Slippery-Slope (Domino Effect) Fallacy:*** In this fallacy there is an objection to an argument on the grounds that once a step is taken, other events will occur (Walton, 1992b). Tindale (2008) includes this under his discussion of correlation and cause. This is a common ploy designed to discourage acceptance of a disliked position. The fallacy often lies in the assumption that the events alluded inevitably follow from the initial action (when they may not). No good reasons are provided for assuming further events will follow.

Example: If we adopt socialized medicine in this country, all other areas will become socialized including even where we live. I certainly don't want to live in a country like that.

Countermeasures: Point out that the further alleged events do not necessarily follow from the initial action.

11. ***Nonfallacy Items: Items that Do Not Include a Fallacy:*** Be ready for a few examples of sound reasoning. Use the list of fallacies as a reminder when playing Game B.

Practice Exercise 7   Vignettes for Game B: Group and Interpersonal Dynamics

Your Name _____ Date _____

Course _____ Instructor's Name _____

REMINDER

The vignettes are more vivid if each item is read aloud. The starred (*) items may be more effective and fun if class members act out the parts. Refer to Box 8.1 for a summary of fallacies.

*1. *Situation*: A multidisciplinary team (special-education teacher, school psychologist, speech therapist, social worker, school nurse, and child's parent) meet to decide if Jason, age four, should be admitted to an Early Childhood-Exceptional Education Needs (EC-EEN) program.

Special-education teacher: I know that Jason's score on the Battelle Developmental Inventory was above the cutoff score for admission to your program, but I think that Jason's behavior, as I saw it during his visit to my classroom, qualifies him for admission to the EC-EEN program. He ran around the room almost all the time, was not task-focused, and did not follow instructions.

School psychologist: Maybe you're right. Why didn't you say something about this during the team meeting?

Special-education teacher: Nobody including the parents, seemed to think that Jason's behavior was a problem except me.

School psychologist: It's really too bad that you didn't feel comfortable enough to bring this up. You were the team member who had the best chance to observe him.

*2. *Situation*: Monthly meeting of agency administrators.

First administrator: I think your idea to give more money to work with the elderly is a good one but in the long run is not a good idea because we would then have to allot more money to services for all other groups.

Second administrator: Why do you think that?

First administrator: Gee, I didn't think of that.

3. *One psychologist to another*: From what I can see, solution focused therapy is more effective than play therapy for helping child abusing families in the best study I could find. Here's its summary:

> **Two contrasting therapies for the treatment of child abuse were compared in a randomized design: solution focused therapy (SFT) including the whole family**

and structured play therapy (SPT) for the child. The Patterson coding system was used as an outcome measure to assess family interaction. There was a high drop-out rate in both groups, but of those who completed the treatment, there was greater improvement in the solution focused therapy group on some comparisons made.

*4. *Situation*: Case conference at a mental health clinic:

Sandra: We may be overusing the category of Borderline Personality Disorder (BPD) when assessing our clients. We might be using this as a catch-all category.

Diana: I don't think so. This diagnosis is included in the DSM-IV (2000). If it is described in the DSM, it must be valid category.

Sandra: But I have read critiques of this classification system and there are real problems with reliability and validity of the system. For example continuous variables such as social anxiety are transformed into dichotomous ones ("social anxiety disorder" or not), many terms are vague (such as "often"), and complaints such as "insomnia," included for example, as a sign of depression, could have many different causes (e.g., see Houts, 2002; Kutchings & Kirk, 1997).

Rubert (Whispering in Roger's ear): There goes Sandra again. She's a real "know-it-all." She even tries to look like Einstein with those cowlicks in her hair.

*5. *Situation*: Discussion of whether to release a client from an inpatient psychiatric facility:

Clinical psychologist: I don't know if Mr. Myers should be released so early. I am concerned that, now that his depression is lifting, he may still have great potential for suicide.

Social worker (interrupting): I noted that Mr. Myers cracked a joke in group this morning.

Nurse: Yes, I recall that joke. It was something about how the president's great expectation had unraveled into great expectorations

*6. *Situation*: Juvenile court worker talking to her supervisor:

Juvenile court worker: I just read a study that suggests that early intervention may reduce the number of kids needing institutional placement. The study did not involve random assignment, but maybe we could conduct a trial here for some of our clients. We could offer more intensive services to some clients and standard services to others, then compare the outcome.

Supervisor: Thanks for sharing this. Let's do a more systematic search for related evidence after we formulate a clear question. For example, what age children are we most interested in? And what are characteristics of these children; for example, are they from poor families?

7. *Hospital administrator speaking to St. Joseph's Hospital Board*: Many hospitals now use resident care technicians and nursing assistants, but we employ LPNs and RNs exclusively. Don't you think we should adopt a model of treatment that so many other hospitals now use?

8. *Situation*: Case conference at a protective service agency:

Chairperson: The Armejo Family presents us with a dilemma: Should we conduct an investigation for potential child abuse or not?

Polly: As I understand the situation, we are in a gray area. A friend of one of their neighbors said that another neighbor reported that they heard children screaming and worried that the children might be abused. I understand that the family has undergone some hard times lately. The father, a custodian at a local Air Force base, has been laid off from work. We have a report from a fellow worker at the base that the Armejos are having marital difficulties.

Jennifer: I am uncomfortable with initiating an investigation for child abuse on the basis of such shaky evidence. I think we should do nothing at this time. What do you think? We must file a formal complaint (initiate a full investigation) or leave the family alone – which is it?

9. Two psychiatric nurses discussing a patient:

First nurse: His behavior on the ward is erratic and unpredictable. He warrants a diagnosis of bipolar.

Second nurse: What makes you think so?

First nurse: Because of his behavior on the unit.

10. All staff in the Methodist Hospital Social Service Department are female. Members of the Department will interview three job candidates, one of whom is male.

One staff member to another (as they walk down the hill): Just between you and me, I think that male social workers are out of their element in hospital social work. They lack the empathy and patience required to do this job well. I am not optimistic about our male candidate's ability to do the job.

*11. *Situation*: Discussion among alcohol and other drug-abuse counselors:

Richard: One study I read suggested that the best hope for improving services for alcohol-dependent persons is to classify alcoholics systematically into types and to match each type with its most effective treatment. It seems there are interactions between treatment and type for mean level of sobriety, but no differences for mean success across treatments. What do you think?

Onesmo: The idea that alcoholics are all unique (each one is different) seems wrong to me. If they were all unique, how would they all experience the same physiological symptoms of withdrawal after they have built up a tolerance for alcohol?

12. *Comment in an interdisciplinary case conference*: I notice attention deficit disorder more and more frequently in records from children referred to us. Perhaps we should classify our children into this category more often.

13. *Situation*: An interdisciplinary case conference in a nursing home:

Psychologist intern: I don't think you should use those feeding and exercise procedures for Mrs. Shore. They don't work. Since she has Parkinson's, she'll often spill her food. I also don't think you should walk her up and down the hall for exercise. I have read reports that argue against everything you're doing.

Nurse: I am not sure you are in the best position to say. You have not even completed your degree yet.

*14. *Situation*: Two nurses are attending a professional conference. Their hospital has sent them to the conference for continuing education. There are about one hundred people attending the two-day conference, for which all paid a hundred-dollar fee:

First nurse (whispering in friend's ear): I wonder if this imaging method affects the longevity of cancer patients, and what kind of evidence these presenters might give us.

Second nurse: Why don't we ask the presenter?

First nurse: That's a good idea. How does this sound: Could you tell us if any controlled trials have been conducted testing the effectiveness of imaging in decreasing morality of cancer patients and if so, could you describe them?

*15. *Situation*: Two geriatric physicians attending a conference on validation therapy as a method for helping the confused elderly:

First physician: I wonder if validation therapy really helps elderly people to become more oriented to time, place, and person?

Second physician: You'll enjoy this presentation by Diggelman this afternoon. He presents reality therapy so well that the time just flies. He is sincere, he gets the audience involved in learning. He walks into the audience and jokes with us during the breaks. His enthusiasm is exciting. Anyone so sincere and enthusiastic must be giving us accurate information.

*16. *Situation*: Confrontation between supervisor and worker:

Supervisor (to worker): You're late for work.

Worker: So, you're telling me that Bill saw me come in late. I don't think it is ethical to have one worker report on another.

17. *Psychiatrist says to himself at a team meeting*: Oh no! Here comes Ms. Carey again. She's well prepared and knows the evidence about teen suicide, but I know I'll go to sleep when she starts talking. Her monotone and soft voice put me out every time.

*18. *Situation*: Judge consulting with a social worker:

Judge Calhoun: The Chicago Police have referred a family to social services. The police found the parents and their two children living in their car without food, adequate clothing—and it's November! Which should we do, put the children in foster care or leave the family alone to fend for itself?

Social worker: I think that in such a situation, I would have to place the children in foster care.

19. *Hospital administrator*: There have been a lot of conferences and presentations about clinical decision making and judgment. I think that we should send our workers to an upcoming conference on the topic. We wouldn't want to be left out of the movement.

*20. *Situation*: Case conference at a juvenile court probation agency:

Ron: This boy has committed a very dangerous act. He constructed an explosive device and set it off in the field next to town. There wasn't anyone, other than the stone deaf, who didn't hear the boom!

Jonathan: Yes, that's true, but he has no prior delinquent act on his record.

Ron: We have to either place him in juvenile detention to protect society or let him off. Which is it?

*21. *Situation*: Case conference regarding juvenile court clients:

Gloria: The Einhorn boys were apprehended for vandalism again. They let the dogs out of the local dog pound, rewired the back of the high-school athletic field scoreboard, altered the controls on the dam, and took a sledge hammer to Mr. Winters' old car out in the wood in the back of his farm. I plan to draw up a bar chart showing in dollars the total value for all that vandalism. Then we'll work on restitution to repay the victims until the chart is filled in completely. What do you think of the bar chart for restitution and goal setting?

Albert: You know, that Winters is a con artist. I bet he claimed that the old wreck of a car in his woods is worth what a rolling vehicle would be.

Sandy: I don't know. Some of those old vehicles are worth a lot to collectors these days. I heard of a '49 Ford that went for $15,000 and that was three years ago.

*22. *Situation:* Child Protective Service case conference:

Mike: A police officer and I interviewed Janie, aged three, four times at Sunnyside Day Care Center. We used anatomically correct dolls to get her story. The officer and I become more and more certain with each interview that Janie has been sexually abused by one of the staff at Sunnyside.

Antonio: I read an article by Ceci and Bruck (1993) reviewing research about suggestibility in young children. It seems that small children, especially if interviewed repeatedly, may construct an untrue story. For example in one study 38% of the children who went to the doctor for a routine examination in which no pelvic examination was done reported that their genitals were touched. In successive interviews with the same children, the children gave successively more elaborate descriptions of acts that the doctor did not perform. I am worried that the same thing might have occurred here. Is there any clue in the progression of her ideas, from interview to interview, that Janie might have picked up unintentional cues to shape her story?

Mike: You're saying that I would intentionally mislead a child into giving false testimony is ridiculous. I would never help a child to lie.

23. *Faculty member speaking in a medical school to faculty*: Problem-based learning (PBL) is used ever more frequently in medical schools around the world to teach clinical reasoning skills. We should use PBL with our students to teach them clinical reasoning skills.

FOLLOW-UP QUESTION

Do any of this game's vignettes reflect real situations particularly well? Which one(s)?

_____

_____

_____

_____

Purpose

To learn to identify and avoid common cognitive biases that influence practice beliefs and actions

Background

Practice or clinical reasoning, refers to the process by which professionals structure problems and make decisions. They make decisions based on certain premises (beliefs, evidence) about what kind of data to collect, how to organize and integrate it, and what intervention methods to use. For example, a child-welfare worker may have to decide whether to leave a child in a foster home for another six months or return the child to its father. She will have to decide what factors to consider when making this decision. These may include characteristics of the child as well as those of the father and the environment in which he lives. Staff may be required to use a risk and/or safety assessment measure that includes characteristics associated with placement outcome.

Research related to judgment and decision making highlights biases and errors that may lead us astray as well as the role of experience in providing corrective feedback (for example see Chapman, 2005; Gambrill, 2005; Jenicek & Hitchcock, 2005; Klein, 1998; Koehler & Harvey, 2005). In their 1980 summary of research on social judgments and errors, Nisbett and Ross emphasized two heuristics (simplifying strategies): (1) availability (e.g., vividness, preferred theory, ease of recalling material), and (2) representativeness (e.g., depending on resemblance, for example similarity of causes to events). It was argued that these often lead us astray. For example, vividness may mislead us such as witnessing severe temper tantrums and making assumptions concerning potential for change based just on such data. We may be mislead by initial impressions that give an incorrect view of a client's characteristics and life circumstances. Because of these initial impressions, we may not change our views in light of new evidence (anchoring and insufficient adjustment)

(Tversky & Kahneman, 1982). For example, when interviewers were told beforehand that the interviewee was either "extroverted" or "introverted," they asked questions that encouraged confirming data (Snyder & white, 1981). There is a self-fulfilling prophecy effect. (See discussion of confirmation biases in Exercise 6.) Gender, race, and personal attractiveness may influence decisions (Garb, 1998). Representativeness refers to making decisions based on similarity. For example, people tend to believe that causes are similar to their effects. Stereotyping is another example; people treat a description as if it represents all the individuals in a group, even when it does not.

Relying on cues, that readily come to mind, is valuable if such cues contribute to sound decisions. If they do not, poor decisions may be made. (See discussion of intuitive and analytic thinking in Part 1.) Fast and frugal heuristics (making decisions based on cues that first come to mind) is a sound guide when such cues are indeed accurate (Gigerenzer, 2008). Simplifying strategies such as the satisfying heuristic (search through alternatives and select the first one that exceeds your aspiration level) (Gigerenzer, 2008, p. 24) often result in rapid adaptive choices. Although such strategies may often be a sound guide, especially when they are based on specific and recurrent characteristics of our environment (cues have ecological rationality), when misleading cues are relied on, they can result in incorrect judgments and poor decisions. Analytic thinking provides a check on the accuracy of intuitive thinking (Kahneman, 2003) as discussed in Part 1. The vignettes in Game C illustrate misleading biases. (See also discussion of confirmation bias and oversimplifications in Exercise 7.) Many others could be added such as "naturalism bias" ("a preference for natural over artificial products even when the two are indistinguishable") (Chapman, 2005, p. 590). (See list in Exercise 10.)

Instructions

1. Review the instructions that precede Exercise 6 before playing this game.
2. Read the description of each fallacy.
3. Read each vignette aloud when playing the game. Act out starred (*) items.

Definitions, Examples, and Countermeasures

1. **Hindsight Bias:** This refers to the tendency to think that you could have predicted an event "before the fact" when indeed you could not have done so (often because you did not have the information at the time in the past that you now have); the tendency to remember successful predictions of client behavior and to forget or ignore unsuccessful predictions (Fischhoff, 1975; Fischhoff & Beyth, 1975; Hoffrage & Pohl, 2003). There is a false sense of predictive accuracy even among experts (Tetlock, 2003). "People who know the nature of events falsely overestimate the probability with which they would have predicted it" (Dawes, 1988, p. 119). (See also Hastie & Dawes, 2001.) Those who fall prey to hindsight bias will often say, "I told you so!" or "Wasn't I right?" But they will not say, "I told you this would be true. I was wrong." Hindsight bias may result in unfairly blaming yourself or other practitioners for not predicting a tragic client outcome (murder, suicide, return to drug abuse). You review the person's history, searching especially for something you "should have noticed," and then hold yourself (or someone else) responsible for not taking timely action, all the while ignoring cases where the same events occurred, unaccompanied by the tragic outcome. This fallacy wins lawsuits for attorneys.

    Example:

    First supervisor: That story about the client who shot his wife, his children, and then himself was a tragic one.

    Second supervisor: Yes, I understand that he attempted suicide once before. Wouldn't you think his counselor would have noted this and had him hospitalized?

    Countermeasures: When looking back, people tend to over estimate the accuracy of their predictions. Keep records of your predictions as you make them, not after the fact. Consult material that clearly describes how to assess risk (e.g., Gigerenzer, 2002; Paling, 2006). (See also Exercise 22.)

2. **Fundamental Attribution Error:** This refers to the tendency to attribute behavior to enduring qualities (personality traits) considered typical of an individual and to overlook environmental influences (Kahneman, Slovic, & Tversky, 1982). In practice, this results in focusing on client characteristics and overlooking environmental factors related to hoped-for outcomes. For example,

we may overlook police pressures in gaining coerced confessions. We may not be aware of the conditions that encourage people to confess. Asymmetries in attribution (to person or environment) between actors and observers may create a self-serving pattern (attributing personal lapses to environmental variables and those of others to their personality characteristics). For a description of the complexities of findings in this area see Malle (2006).

Example: A family therapist says,

I know that the couple has faced severe financial hardships because of the husband's being laid off, the flood destroying much of their furniture and household goods, and the wife's illness and surgery, but I still think that their personality clash explains their problem. He is aggressive and she has a passive personality.

Countermeasures: Always ask, "Are there influential environmental variables?" The environments in which we live influence our behavior. Mirowsky and Ross (2003) argue that psychological problems such as depression are often related to stressful environmental circumstances, including discrimination and oppression. See also critiques of claims regarding the role of genes (e.g., Joseph, 2004; Oliver, 2006; Strohman, 2003). Contextual views emphasize the role of environmental influences (Gambrill, 2006; Lewontin, 1994; Reid, Patterson, & Snyder, 2002).

3. *Framing Effects:* Posing a decision in a certain way influences decisions. For example, framing a decision in a way that emphasizes potential benefits increases the likelihood that the decision maker will say "yes." On the other hand, we are more likely to say "no" when a decision is posed in a way that emphasizes possible adverse consequences. (See discussion of framing effects in Paling (2006.) Framing effects are more powerful when life-affecting decisions are being made such as whether to undergo a complex surgical procedure.

Example:

Counselor: Perhaps I can help you with your decision. We know that two-thirds of those who get treatment at Anderson Hospital for the Alcohol Dependent remain alcohol-free for two years. We also know that one-third of those treated at Luther Hospital's Alcohol Dependency Unit return to drinking within 2 years.

Client: I think I'll choose Anderson because, from what you have said, my chances seem better there.

Countermeasures: Describe negative as well as positive consequences for all alternatives.

4. *Overconfidence:* An inflated (inaccurate) belief in the accuracy of your judgments. We often have inaccurate beliefs about the accuracy of our predictions. Self-inflated assessments of our skills and knowledge (Dunning, Heath, & Suls, 2004) may result in offering clients ineffective or harmful services. David Burns (2008) collected data concerning degree of agreement between clients and professionals regarding the helpfulness of each therapy session for hundreds of exchanges. The correlation was zero. Overconfidence is encouraged by confirmation biases which encourage a focus only on data that support a preferred view. (See discussion of such biases in Exercise 7.) Overconfidence is encouraged by *the illusion of control*—a tendency to believe we can influence outcomes when we cannot.

5. *Overlooking Regression Effect:* Ignoring the tendency for people with very high or very low scores on a measure or variable to have scores closer to the center or mean of the distribution when measured a second time. Let us say that an individual scores very low or high on some assessment measure or test and is given a program designed to improve performance. If the client's posttest score is different, the regression fallacy lies in assuming that the treatment accounts for the change. Extreme pretest results tend to contain large errors that are corrected at posttest. Consider an average student who took a test and got one of the lowest scores in the class. In subsequent testing, the student will probably do better (regress toward the mean or average). Why? Perhaps during the pretest the student was ill or distracted, failed to understand instructions, or didn't see the items on the back of the last page, The test may have included questions about content in the one area he or she did not study.

The same principle holds for extremely high scores on a pretest that may have been due to unusually effective guessing or chance study of just the right topics for the test. Regression can account for the apparent effectiveness or ineffectiveness of programs designed to help those who pretest unusually low or high in some characteristic.

Example: A school social worker says,

We pretested all the fifth graders at Lowell Middle School on social skills, then involved the 10% who scored lowest in a five-week Working Together Program. This program models better social skills and provides practice for all participants. At posttest, the fifth graders scored much higher on the same measure of social skills. This program seems to work.

Countermeasures: Be wary of studies that single out extreme groups for observation. One way to avoid the regression error is to submit half the extreme group to treatment, the other half to an alternate treatment or none; then posttest both groups and compare them.

6. ***The Law of Small Numbers:*** The belief that because of a person has intimate knowledge of one or a few cases, he or she knows what is generally true about clients. This fallacy involves an insensitivity to sample size (mistakenly placing greater confidence in conclusions based on a small sample than on a much larger one). (See also discussion of case examples and testimonials in Exercise 6). The misleading law of small numbers is the reverse of the empirically based *law of large numbers*, which states that as samples include successively larger proportions of a population, the characteristics of the sample more accurately represent the characteristics of the population (unless the variance is very low). In other words, many observations provide the basis for more accurate generalizations.

Example: A child-care worker says,

Thanks for summarizing the study of 421 children that reported significantly lower intelligence among children whose mothers drank three drinks per day, but I doubt those findings. My sister regularly drank more than three drinks per day, and her children are fine.

Countermeasures: Give greater weight to conclusions based on randomly drawn, representative samples; give less weight to experience with one or a *few* clients.

7. ***Ignoring Prevalence Rate:*** This refers to the mistaken belief that the same assessment or screening tool will identify individuals just as well in a low prevalence group (where few people have the problem) as it will in a high prevalence group (where many people have the problem).

Example: A mental-health worker says,

Did you know among those hospitalized for a serious mental illness (high prevalence group) who took a Suicide Prediction Instrument (SPI), 10% of those who scored in the high risk category committed suicide within two years of their release from the hospital? If we administer the SPI to all outpatient mental-health clients (low prevalence) at the Apple Valley Clinic, we can be sure that if a client scores as high risk on SPI, then that client has a 10% chance of committing suicide in the next two years.

Countermeasures: In the low base-rate situation, there will be many more false positives (persons judged to have the problem who do not) than in the high base-rate situation. Seek information about base rate regarding topics of discussion. What is regarded as "abnormal" behavior may indeed be normative as reflected in base rate data.

8. *Omission Bias*: The tendency to judge harmful actions as worse, or less ethically questionable compared to equally harmful omissions (inactions). Clients may be harmed by not receiving adequate services as well as by offering services that harm them. The latter are more vivid.

    Example: Mr. A., a social worker rarely follows up on referrals to determine whether his clients were helped or harmed and he does not check out the quality of parent training programs offered by agencies to which he refers his clients.

    Countermeasures: Seek information regarding the outcome of all decisions.

9. *Gambler's Fallacy:* The mistaken belief that in a series of independent events, where a run of the same event occurs, the next event is almost certain to break the run because that event is "due." For example, if you toss a coin fairly, and four heads appear, then you tend to believe that the next coin tossed should be a tail because the tail is "about due" to even things out.

    Example:

    My husband and I have just had our eighth child. Another girl, and I am really disappointed. I suppose I should thank God she was healthy, but this one was supposed to have been a boy. Even the doctor told me that the law of averages were [sic] in

our favor 100 to 1 ("Dear Abby," June 28, 1974; cited in Dawes, 1988, p. 275).

The doctor's advice was in error, because on the eighth trial, the chance was essentially .5, as it was for the other births. "Like coins, sperm have no memories, especially not for past conceptions of which they know nothing" (Dawes, 1988, p. 291).

Countermeasures: Remember that for truly independent events—tosses of a fair coin, birth of boy or girl in a given hospital—what happened previously cannot affect the next in the series. No matter how many times you enter the lottery, your chances of winning the next time you play will be the same no matter how many times you have played in the past. This is important to understand and to convey to those clients who spend money they can ill afford on gambling.

10. *Anchoring and Insufficient Adjustment:* The tendency to base estimates of the likelihood of events on an initial piece of information and then not adjust this estimate in the face of new and vital information (Tversky & Kahneman, 1982). (See also number 11 that follows.) There are several reasons for anchoring, including the order in which information is given, and the tendency of observers to overestimate or underestimate probabilities.

Example:

Physical therapist: I always base decisions about a patient's chances for rehabilitation on my first few moments with the patient.

Countermeasures: Use strategies that encourage alternative hypotheses. For example, when you begin a group meeting, you could resolve to consider several hypotheses about what may be the principal interest of the group at the meeting. Resolve not to form an opinion until each member of the group has had a chance to speak. Also, you could select a hypothesis "at the other end of the pole," or that directly counters your initial estimate or belief.

11. *Availability:* This refers to the tendency to judge as most likely those events that can be readily imagined or recalled, perhaps because they are recent or vivid (Nisbett & Ross, 1980; Tversky & Kahneman, 1973). (See number 10.) We tend to make judgments based on the accessibility of concepts/memories—how easy it is to think/see/hear them. For example, the probability of an event is often judged by how easy it is to recall it. People judge events to

be more likely if they are vivid, recent, familiar, or have for some other reason caught their attention. Often, reliance on availability is successful as emphasized by Gigerenzer (2008) in his discussion of fast and frugal heuristics. However, at other times available theories or vivid data may lead us astray.

Example: I think she has Asperger's Syndrome. I just read a book about this complex disorder.

Countermeasures: Try to think of alternatives that do not come to mind readily. When possible, consult surveys that describe the relative frequencies of events (see Arkes, 1981).

12. *Nonfallacy Items:* Items that do not contain fallacies. These items illustrate examples of persons who use sound premises to reach a conclusion about the effectiveness of a treatment or what is generally true of clients. Nonfallacy items also show someone pointing out or avoiding a fallacy.

Refer to the list of fallacies in Box 8.1 as needed when playing Game C.

Box 8.1   Fallacies in Game C

1. Hindsight bias
2. Fundamental attribution error
3. Framing effects
4. Overconfidence
5. Overlooking regression effects
6. Law of small numbers
7. Ignoring prevalence rate
8. Omission bias
9. Gambler's fallacy
10. Anchoring and insufficient adjustment
11. Availability (misleading)
12. Nonfallacy item

Your Name _____ Date _____

Course _____ Instructor's Name _____

REMINDER

We think that the starred (*) items work best if the narrator reads the background and several actors act out the parts. Acting out the situation vividly portrays the content of each vignette. We hope this active participation will help you to retain the lesson in memory and transfer new knowledge and skills to practice. Consult the general instructions for playing the Reasoning-in-Practice Games as well as list of fallacies for Game C as needed.

*1.   *Situation*: A new supervisor has just been hired as an early childhood/special-education director. The school administration is concerned that too many children who don't need special education are admitted into the school's special-education program; then, in the spring when the program fills, too few children are admitted into the program who really need it.

New supervisor: I think that we need to administer standardized tests to see which children should be admitted into the new program.

First special-education teacher: We haven't used standardized tests before, and we have done a good job of identifying those needing the program. Think for example of the Williams boy. We admitted him, and he clearly needs our services.

Second special-education teacher: Yes! And there's the Gordan girl, and she clearly needed speech therapy.

*2.   *Situation*: School officials have requested a study to evaluate their district's preschool enrichment program. The child-care worker responsible for the study is reporting.

Child-care worker: We administered the Bailey's Developmental Inventory to all 4-year-old children in the Washington County School District. Those who scored in the lowest 5% were enrolled in the District's Preschool Enrichment Program. The children in the Enrichment Program scored 25% higher 1 year later, just prior to kindergarten.

School official: The Enrichment Program really helps preschool kids approach the average level for children starting kindergarten.

*3.   *Situation*: Orthopedic surgeon speaking to his patient:

Doctor: If you have orthoscopic surgery on your knee, you will have a good chance for full use of your knee.

Patient: How good a chance?

Doctor: In about 75% of such cases, the operation is a complete success.

Patient: And what about with cortisone treatment?

Doctor: About a quarter of those who get cortisone do not improve to full use of the knee.

Patient: Lets do the knee surgery.

*4. *Situation*: Two psychologists discussing the grade-school performance of children from a local low-income housing area.

Maria: Remember that envelope full of paint chips that I sent to the county health department? I got the chips off the window sills and floors of the tenement housing on Bridge Street. The county health nurse called today to tell me that the paint chips are toxic—full of lead! The nurse said that anyone breathing dust from the paint or ingesting food contaminated with the lead, or infants and toddlers eating the chips as they crawl around the floor, could suffer long-term cognitive deficits and other health problems.

Joe: I was a little worried about that as a factor in school performance. Still, I think that the major determinant of performance is cultural: The Bridge Street people just don't value education. They are simply not motivated enough to do anything about education in their area.

5. *Situation*: Two psychologists at lunch:

First psychologist: Now that I have been practicing for 2 years I can tell just how much my client likes me and feel my sessions helped.

Second psychologist: Me too. but I do wonder sometimes about why so many of my clients drop out early.

6. *Nurse administrator*: I looked for the best evidence I could find regarding the value of decision aids for people facing health treatment and screening decisions. I found a systematic review by O'Connor and her colleagues (2003) in the Cochrane database. In the absence of counterevidence, which I looked for, I support the use of decision aids for clients.

*7. *Situation*: Two alcohol and drug abuse counselors are talking in their office over a bag lunch.

Maureen: Who would have thought that Rodrigues would be first among the eight in the recovery group to start using drugs again?

Penny: Oh, it didn't surprise me. There was something about him that tipped me off. I still can't put my finger on it. But I would have guessed it.

8. *Client*: I'd much rather have a slim (10%) chance to overcome the problem than face a likely failure (90%).

9. *School social worker*: Your study of fifty high-school boys that found no relationship between level of knowledge learned in a sex education program and more permissive attitudes toward sex does not impress me. I know a student at King High School who took the same kind of program who swore that his permissiveness began because of it. He just found out that he has AIDS, and he has transmitted it to at least one female student.

10. *Social-work supervisor*: We arranged that all 100 social workers employed by Megalopolis County would take the State Social Work Competency Examination. The top ten were given engraved gold plaques with their name on them for their offices. During the year immediately after the examination, we arranged a series of in-service

training programs for all 100. Then we administered the same examination to all 100 a year later. Much to our surprise, the top ten on the prior test averaged 12% worse on their second test. These top ten must have relaxed during the training and not paid much attention.

*11. *Situation:* Two girls-club leaders are talking about Kisha, a new club member.

Ginny: I don't think Kisha is going to graduate from Washington High School. Both of Kisha's parents are illiterate. Her father is absent from the home. Her mother is on AFDC. Her school is notorious for not graduating its students. She's attractive and bright, but there are pimps in her neighborhood.

Pat: Yes. I don't think she has the strength of character needed to stay with her studies.

12. *Caseworker planning to visit an Aid-for-Dependent-Children case in a dangerous area of the city.* Three from our office have gotten through to their cases with backup support in the past with only minor confrontations: I'm sure the next one will have trouble.

13. *Situation:* A researcher is describing a risk-assessment instrument to an audience of protective-service workers.

Researcher: My child-abuse prediction instrument accurately identified 90% of protective-service clients who reabused their child within a year.

Protective-service worker: Wow! If we could administer your test to all families in the community, we could identify 90% there, too.

14. *Surgeon:* I evaluated a 78-year-old man for lethargy, stomach pain, and sleep disturbance after he retired and his wife died. I conducted elaborate and costly tests to investigate physiological causes, including lung cancer, thyroid disease, and an infection of the stomach and intestines. I am sure that I did not overlook anything.

15. *Psychiatrist:* Typically, when I have a little information about the client, I find that no amount of additional history taking and information from other sources can change my mind about what to do.

*16. *Situation:* Two university instructors discussing teaching over their lunch break:

First instructor: I can tell on the first day of class who the stars will be. The star students just shine out somehow.

Second instructor: I think you might be guilty of forming an initial opinion hastily, then not revising your opinion as the semester wears on. I would be worried also about bias in grading if you're not careful.

17. *Hospital physician:* I try to get a good look at a patient's chart before seeing the patient. Usually, all I need to know about whether the patient should be discharged to a community program, a nursing home, or some other program, is in the chart. Then, I look for these indicators when I see the patient.

*18. *Situation:* Two psychologists discussing how to help poor readers in an elementary school.

First child psychologist: I have some information that might help your poor reader and his parents. Miller, Robson, and Bushell (1986) studied thirty-three failing readers and their parents. The children were ages 8 to 11 and had reading delays of at least 18 months. The parents read with their kids over 6 weeks for an average of 7.6 hours per family. Reading accuracy and comprehension scores for the paired reading-program kids were compared with those of kids who did not participate in the program. Results favored kids in the program. You might try paired reading.

Second child psychologist: About a year ago, one of our psychologists tried paired reading. The reading developed into a battle ground. The kid bugged his parents constantly while they tried to read with him. The kid was real innovative when it came to distractions during the paired reading: He even ate a goldfish. I don't think I'll try paired reading.

19. *One pro\bation officer to another*: My most recent three sex offenders have been apprehended for a new offense within two months of when their cases were assigned to me. This next one is bound to be a success.

*20. *Situation*: Two occupational therapists talking at lunch.

First occupational therapist: I think it is important to kept track of harms to clients in our work. I keep track of each time a client seems worse off with a treatment. I have found few instances of harming my clients.

Second occupational therapist: That's a good idea. I'm going to keep track of times the methods I use harm clients.

*21. *Situation*: A psychologist is telling an audience about a new instrument to predict outcome for parolees. (In the United States, parole is a conditional release from prison; probation is a suspended prison sentence to be served in the community provided that the probationer follows certain rules.)

Psychologist: Our parole-prediction study found that 95% of criminal offenders who scored in the high-risk group and were released from our maximum security prison went on to commit a new offense within a year.

Community probation officer: I would like to give your parole prediction measure to my clients so I can identify high-risk clients, too. I'll be able to tell the judge in my presentence report which offenders should be handled more conservatively.

22. *Situation*: Two social workers talking about a client at lunch.

Social Worker 1: I took a continuing education course on trauma last week. This client is clearly traumatized and we should seek out more information related to this history.

FOLLOW-UP QUESTION

Do any of this game's vignettes reflect real situations particularly well?

Which one(s)?

_____

_____

_____

Purpose

1. To become familiar with a practice fallacy that you and a partner have chosen to demonstrate before the class in a brief vignette
2. To learn more about other fallacies by watching others demonstrate theirs

Background

The credit for devising an exercise in which professionals *purposefully* mess up for instructional purposes may go to clinical scholars at the University of North Carolina (Michael, Boyce, & Wilcox, 1984, p. xi). Apparently, a clinical scholars' skit in "Clinical Flaw Catching" left such an impression on Max Michael and his colleagues that they wrote the delightful book, *Biomedical Bestiary,* complete with humorous illustrations of thirteen fallacies from the medical literature. In this exercise, student presentations illustrate each fallacy, much as the cartoons in *Biomedical Bestiary* do.

Instructions

1. Sign up with a partner for one practice fallacy from the List of Practice Fallacies and Pitfalls at the end of this exercise. (See Box 9.1.) These fallacies are defined in the Reasoning-in-Practice Games, Professional Thinking Form, and the professional literature.
2. Read about your chosen fallacy (see References at the back of this workbook) and note important points. Consult references to additional literature in sources you locate. Keep a record of sources by noting complete references for each using the American Psychological Association's reference style. Consult books on critical thinking and informal fallacies cited in our workbook. Consult Internet sources such as fallacyfiiles.com, skepdic.com, and Carl Sagan's *Baloney Detection Kit* and *Guide to Logical Fallacies* (Downes).

3. First, in no more than two pages, define the fallacy, using literature to document your definition, and describe how you would avoid the fallacy in practice and policy situations. You may use conceptual definitions, examples, or even measures to define your fallacy. Second, attach a reference list using APA style. Third, attach a script for actors to follow, including descriptions of props (see sample vignette script included in this exercise) (Box 9.2). Your vignette should last, at most, about a minute. Vignettes seem to work best if they are brief (about 30 seconds), are a bit overdone, make use of props, and clearly demonstrate just *one* fallacy.

4. Demonstrate your chosen fallacy to the class with your partner or with help from other students whom you direct. (They'll volunteer because they'll probably need help with *their* vignettes.) And, post your example of a fallacy on YouTube so other students can see and comment on it. Your demonstration should include a short introductory statement describing who is involved, where it takes place, and what is going on so that your audience can get the gist of what they will see. Your vignette can either be highly realistic or be overacted and humorous, with overdressing, engaging props, or eccentric mannerisms.

FOLLOW-UP QUESTION

What have you learned from this exercise?

_____

_____

_____

_____

Box 9.1 Examples of Practice Fallacies and Pitfalls*

1. Ad hominem, focusing on the person (attack, praise) rather than the argument
2. Anchoring and insufficient adjustment
3. Appeal to unfounded authority, *ad verecundium*. Uncritical documentation, such as relying on citation alone (See Walton, 1997a)
4. Appeal to experience; all evidence is equally good, experience
5. Arguing from emotion; appeal to pity/anger
6. Arguing from ignorance: assuming that an absence of evidence for an assumption indicates that it is not true (e.g., see Walton, 1996)
7. Assuming hard-headed therefore hard-hearted
8. Begging the question (see Walton, 1991)
9. Case example
10. Confirmation bias; searching only for confirming evidence; focusing on successes only, lack of objectivity, not objective, bias, vested interests
11. Confusing cause and effect; does depression cause drinking or does drinking cause depression?
12. Confusing correlation and causation
13. Diversion, red herring, drawing a red herring across the trail of an argument
14. Egocentric (self-serving) bias: accepting more responsibility for success than for failure
15. Ecological fallacy: assuming that something true for a group is true of an individual
16. Either-or, only two sides, only two alternatives, false dilemma
17. Emotive language; using emotionally loaded words to influence decisions
18. Fallacy of Accident: applying of a general rule to a particular person to which it does not apply
19. Fallacy of composition: assuming what is true of the parts is true of the whole
20. Fallacy in labeling
21. Framing effects
22. Fundamental attribution error
23. Gambler's fallacy
24. Groupthink
25. Hasty generalization, biased sample, sweeping generalization
26. Hindsight bias, i knew it would be so, hindsight does not equal foresight
27. Ignoring base rate, ignoring prior probability, ignoring prevalence rate
28. Is-ought fallacy: assuming that because something *is* the case, that it *should* be the case
29. Jargon
30. Leading, loaded, biased question
31. Manner, style, charisma, stage presence
32. Naturalism bias: a preference for natural over artificial products even when the two are identical
33. New, newness, tried-and-true, tradition
34. Oversimplifications
35. Overconfidence
36. Overlooking regression effects, regression to the mean, regression fallacy
37. Popularity, peer pressure, bandwagon, appeal to numbers, because everybody...

(continued)

Box 9.1   Continued

38. Post hoc ergo propter hoc, after this, therefore because of this
39. Representativeness: making decisions based on similarity (E.G., Believes Causes Are Similar To Their Effects)
40. Selection bias, biased selection of clients
41. Slippery slope: assuming (mistakenly) that if one event occurs, others will follow when this is not necessarily true
42. Stereotyping
43. Straw man argument
44. Tautology, word defines itself
45. Testimonial
46. Two questions, double-barreled question, ambiguous
47. Vagueness, unclear term, undefined term, vague outcome criterion

*Described in Reasoning-in-Practice Games, Professional Thinking Forms' key, and literature concerning judgment and decision making.

Box 9.2   Sample Vignette Script

FOCUSING ON SUCCESSES ONLY
by Michael Werner and Tara Lehman
University of Wisconsin, Eau Claire

Situation: Four patients sit bedraggled with spots painted on their faces.

[Hold up a sign that reads "9:00 A.M. "]
Doctor: Today we are trying an experimental drug for people such as
yourselves, who have blotchy skin disease. This should take care of your disease in a matter of seconds. *[Pours water into four glasses containing dry ice, i.e., solid carbon dioxide. Everybody appears to take a drink. (Don't drink, it will burn the mouth.)]*

[Hold up a sign that reads "9:01 A.M.")
Doctor [looking at first patient): Wow! Your skin really cleared up.
How do you feel?
First patient: I feel great!
Doctor: This stuff really does work: At last, a new miracle drug!
First patient [looking at the other three patients): But what about these
other three uncured, sickly, sorry-looking specimens? *[The other three hang their heads.]*

Doctor: That's OK. It doesn't matter. We did have one great success! It really works.
What a breakthrough! I must tell all my colleagues to use it.

EXERCISE 10   FALLACY SPOTTING IN PROFESSIONAL CONTEXTS

Purpose

To hone your skills in spotting fallacies in professional sources

Background

This is one of our students' favorite exercises. Students select some quote relevant to their profession and critique it (see items below). You could select quotes from one of your professors. You could critique a statement in this very book. Although we have tried to avoid fallacies, we are sure that we have been guilty of some. In fact, we would be grateful if you would inform us about them so we can correct them.

Instructions

1. Review the fallacies described in the Reasoning-in-Practice Games and in the Professional Thinking Form's scoring key.
2. Identify an example of professional content that you think illustrates a fallacy.
3. Note the complete source on the Fallacy Spotting in Professional Contexts Form using the APA reference style used in this book.
4. Give verbatim quote that states a claim (include page numbers as relevant). You could duplicate relevant portions of an article/chapter and attach a copy highlighting the quote of concern. To be fair, do not take a sentence out of its context in a way that alters its meaning.
5. Identify (name) the fallacy involved and explain why you think it represents this fallacy in the critique section of the worksheet.

Your Name _____ Date _____

Course _____ Instructor's Name _____

Source *

_____

_____

Claim. Give verbatim description or attach a copy noting content focused on.

_____

_____

_____

_____

_____

Critique. Identify the main fallacy, describe why you think this applies to the quoted material, and describe possible consequences of believing an inaccurate claim. Have there been any critical tests of the claim? If so, what was found? (Consult relevant databases. See Exercises 12, 19, and 20.)

Main Fallacy: _____

How it applies to quote: _____

_____

_____

_____

_____

_____

*If newspapers, give correct date, title of article, author, and page numbers. If journal, give title, author, volume number, and page numbers. If book, give full title, author, date, publisher. Use APA style. If in a conversation, describe context and position of person. If Internet, give website address and date accessed.

FOLLOW-UP QUESTION

What have you learned from this exercise?

_____

_____

_____

EXERCISE 11   AVOIDING GROUP THINK

Purpose

To learn about and practice avoiding strategies used in team meetings and case conferences that decrease the likelihood of making well-informed decisions

Background

Team meetings and case conferences are everyday occurrences in professional practice. As Meehl (1973) suggests in his classic chapter "Why I do not attend case conferences," discussions do not always forward careful appraisal of alternatives. One tendency he notes is the "buddy-buddy" syndrome in which we are reluctant to raise questions about other people's comments because of the false belief that this requires harsh or discourteous methods. Group think, the tendency to prematurely choose one alternative and to "cool out" dissent, has resulted in grievous consequences as described by Janis (1982) and others (Tuchman, 1984) (see also Baron, 2005). Conditions that encourage groupthink include high cohesiveness, insulation of the group, lack of procedures to critically appraise judgments and decisions, an authoritarian leader and high stress with little hope of discovering and forwarding a choice that differs from the one preferred by the leader of the group. These conditions encourage seeking agreement among group members. Indicators of group think include the following:

- An illusion of invulnerability that results in overoptimistic and excessive risk taking.
- Belief in the group's inherent morality.
- Pressure applied to any group member who disagrees with the majority view.
- Collective efforts to rationalize or discount warnings.
- A shared illusion of unanimity.
- Self-appointed "mind guards" who protect the group from information that might challenge the group's complacency.

- Self-censorship of deviation from what seems to be the group's consensus.
- Stereotypical views of adversaries as too evil to make negotiating worthwhile or too stupid or weak to pose a serious treat (Janis, 1982).

Results of groupthink include poor decisions as a result of lack of consideration of well-argued alternatives, vague or incomplete description of objectives, overlooking risks of preferred choices, confirmation biases (seeking only data that confirm preferred views) and failure to critically appraise choices and alternatives (Janis & Mann, 1977; Myers, 2002).

Methods Janis (1982) suggests for avoiding group think include the following:

- The leader should assign the role of critical evaluation to each member. Every member should be encouraged to air objections and doubts and to look for new sources of information.
- The leader should not state his or her own judgments or preferences at the outset.
- Several independent policy planning groups should be established, each with a different leader.
- The group should divide into subgroups and meet separately and then later come together to work out differences.
- Members should discuss deliberations of the group with qualified outsiders.
- Qualified outsiders should be invited in for group deliberations.
- One member of the group should be assigned the role of devil's advocate. (Assigning just one devil's advocate in a group may not be effective because of the strong tendencies of groups to persuade a lone dissenter, see for example the classic study by Asch, 1956).
- After the group has reached an agreement, another meeting should be held in which every member is encouraged to express any doubts and to rethink the issue.

Instructions

Step 1

Keep track of the kind and frequency of group think indicators in conferences and/or team meetings (or class) for one week using the form in this exercise. What was the most common group think ploy? Who used group think ploys most often? What was the baseline of each group think indicator? (Divide time into number for each indicator to obtain rate.)

Step 2

Select a method designed to decrease group think (see background material), encourage other members of a group to adopt it and record what happens.

Situation (group): _____

Remedy selected: _____

_____

Percentage of times used compared to opportunities to use _____

Rate of group think ploys before implementation of remedy: _____
Rate of group think indicators after implementation

Discussion: _____

_____

_____

_____

_____

Other Practice Opportunities

• Practice using specific group think ploys in an exaggerated manner in a group of other students to highlight their character.
• Together with seven students, practice countering group think ploys in a role-played team conference using the fishbowl technique in which class members observe a role play. Observers will keep track of ploys used, whether effective responses followed, and with what consequences using the form in this exercise.

Practice Exercise 11   Nature and Frequency of Group Think Indicators

Your Name _____ Date _____

Course _____ Instructor's Name _____

INSTRUCTIONS

Keep track of indicators of group think for one week. Be sure to note overall time observed: _____

Situation	Source	Statement	Kind of Ploy	Consequences

Key: *Situation*: T (team meeting), CC (case conference), C (class), O (other _____).

Source: L (leader), M (member), V (visitor), O (other _____)

Kind of ploy: Please describe (e.g., buddy-buddy, ad hominem, etc.). See also background information in Exercises 6, 7, and 8.

Consequence: + (contributed to a sound decision); − (detracted from making a sound decision)

PART 4
Evidence-Informed Decision Making

The process and philosophy of evidence-based practice (EBP) was introduced within the health area and has spread to other professions. Both the process and philosophy and the origins are described in the introduction to this book. The exercises in Part 4 provide guidance in carrying out the steps involved in the process such as posing well-structured questions that guide an efficient, effective search for related research findings. Exercise 12 describes the process of EBP in greater detail and provides an opportunity for carrying out this process. Exercises 13 and 14 offer opportunities to apply the process of EBP in team meetings and case conferences. Exercise 15 provides instructions for preparing Critically Appraised Topics (CATs) and guides you in preparing a CAT for your supervisor. Exercise 16 describes a form for honoring informed consent guidelines described in professional codes of ethics. Suggestions for asking questions regarding the evidentiary status of services that must be raised if we are to draw on research findings related to decisions we make are provided in Exercise 17. Exercise 18 offers an opportunity to review the evidentiary status of an agency's service. We hope these exercises will enhance your skills in integrating ethical, evidentiary, and application concerns in helping clients make informed decisions that affect their well-being.

Purpose

To describe the steps involved in evidence-based practice and to offer practice in implementing these steps including sharing ignorance as well as knowledge (e.g., see DUETs and jameslindlibrary.org).

Background

Part 1 offers an overview of EBP. Here we describe the steps in detail as well as the variety of questions to which they may be applied. Ethical obligations described in professional codes of ethics require practitioners to draw on practice- and policy-related research findings and to involve clients as informed participants concerning the costs and benefits of recommended services and of alternatives. EBP provides a process and a variety of related tools designed to fulfill these obligations (Straus, Richardson, Glasziou, & Haynes, 2005). The steps in EBP illustrate the close connection with values, skills, and knowledge related to critical thinking. They are designed to help professionals make conscientious and judicious use of current best evidence in making decisions concerning clients.

Questions EBP can Help Answer

Types of Questions That May Occur in Your Work with Clients

1. *Effectiveness* questions concern how effective an intervention might be for a particular client (e.g., "What feeding method(s) will work best for infants born with a cleft lip/palate?" "What method, if any, will most effectively forestall the onset of Alzheimer's disease among nursing home residents like those here at Lakeside?" "Which method is most effective in helping interdisciplinary teams to work effectively?").
2. *Risk/prognosis* questions concern the likelihood that a particular person will engage in a particular behavior or experience a certain

event in a given period. For example, "What is the likelihood that a sex offender like Joe will commit a new offense within the two years of his parole?" "If I place sexually abused siblings in the same adoptive home, how likely is it that they will continue to abuse each other?"

3. *Description* questions may concern base rate and other descriptive data about clients (estimate of the frequency of a problem in a given population based on a sample of individuals from that population) or what has been found regarding similar clients. Examples are "What are the most common reasons for readmission to a hospital for aged persons who had been discharged to community support services?" "What is the base rate of teenage pregnancy in this city?" "What environmental and personal characteristics are associated with delinquent behavior of teenage boys?"

4. *Assessment* questions concern descriptions of clients' problems, alternative competing behaviors, and their contexts. For example, "What is the most accurate assessment tool to determine pain in the neonate (newborn infant less than six weeks of age)?" "Is there a reliable, valid measure of depression or substance abuse, or parenting skills that will be valuable with my client?" "What is the quickest, easiest to administer, least obtrusive, and most accurate assessment tool to see whether a client here at Sacred Heart Hospital has an alcohol abuse problem?" "What is the best instrument to screen for depression among the elderly at Syveresn Lutheran Home?"

5. *Prevention* questions concern the most effective way to prevent the initial occurrence of a problem or undesirable event, for example, "What is the most effective way to prevent SIDS (sudden infant death syndrome)?" "What is the most effective way to prevent skin breakdown in the diaper area of newborns having watery stools?" What is the most effective say to prevent teenage pregnancy among students at South Middle School?" "Which is the most effective way to teach kindergarteners and first graders not to wander off with someone not authorized to take the child from school?"

6. Other kinds of questions include those regarding harm, cost-benefit of different practices and policies (e.g., see Gray, 2001a; Guyatt, Rennie, Meade & Cook, 2008) and self-development (e.g., see Exercise 36).

Gibbs (2003) suggests a first step regarding motivation (Step 1). Steps described by Sackett et al (2000) and Straus et al. (2005) can be seen in Steps 2 to 6.

Step 1

Become motivated to offer clients evidence-informed services. The history of the helping professions provides many examples of iatrogenic (harmful) effects produced inadvertently by caring practitioners across the helping professions. Examples include

- The juvenile awareness delinquency prevention program that led to higher delinquency levels among program participants than among controls (Petrosino, Turpin-Petrosino, & Buehler, 2003) (see Exercise 4).
- Retrolental fibroplasias caused by excessive oxygen levels for premature babies (Silverman, 1980).
- Frail and elderly persons whose death rate was higher among those receiving intensive casework than among those not receiving this (Blenkner, Bloom, & Nielsen, 1971).

Good intentions do not protect us from harming clients, as these examples show. Beware of the *hard-headed-therefore-hard-hearted* fallacy—the fallacy that we cannot be both empathic and warm-hearted professionals, and be critical thinkers. Ideally, we should be *both* soft-hearted and analytical (hard-headed). For a more detailed discussion of this fallacy see Exercise 6.

Step 2

Convert the need for information into an answerable question of practical importance regarding a client (see earlier description of different kinds of questions).

1. Briefly describe your client and an important decision you must make in the relevant spaces on Exercise 12.
2. Describe a well-structured question related to your information needs in the next space in Exercise 12 and note the question type. Well-structured questions state the client type (e.g., depressed elderly), identify an intervention (which may be an assessment

method), describe some alternative course of action (e.g., watchful waiting), and describe a hoped-for outcome (e.g., decrease depression). This is called a PICO question. Gibbs (2003) refers to these as COPES questions: they are client oriented, of practical importance, and can guide a search especially, when accompanied by relevant methodological filters such as the term "systematic review." (See Box 12.3.) Other examples of questions:

- In delinquents at risk of further delinquency are "Scared Straight" programs effective in decreasing future delinquency?
- In women with suspected breast cancer, does vacuum assisted core needle biopsy or fine needle aspiration result in fewer hematomas?
- In families in which child abuse is a concern, is a Webster-Stratton Parent Training Program or current agency program more effective in preventing further child abuse?

Thus well-structured questions should:

- relate directly to information needed regarding a decision
- clearly describe: (1) client type; (2) proposed intervention; (3) some comparison, such as watchful waiting; and (4) a desired outcome. When searching, a methodological filter related to appropriate research design should be included in the search terms used.
- concern a decision you are likely to encounter again.

3. Write down your best answer to your question and describe the sources you used in Practice Exercise 12 *before* searching for external research.

Step 3

Track down the best evidence related to your question using the following steps.

1. Underline key terms in your question and place them at the top of each column in the Search Planning Form Box 12.1. Consult a thesaurus to locate synonyms for key terms.

2. Select a search engine or relevant database (e.g., Google scholar, ERIC, Medline, PubMed, Cochrane, or Campbell Library) that is most likely to contain research findings regarding your question (see Box 12.2). Consult a reference librarian as needed.

3. Design a search strategy. Review Box 12.3, Quality filters for Locating Research Findings, to identify descriptors related to your

Box 12.1   Search Planning Form

Your Name _____ Date _____

Course _____ Instructor's Name _____

Well-Structured Question _____

_____

_____

INSTRUCTIONS

1. Circle key words in your well-structured question that will help you limit your search in Practice Exercise 12.
2. Select the most useful database or WWW address (see Box 12.2).
3. Keep a record of your search on the Search History Log (see Box 12.4).

Client Type	Terms Describing the Intervention	Terms Describing an Alternate Option	Hoped-for Outcome(s)	Quality Filter Terms

Note: Include synonyms in each column that may help you to search effectively

BOX 12.2   Some Useful Databases for Practitioners*

DATABASE	CONTENTS
CINAHL	Nursing and Allied Health
ERIC	Documents on microfiche regarding issues in education (accessible free on the World Wide Web under: ericir.syr.edu/)
PsychInfo	Psychological literature regarding behavior, learning theory, therapy
Bandolier Center for Reviews and Dissemination Cochrane and Campbell Databases of systematic reviews DUETS Equator Essential Evidence Plus Medscape Netting the Evidence PubMed TRIP database.com Research into Practice	Medicine, Nursing, Psychology, Social Work
pages.nyu.edu/~holden/gh-w3-f.htm	Social Work

question. If your initial search yields no hits, use less restrictive search terms.

4. Keep a search history log in Box 12.4.

Let us take an example. Consider this question. In elderly depressed clients, is cognitive behavioral therapy compared to no intervention effective in decreasing depression? First, circle key words in the question: elderly, depressed, cognitive behavioral, decrease depression. Insert each word in the appropriate spaces in Box 12.1. Thus, in the first column (client type) you would place "elderly, depressed in the second, cognitive behavioral, in the third (no intervention), in the fourth (decreased depression) and in the fifth, insert a quality filter (effectiveness) (See Box 12.3.) Next, identify the type of question in Practice Exercise 12. Useful descriptors for locating evidence can be seen in Box 12.3. Combine the columns in a single row in Box 12.1 using Boolean search terms ("and," "or"). Terms in your search may include (elderly, depressed or geriatric depression), and

Type of Practice Question	Useful Terms to Find Best Evidence
Assessment (assessment or diagnosis or client evaluation) AND (descriptors to the right).	(Inter-Rater Reliability or Inter-Rater Agreement or Assessment or Diagnosis* or Kappa or Sensitivity or Specificity or Positive Predictive Value or Negative Predictive Value or Likelihood Ratio* or Pretest Odds).
Description (survey or needs assessment or client satisfaction) AND (descriptors to the right)	(Random* Select* or Stratified Random or Representative Sample* or Pretested or Response Rate)
Effectiveness	(Random* or Control Group* or Statistical* Significant* or Experimental Group* or Randomized Control Trail* or RCT or experimental*design)
Prevention (prevent*) AND (descriptors to the right)	(Random* or Control Group* or Statistical* Significan* or Experimental Group* or Randomized Control Trial* or RCT or experiment* design)
Risk/Prognosis (risk or prognosis* or predict*) AND (descriptors to the right)	(Validation Sample or Gold Standard or Positive Predictive Value or Negative Predictive Value or Predictive Validity or Risk Reduction or Estimating Risk or Risk Estimation or Prediction Study)
Synthesis of Studies	Meta-anal or systematic review or synthesis

"*" is a symbol that means "Search for any word that has the root word to the left of the symbol." For example, "prevent*" means *prevention, preventing, preventable*, as well as *prevent*. Such terms are called "*methodologic search filters*" (Sackett, Richardson, Rosenberg, & Haynes, 1997). See also Gibbs (2003).

(cognitive behavioral therapy or behavior therapy), and (controlled trial or systematic review).

Step 4

Critically appraise the best evidence regarding your question "for its validity (closeness to the truth), impact (size of the effect), and applicability (usefulness in clinical practice)" (Straus, et al., 2005, p. 4). What is the likelihood that the research method used in a study can answer the question

Box 12.4 Search History Log

Your Name _____ Date _____

Course _____ Instructor's Name _____

Question: _____

_____

Search Number	Database Searched	Search Terms	Number of Hits	Comments

(continued)

Box 12.4 Continued

Search Number	Database Searched	Search Terms	Number of Hits	Comments

Describe what you learned from your search.

_____

_____

_____

posed, 0 (none), 1 (slight—10%), 2 (fair—30%), 3 (moderate—50%), 4 (good—70%), 5 (very good—90%)? Valuable guides include Ciliska, Thomas, and Buffett (2008); Guyatt et al. (2008); Henegan and Badenoch (2006), Moore & McQuaid (2006); and Straus et al. (2005). Criteria for appraising different kinds of research reports are included in subsequent Exercises. Please consult these as needed. See also checklists and flow-charts developed to assist in the critical appraisal of different kinds of research. These include

- CONSORT (Consolidated Standards of Reporting Trials) www. consort-statement.org (Moher, Schulz, Altman, & the CONSORT Group, 2001). See also Zwarenstein, et al., 2008.

- MOOSE (Meta-Analysis of Observational Studies) (Stroup, et al., 2000)
- Qualitative Checklist (see e.g., Greenhalgh, 2006). See also Bromely, et al., 2002
- QUORUM (Quality of Reporting of Meta-Analysis) (Moher, Cook, Eastwood, Olkin, Rennie, & Stroup, For the QUORUM Group, 1999)
- STARD (Standards for Reporting Diagnostic Accuracy) (Bossuyt, et al., 2003)
- STROBE (Strengthening the Reporting of Observational Studies) www.strobe-statement.org
- TREND (Transparent Reporting of Evaluations With Nonrandomized Designs) (Des Jarlais, Lyles, Crepaz, & the TREND Group, 2004)

Step 5

Integrate your critical appraisal with other vital information including your clinical expertise and information regarding your client's unique characteristics and circumstances including their values and expectations and, together with your client, make a decision about what to do. Complete Practice Exercise 12 as well as appropriate evidence ratings and prepare an Action Plan (two to four pages). Include a client description which may pertain to the following (choose one):

An individual: Client name (use a pseudonym to protect confidentiality), age, gender, occupation and work history, brief social history, when they sought help at your agency, presenting concerns, brief history including efforts to alleviate concern(s), how the client and significant others (e.g., family members) view concern(s), how you view them, client strengths, environmental resources, including social supports

A group: Specific goals of group (desired outcomes), number in group, members' ages, gender, occupations/social roles, history of group efforts

An organization: Purpose, structure, culture and climate, resources, goals

A community: Geographical area, demographics (race, ethnicity, age distribution), businesses, recreational opportunities, political climate, medical facilities, hoped-for outcomes

A policy: Aims, involved parties, methods used, resources for implementation, consequences, current goals

You may learn that no high-quality research is available. This is an important finding to share with your client. Does a systematic review or careful meta-analyses show that an intervention is ineffective or harmful? You could use the following scale:

−3	−2	−1	0	+1	+2	+3
Strong harmful effect	Moderate harmful effect	Slight harmful effects	No effect	Slight positive effect	Moderate positive effect	Strong positive effect

Step 6

Evaluate the outcome of this process and seek ways to improve it in the future. Were outcomes pursued specific and relevant to your client and/or their significant others (such as family members)? How did you assess progress? What did you find? Be as clear as possible so that both you and your clients can accurately determine if valued goals have been attained and to what degree or if harm occurred. Compare data collected during intervention with baseline data (the preintervention level of performance) if you have them. Consult sources describing single-case studies as needed (e.g., Bloom, Fisher, & Orme, 2005).

Next Steps

Teach others to do EBP. Share this exercise with others in your agency. Advocate that the agency use the WWW and databases that concern your clients and their hoped-for outcomes. Exchange practice action summaries with others. Encourage your fellow workers to prepare summaries addressing their questions regarding practices and policies. Seek out advances in diffusing innovations (e.g., Greenhalgh, et al., 2004).

Your Name _____ Date _____

Course _____ Instructor's Name _____

Brief description of client including presenting concerns: _____

_____

_____

_____

Important decision that you must make: _____

_____

_____

_____

Well-structured question related to this decision: _____

_____

_____

_____

Question type   ☐   Effectiveness   ☐   Risk/Prognosis   ☐   Description
                ☐   Assessment   ☐   Prevention

Your best answer before searching for external evidence: _____

_____

_____

_____

Resource(s) used (e.g., supervisor, intuition): _____

_____

_____

_____

_____

_____

Your answer based on a review of external research. Summarize your search (databases and descriptor terms used, hits), and the quality of evidence found. Attach a copy of your best source. Briefly summarize what you learned regarding your question (Attach your search planning form and search log).

_____

_____

_____

_____

_____

Action Plan. Please describe what you will do based on your search.

_____

_____

_____

_____

_____

_____

_____

_____

_____

_____

_____

_____

_____

_____

_____

Did the results of your search improve the quality of services offered to your clients?

_____ Yes _____ No

If yes, describe exactly how it influenced your work.

_____

_____

_____

_____

_____

_____

If no, please describe why.

_____

_____

_____

_____

_____

_____

Purpose

To acquaint you with EBP

To give you immediate feedback by comparing your performance with that of an interdisciplinary EBP team's performance

Background

Interdisciplinary teams have also been called *multidisciplinary, interdisciplinary, cross-disciplinary, transdisciplinary, or interprofessional teams*. Aron Shlonsky and Mike Saini at the University of Toronto (2007) prepared a systematic review. We have here only preliminary results of this review. They proposed that a multidisciplinary EBP team must have two or more helping professions represented and must be working directly with individual clients or patients. Setting policy only would not meet this criterion. To be included in their review, a source had to summarize observations of the impact of the team's intervention with clients or patients and had to reflect the evidence-informed process (see Exercise 12). This includes the following:

- Posing well-structured questions: Converting information needs into a well-structured question called a *PICO question* (i.e., one that states the Patient type, Intervention or course of action, alternate Course of action, and intended Outcome).
- Evidence Search: Finding, with maximum efficiency, the best evidence with which to answer the question (generally this means using electronic search techniques and specific search terms).
- Evidence Critique: Determining the merit, feasibility, and utility of evidence (i.e., applying criteria for good study methodology and indices of treatment effect size).
- Integration/Synthesis: Combining findings from all relevant sources of information to make a decision (i.e., deciding what to do based on external research findings as well as client characteristics and circumstances including client preferences).
- Evaluating what happens.

Only one of 2045 documents located met their criteria for inclusion. This was an article by Akobeng (2005) titled "Evidence in Practice." Akobeng (2005) described efforts of a team (junior doctors, nurses, and a pharmacist) to help Laura, a 16-year-old girl with her chronic Crohn's disease (bloody diarrhea, abdominal pain, and weight loss). Her symptoms were not relieved by conventional treatment, including corticosteroids and diet. One member of the team, Dr. B, suggested that the team consider use of "infliximab" based on information he obtained at a conference. The team posed this PICO question, In a 16-year-old girl with active Crohn's disease unresponsive to conventional therapy, is infliximab effective in inducing remission? The team looked into PubMed (http://pubmed.gov/) and the Cochrane Library for systematic reviews and meta-analyses of randomized clinical trials and for individual randomized trials using search terms: (Crohn's disease OR Crohn disease) AND (infliximab OR remicade) AND remission (......) (p. 849). They found one relevant meta-analysis in the Cochrane Library, no meta-analyses in PubMed, but two relevant studies in PubMed. Their best evidence was a meta-analysis that narrowed to a single study. In this study, 108 subjects, aged 26 to 46 years, with Crohn's disease that resisted conventional treatment, were randomly assigned to placebo or to infliximab given intravenously. The team concluded that results for a dose of 5mg/kg favored the infliximab on both symptom-rating scales.

Dr. B appraised the study's quality and computed the "relative risk" by subtracting the percentage in remission in the placebo from the percentage in remission in the infliximab group. In the infliximab study cited by the Akobeng (2005) team, relative risk was 28.5% favoring the infliximab patients. *Note*: Relative risk should *never* be used alone; absolute risk should also be given. See Exercise 22 for discussion of problems using relative risk. The team discussed the evidence's applicability to Laura. The study located involved subjects aged 26 to 46 years, but the team saw no reason that its results would not apply to Laura, the 16-year-old. After determining that the drug would be available to Laura, members of the team discussed the effects of the drug and its potential side effects with her. She and her family decided that Laura should take the infliximab. She did, and three weeks later her symptoms had "settled." It seems she was *not* informed about *absolute risk*, which is vital information required to make informed decisions. Other questions pertain to side effects and length of follow-up.

Enhancing Team Effectiveness

Since little has been written specifically about effective EBP teams, we rely on our own experience teaching interdisciplinary EBP courses and on the summary of research by Kozlowski and Ilgen (2006) (see also Cooke, Gorman, & Winner, 2007; Nemeth & Goncalo, 2005 as well as Exercise 12). Suggestions for making teams effective, both in skill development and in organizations, include the following:

- *Sense of Mission*: There is a focus on helping clients and avoiding harm and making informed decisions. Indicators include client's perception that they are central to what is going on and staff making every effort to help each other to serve clients.

- *Shared Problem-Solving Process*: The team needs a shared process that guides problem-solving—one in which a search for evidence pertinent to decisions and controversy are viewed as vital for discovering possible solutions. Team members should know (1) how basic technologies and procedures work, (2) how to carry out team tasks, (3) know which team members have particular skills and knowledge, and (4) understand how the EBP team process can be used to seek solutions together (Suggested by Kozlowski & Ilgen, 2006, pp. 81–83).

- *Team Environment*: The team needs a climate that reflects the team's mission of helping clients and avoiding harm and that supports efforts to contribute to that mission. The team needs a supportive organizational environment that will provide time and material support for efforts to identify and answer life-affecting questions. Organizations resist change. An interdisciplinary EBP team may arrive at conclusions at odds with organizational policy.

- *Team Learning*: Members need to be trained to apply EBP skills within the context of their organization. The Instructors' Manual that accompanies this book contains course outlines designed to help students to acquire competencies demonstrated in the audiovisual material that accompanies these exercises.

- *Leadership*: Team leadership should not be based on the relative status of the disciplines represented on the team, but rather, on which member of the team wants to take on a problem, assuming that all team members have equal skill in applying the EBP process. The audiovisual material that accompanies these exercises shows leaders who were selected by the team.

- *Necessary Support and Equipment*: Exercises 13 and 14 took place in a computer laboratory with up-to-date equipment. Each team member was able to contribute to the team's effectiveness within restricted time allowed.

Instructions

Please complete Practice Exercise 13. Part of this exercise was given as a final examination counting toward a grade in a course that taught students to think critically and to work as a team to apply EBP skills. Students, who had practiced the EBP process as a team before, were given thirty minutes to work as a group to answer the question. If you work as a team in a computer laboratory to do this exercise we suggest that you try to complete the exercise in thirty minutes also. You might give yourself more time if you work alone. The web-based material that accompanies this exercise illustrates how students from multiple disciplines can apply team skills to pose and answer a well-built (PICO) question. The teams did their work in a computer laboratory, not in a human service agency. Still, the video may be helpful to suggest how such teams may function effectively within organizations.

Practice Exercise 13 Working in Evidence-Based Teams

Instructor's Name _____ Course _____ Date _____

Names of Group Members _____

This exercise tests your thinking and skills regarding a complex social problem: how to prevent alcohol misuse in young people. It assumes rudimentary knowledge regarding the process of EBP including how to pose and answer questions to make well-reasoned judgments and decisions. You will apply this process to make your recommendations. You will need to work as a team to accomplish your task with maximum success. Work through the problem answering each question in sequence.

TOPIC: Preventing Alcohol Misuse in Young People (thirty minutes, no more)

Assume that one of you has taught for several years, and you now are the principal of a middle school and high school that includes grades 7 through 12. You are concerned about alcohol misuse among young people through direct experience with several tragic situations. One group of students experimented with vodka and one drank a fatal dose. Others will not live to graduate, because they were involved in another mishap related to alcohol misuse such as a fatal car accident. You wonder what primary prevention program (preventing the initial occurrence of a problem) would most effectively prevent alcohol misuse among young people. You have been given a mandate by the school board that you must try something. What approach would you try?

1. Describe your PICO question here. (Include all three or four elements of a PICO question.)

    _____

    _____

    _____

    _____

2. Record your search plan in Box 13.1 including terms to mark key concepts and include relevant search terms ("methodogic search filters") (Sackett, et al., 1997, p. 62) or MOLES (Gibbs, 2003, p. 100).

3. Record your search histories or history for your group including the databases searched, terms used, and numbers of hits to locate your best document on Box 13.2.

4. How sound is your best source relative to criteria on the appropriate evidence rating form? Summarize your assessment of the evidence quality here in a brief paragraph.

    _____

    _____

    _____

    _____

    _____

5. What intervention does this source support? Can you determine Number Needed to Treat? (See Bandolier's guide for calculating NNT; see also Glossary.) (Attach Boxes 13.1 and 13.2 to your exercise.)

    _____

    _____

    _____

    _____

    _____

BOX 13.1 Search Planning Form

Client Type	Terms Describing the Intervention	Terms Describing an Alternate Option	Hoped-for Outcome(s)	Quality Filter Terms

BOX 13.2 Search History Log

Search Number	Database Searched	Search Terms	Number of Hits	Comments

EXERCISE 14   WORKING IN EVIDENCE-BASED TEAMS 2

Purpose

To give you practice in a team in applying the process of evidence-informed practice. You can also compare your team's performance with that of another team

Background

Please read material in Exercises 12 and 13 first.

Instructions

This exercise was given as a final examination in a course designed to teach students to think critically and to work as a team to apply the process of EBP. Students who had practiced the process as a team were given thirty minutes to work as a group to answer two questions. If you work as a team in a computer laboratory, try to complete this exercise in thirty minutes as did the team you will see. Give yourself more time if you work alone. In either case, the audiovisual material for this exercise demonstrates how the team accomplished the tasks in this exercise.

Practice Exercise 14   Working in Evidence-Based Teams 2

Instructor's Name _____ Course _____ Date _____

Names of Group Members _____

Assume that you have taken a job as a probation-parole officer working with juvenile clients who have been adjudicated by a local juvenile court. Your supervisor at your agency has asked you for your opinion about whether juveniles, who are served by your probation-parole agency should participate in a delinquency prevention program patterned after a one in the popular video titled: "Scared Straight." This video shows an innovative program put on by "lifers" serving a life sentence that is intended to literally scare the delinquents straight.

1. Describe your PICO question here. (In the accompanying audiovisual material you will see, the class calls it a Client Oriented Practical Evidence Search (COPES) Question (Gibbs, 2003). (Include all four elements of a PICO question described in Exercise 12.)

_____

_____

_____

_____

2. Record your search plan on a copy of Box 13.1 here including appropriate search terms to mark key concepts as well as "methodogic search filters" (Sackett, et al., 1997, p. 62) or MOLES (Gibbs, 2003, p. 100).

3. Record your search histories or history for your group including the databases searched, terms used and number of hits, to locate your best document on a copy of Box 13.2.

4. How sound is your best source relative to criteria on the appropriate evidence rating form? Please summarize your assessment of the evidence quality in a brief paragraph.

_____

_____

_____

5. What advice would you give to your supervisor about using the "Scared Straight" program to prevent delinquency careers?

_____

_____

_____

_____

_____

_____

6. Can you calculate Number Needed to Treat (NNT) for any studies? If so, please give results here.

_____

_____

_____

_____

_____

EXERCISE 15 PREPARING CRITICALLY APPRAISED TOPICS

Purpose

To acquaint you with elements in a critically appraised topic (CAT)

To give you feedback by comparing your CAT with one presented by a nursing student in response to a question from a public health nurse

To prepare a CAT for your supervisor

Background

CATs are short (one to two page) summaries of the available evidence related to a specific clinical question or situation encountered in practice. A CAT summarizes a process that begins with a practice question, proceeds to a well-built question, describes the search strategy used to locate the current best evidence, critically appraises what is found, and makes a recommendation based on what is found (the clinical bottom line). Cost effectiveness of different programs should be considered as well as evidentiary concern (see e.g., Guyatt, et al., 2008; Straus, et al., 2005.) CATs may be prepared for journal club presentations (see Exercise 35). First review the process of EBP in Exercise 12. You can learn more about how to construct CATs and how to locate ones that have been prepared by consulting sources on the Internet. (See e.g., evidence-based purchasing www.cebm.utoronto.ca/syllabus.) The Centre for Evidence-Based Medicine (CEBM) has a website that provides an outline and criteria for a CAT. Go to http://www.cebm/net/index.aspx then to EBM tools. On this page you will find "Level of evidence" that can help you to rate the quality of evidence specific to different types of questions; you will find "Critical appraisal worksheets" that can help you to evaluate the quality of evidence and a program called *CAT maker*. This program

- prompts you for your clinical question, your search strategy, and key information about the study you found;
- provides online critical appraisal guides for assessing the validity and usefulness of the study;

- automates the calculation of clinically useful measures (and their 95% confidence intervals);
- helps you formulate clinical "Bottom Lines" from what you have read;
- creates one-page summaries (CATs) that are easy to store, print, retrieve, and share (as both text and HTML files);
- helps you remember when to update each CAT you create; and
- helps you teach others how to practice EBM (CEBM Centre for Evidence-Based Medicine. CATmaker http://www.cebm.net/index.aspx?o=1216. Retrieved 11/17/2007).

If the CEBM site is unavailable, you can find a CAT tutorial at this address through the University of Alberta:

http://www.library.ualberta.ca/subject/healthsciences/catwalk/index.cfm

Sources for locating CATs that have already been prepared include the following:

- University of North Carolina
  http://www.med.unc.edu/medicine/edursrc/!catlist.htm+
- University of Western Sydney (Occupational Therapy)
  http://www.otcats.com/
- University of Michigan
  http://www.med.umich.edu/pediatrics/ebm/
- Middlesex University
  http://www.lr.mdx.ac.uk/hc/chic/CATS/index htm

Instructions

1. Please read the following example first.

This example is from an interdisciplinary course titled, Practical Applications of EBP. Students included those in social work, nursing, psychology, premedicine, special education, health care administration, and public relations. Each student was asked to solicit a question from a helping professional and then to follow the steps described subsequently. One student, Kathryn Forkrud, contacted a public health nurse working for Eau Claire County in Wisconsin (Anita Schubring). Anita told Kathryn that she was concerned about a high rate of tooth decay in Altoona, a town near Eau Claire. Altoona does not have fluoridation in the town's drinking water. Anita told Kathryn that she wanted evidence to present to the Altoona city officials that might persuade them to put fluoride in Altoona's water as a way to safely reduce tooth decay among Altoona's children. (Note the premature assumption that fluoridation of the water supply is a good idea.) Please view related material on the book's website.

2. Complete Practice Exercise 15 regarding preparing and presenting a CAT.

    Use visual aids. Your presentation should be no more than six minutes. You can follow the steps used by Kathryn in her presentation and recorded search on the workbook's website to check your work. If you are unfamiliar with the process of EBP, prepare for this exercise by reading background information in Exercise 12. (For a description of controversies regarding fluoridation see Cheng, Chalmers & Sheldon (2007).)

Practice Exercise 15   Preparing and Presenting a Critically Appraised Topic

Your Name _____ Date _____

Instructor's Name _____ Course _____

1. State who you are, who generated your question, where that person works, and why their question is important.

   _____

   _____

   _____

   _____

   _____

2. Describe your well-structured question on an overhead or PowerPoint slide (see Exercise 12). This describes the client type, intervention or course of action, alternate course of action, and hoped-for outcome.

   _____

   _____

   _____

   _____

   _____

3. Present your search plan including search terms and databases you plan to search.

   _____

   _____

   _____

   _____

4. Present your search history including the databases you searched, search terms used, and number of documents retrieved for each search string.

    _____

    _____

    _____

    _____

    _____

5. Present your best source.

    _____

    _____

    _____

    _____

    _____

6. Based on critical appraisal of this source, how would you answer this question? The evidence may not be sufficiently clear to make a recommendation. There may be contradictory results. The results may be clear regarding positive effects, but the intervention may also have harmful effects. If so, how do you weigh their relative impact?

    _____

    _____

    _____

    _____

    _____

Preparing a CAT For Your Supervisor

Agency staff often donate their time to students as field instructors. One way students can reciprocate is to help staff acquire information they need. The exercises offer such an opportunity.

INSTRUCTIONS

Step 1 Give Practice Exercise 15.2 to your field instructor and, when completed, bring this to class.

Step 2 What kind of question did your supervisor pose? _____

Step 3 Prepare a CAT (critically appraised topic) regarding your supervisor's question and e-mail this to your instructor and all other class members. Include cost-benefit information if possible noting both short- and long-term costs and benefits.

Step 4 Present your CAT in class.

Step 5 Integrate class feedback regarding your CAT including further search and appraisal as needed. E-mail the revised CAT to your instructor and class members and give a copy to your supervisor.

Step 6 Seek your supervisor's feedback regarding the usefulness of your CAT and describe this here.

_____

_____

_____

_____

Practice Exercise 15.2

TO: Field Instructor _____

FROM: _____

RE: Request for Practice or Policy Question

Field instruction and internships are a key part of the education of professionals. We hope you will help us integrate such instruction more closely in our courses by suggesting a practice or policy question directly related to work for students to pursue and provide feedback to you.

The attached form asks you to pose a question about some method or procedure you currently use or are considering using. Any question regarding the effectiveness of a method or procedure you use or plan to use would be appropriate. A question may concern whether a pregnancy prevention program would be effective in reducing the frequency of pregnancy among girls in a local high school or the effect of daily reassurance calls to elderly persons in the community on the frequency of calls to the agency. Such questions come directly from practitioners who make life-affecting decisions.

Please complete the attached form and return it to the student you supervise so he/she can bring the completed form to class

PRACTICE OR POLICY QUESTION

PLEASE RETURN TO THE STUDENT YOU SUPERVISE.

Name of Agency:_____

Your Name: _____

Address of Agency _____

Agency Phone Number: _____

Type of Client Served by Agency: _____

What important question concerns you about your agency and its effectiveness? You may wonder which of two approaches to treating residents who have Alzheimer's disease results in a longer period of self-sufficiency for residents; you may wonder if preschool children who are exposed to sex education films falsely report sexual abuse more frequently than children not exposed to such material.

Please describe your question here as clearly as possible. If you can, define key words in your question.

_____

_____

_____

_____

_____

_____

_____

_____

_____

_____

Continue as needed.
_____

EXERCISE 16 INVOLVING CLIENTS AS INFORMED PARTICIPANTS

Purpose

To illustrate how clients can be involved as informed participants

Background

Professional codes of ethics require informed consent regarding the risks and benefits of recommended methods and of alternatives. Shared decision making and being informed is a top patient priority (Schattner, Bronstein, & Jellin, 2006). Informing clients about Number Needed to Treat can contribute to involving clients as informed participants. (See *Bandolier Guide to NNT.*) Most clients are not involved as informed participants (e.g., see Braddock, Edwards, Hasenberg, Laidley, & Levinson, 1999; Katz, 2002). Entwistle and her colleagues suggest a format for doing so as shown in this exercise. Lack of skill in accurately communicating risk to clients compromises informed consent as described in Exercise 22. Increased attention has been devoted to involving clients as informed participants in decisions made, including considering their wishes for degree of participation (see e.g., Coulter, 2002; Coulter & Ellins, 2007; O'Connor, et al., 2003, 2007; Stacey, Samant, Bennett, 2008).

INSTRUCTIONS

Complete Practice Exercise 16. Select a client with whom you are working or find a social worker who works directly with clients. Describe a key outcome being pursued as well as the method being used to attain it. Describe the best evidence found regarding how to attain this outcome. Give complete reference and complete Part A of Box 16.1, Evidence-Informed Client Choice Form. Gather information needed to complete Parts B and C of Box 16.1.

Your Name _____ Date _____

Course _____ Instructor's Name _____

1. Key outcome pursued _____

   _____

2. Method used _____

   _____

3. Best evidence found regarding this outcome _____

   _____

   _____

   _____

   Source _____

   _____

   _____

4. Based on above, complete Part A of Box 16.1.

5. Gather the information needed to complete Part B of Box 16.1. This may require visits to the referral agency and review of agency reports. Questions here include the following:

   a. How do staff assess progress with their clients? What criteria do they use?

   _____

   _____

   _____

   _____

b. Do they systematically evaluate outcome of services with clients? _____ Yes _____ No Please describe.

_____

_____

_____

_____

c. How do individual staff members keep track of their success regarding pursuit of different outcomes with clients? Please describe.

_____

_____

_____

_____

6. Describe degree of match between method(s) offered and what research suggests is likely to be effective.

_____

_____

_____

_____

7. Discuss ethical implications of gaps between services offered and what is most likely to maximize the likelihood of success.

_____

_____

_____

_____

8. Should clients receive a copy of a completed "Evidence-Informed Client Choice Form" for each major service recommended? _____ Yes _____ No Please describe reasons for your answers:

_____

_____

_____

_____

_____

9. Do all clients want to be involved in making decisions? Consult related literature and discuss ethical implications of different levels of client involvement.

_____

_____

_____

_____

_____

Box 16.1   Evidence-Informed Client Choice Form*

Agency: _____ Date: _____

Client: _____

Hoped-for outcome(s): _____

Referral agency (as relevant) and department or program within agency: _____

Staff member within agency who will offer (or is providing) services: _____

A.   *Related External Research*

_____   1. This program has been critically tested and found to help people like me to attain hoped-for outcomes.

_____   2. This program has been critically tested and found not to be effective in attaining hoped-for outcomes.

_____   3. This program has never been rigorously tested in relation to hoped-for outcomes.

_____   4. Other programs have been critically tested and found to help people like me attain hoped-for outcomes.

_____   5. This program has been critically tested and been found to have harmful effects (e.g., decrease the likelihood of attaining hoped-for outcomes or make me worse).

B.   *Agency's Background Regarding Use of This Method*

_____   1. The agency to which I have been referred has a track record of success in using this program with people like me.

C.   *Staff Person's Track Record in Use of This Method.*

_____   1. The staff member who will work with me has a track record of success in using this method with people like me.

*See for example "Evidence-informed patient choice," by V. A. Entwistle et al., 1998, *International Journal of Technology Assessment in Health Care*, 14, pp. 212–215.

Note: This form is completed by the professional who gives it to the client. One is prepared for each outcome pursued (e.g., decreasing cocaine use, increasing positive parenting skills, increasing consistency in exercise program).

EXERCISE 17   ASKING HARD QUESTIONS

Purpose

One purpose of this exercise is to give you practice in asking questions such as "Do the services we offer our clients really help them?" A second is to help you to develop diplomatic ways to raise such questions. Asking such questions is vital to the process and philosophy of evidence-informed practice.

Background

Offering clients effective services and honoring ethical obligations requires asking questions such as "Does this service that we offer clients really help them?" "How do we know whether it does more good than harm?" "How good is the evidence?" "What does antisocial mean?" The literature regarding evaluation shows that people often find such questions threatening (e.g., Baer, 2003). Indeed, you may be threatening the financial survival of an agency which offers clients ineffective services or services that have been critically tested and found to be harmful. You will often have to be persistent, that is, raise a question again, perhaps in a different way (see Gambrill, 2006). You will have to acquire effective skills for responding to neutralizing efforts (i.e., raise your question again). We can draw on literature concerning interpersonal behavior and critical thinking to identify and hone related skills. Questions differ in their "threat" level. Using terms such as 'evidence,' or 'research" may "turn-off" others. Let's say that someone claims that multisystemic therapy works. We could ask "What evidence do you have?" (see e.g., Littell, 2005, 2006). Or, we could avoid such terms and ask for example "Does it work for all kinds of problems?"

Instructions

Please complete Practice Exercise 17.

Your Name _____ Date _____

Course _____ Instructor's Name _____

1.   Review the questions Richard Paul suggests for thinking critically about decisions and judgments in Box 17.1 as well as the questions in Box 17.2 related to different kinds of claims.

2.   Select a question you would like to practice raising and write this here:

_____

_____

_____

3.   Describe how you would feel and respond if someone asked you that question:

I would feel_____

_____

I would respond (what I would say) _____

_____

4.   Is there a more diplomatic way to raise this question? Please suggest one example:

_____

_____

_____

5.   Describe obstacles to raising this question.

_____

_____

_____

6.   Describe feasible remedies to obstacles you suggest: _____

_____

_____

_____

7.   Practice asking your question over the next week. Keep track of the following on a chart: situation, question, what happened and describe here.

_____

_____

_____

_____

8.   Practice asking questions about the evidentiary status of agency practices and policies in a small group of other students. What questions seem to work best (result in clear answers with the least negative reactions)? Which questions do not work well?

_____

_____

_____

_____

_____

Questions that are successful. (Describe exact wording):

a. _____

b. _____

c. _____

Questions that do not work well. (Describe exact wording:)

a. _____

b. _____

c. _____

Box 17.1 A Taxonomy of Socratic Questions for Decision Making and Problem Solving[1]

QUESTIONS OF CLARIFICATION

- What do you mean by _____?
- What is your main point?
- How does _____ relate to _____?
- Could you put that another way?
- Is your basic point _____ or _____?
- Let me see if I understand you: Do you mean _____ or _____?
- How does this relate to our discussion (problem, issue)?
- Could you give me an example?
- Would you say more about that?

QUESTIONS ABOUT ASSUMPTIONS

- What are you assuming?
- What could we assume instead?
- You seem to be assuming _____. Do I understand you correctly?
- All of your reasoning depends on the idea that _____. Why have you based your reasoning on _____ rather than _____?
- Is it always the case? Why do you think the assumption holds here?

QUESTIONS ABOUT REASONS AND EVIDENCE

- What would be an example?
- Are these reasons adequate?
- Why do you think this is true?
- Do you have any evidence for that?
- How does that apply to this case?
- What would change your mind?
- What other information do we need?
- How could we find out whether that is true?

[1] Source: Adapted from Paul R. (1993) *Critical thinking: What every person needs to survive in a rapidly changing world (Revised 3nd ed.).* (pp.367–368). Santa Rose, CA: Foundation for Critical Thinking. www.criticalthinking.org. Reprinted with permission.

(continued)

Box 17.1 Continued

QUESTIONS ABOUT VIEWPOINTS OR PERSPECTIVES

- You seem to be approaching this from _____ perspective. Why have you chosen this view?
- How may other people respond? Why?
- How could you answer the objection that _____?
- What is an alternative?

QUESTIONS ABOUT IMPLICATIONS AND CONSEQUENCES

- What are you implying by that?
- When you say _____, are you implying _____?
- If that happened, what might happen as a result? Why?
- What is an alternative?

QUESTIONS ABOUT THE QUESTION

- Do we all agree that this is the key question?
- Is this the same issue as _____?
- What does this question assume?
- Why is this question important?
- How could someone settle this question?
- Can we break this question down?
- Is the question clear? Do we understand it?
- Is this question easy or hard to answer? Why
- Does this question ask us to evaluate something?
- To answer this question, what questions would we have to answer first?

Box 17.2 Examples of Questions Regarding Different Kinds of Claims

1. About a "problem"
   - Exactly how is it defined? Give specific examples.
   - Who says X is a problem? Do they have any special interests? If so, what are they?
   - What is the base rate?
   - What kind of problem is it?
   - What controversies exist regarding this "problem"?
   - Is there a remedy?

2. About prevalence
   - Exactly what is it?
   - Who or what organization presented this figure? Are special interests involved?
   - How was this figure obtained? Do methods used enable an accurate estimate?
   - Do other sources make different estimates?

3. About risk
   - What is the absolute risk reduction? (see Exercise 22).
   - What is the number needed to harm (NNH)?
   - What is the false positive rate?
   - What is the false negative rate?
   - Is risk associated with greater mortality?

4. About assessment and diagnostic measures
   - Is a measure reliable? What kind of reliability was checked? What were the results? Is this the most important kind of reliability to check?
   - Is a measure valid? Does it measure what it is designed to measure? What kind of validity was investigated? What were the specific results (e.g., correlations of scores with a criteria measure). Is this the most important kind of validity for clients?

5. About effectiveness
   - Were critical tests of claims carried out? What were the results?
   - How rigorous were the critical tests?
   - Are reviews of related research of high quality (e.g., rigorous, comprehensive in search and transparent in description of methods and findings)?
   - Was the possibility of harmful effects investigated?

(continued)

Box 17.2 Continued

6. About causes
   - Is correlation confused with causation?
   - Could associations found be coincidental?
   - Could a third factor be responsible?
   - Are boundaries or necessary conditions clearly described (circumstances where relationships do not hold) (Haynes, 1992)?
   - Are well-argued alternative views accurately presented (e.g., see Uttal, 2001)?
   - How strong are associations?
   - Are interventions based on presumed causes effective?
   - Is the post hoc ergo proc fallacy made (see Exercise __)?
   - Are vague multifactorial claims made that do not permit critical tests?

7. About predictions
   - Are key valued "end states" accurately predicted (rather than surrogates)?
   - What percentage are accurate?
   - What is the variance in accuracy?

Purpose

To provide an opportunity to review the evidentiary status of an agency's services (at least in one area) and compare this with what research suggests is most likely to result in hoped-for outcomes (including services purchased from other agencies)

Background

Agency services match what research suggests is effective to different degrees. There may be large gaps between what is offered and what should be offered to maximize the likelihood of success. Variations in services offered to achieve the same outcome raise questions such as: Are they all of equal effectiveness? Are some more effective than others? Are any harmful? Services are often purchased from other agencies and it is vital to review the evidentiary status of such service. (See extensive literature on evidence-based purchasing, for example, www.cebm.utoronto.ca/syllabi/print/whole. htm on evidence-based purchases.)

Instructions

Please complete Practice Exercises 18.1 and 18.2.

Practice Exercise 18.1   Evaluating Agency Service

Your Name _____ Date _____

Course _____ Instructor's Name _____

1.   What is the most frequent presenting concern addressed by this agency?

_____

_____

_____

_____

2.   Clearly describe the service used most often (or attach description) as well as hoped-for outcome(s).

Service used: _____

_____

_____

_____

_____

Hoped-for outcome(s): _____

_____

3.   How does your agency evaluate the success of this service? Please give specific examples.

_____

_____

_____

_____

_____

4. Complete Practice Exercise 18.2. Prepare a pie chart using the categories shown in Practice Exercise 18.2 regarding other key services or programs used if you wish.

Your Name _____ Date _____

Course _____ Instructor's Name _____

Agency _____

Source of Funding _____

Ethical obligations of professionals require consideration of the evidentiary status of services offered, including those purchased from other agencies. Please complete the pie charts below depicting current and optimal distribution for the major service offered to clients in your agency using the following categories (based on Gray, 2001a):

1. Services critically tested and found to be effective; they do more good than harm.
2. Services critically tested and found to be ineffective.
3. Services of unknown effect.
4. Services critically tested and found to be harmful; they do more harm than good.
5. Services are of unknown effect (they have not been tested) but are in a well-designed research study.

Current services

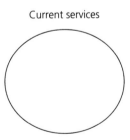

Optimal services

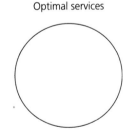

a. If you describe services as falling under #1, give the complete citation for the highest quality study or review reflecting these critical tests here.

_____

_____

_____

b If you checked 2 or 4, cite related study/review here.

_____

_____

_____

_____

c. If you checked 5, give information regarding this in-progress study (e.g., site of study, author, design, etc.)

_____

_____

_____

_____

d. Describe gaps found between the evidentiary status of current and ideal service distribution.

_____

_____

_____

_____

e. Discuss the ethical implications of any gaps found.

_____

_____

_____

_____

Please describe reasons for gaps found.

_____

_____

_____

_____

_____

5. Describe how gaps could be decreased (e.g., involving clients in advocating for more effective services).

_____

_____

_____

_____

_____

PART 5
Critically Appraising Different Kinds of Research

How Good Is the Evidence?

Knowledge and skill in critically appraising research regarding practices and policies allows professionals to fulfill ethical obligations such as involving clients as informed rather than as uninformed or misinformed participants. Exercise 19 provides guidelines for evaluating effectiveness studies. Exercise 20 describes criteria for critically appraising research reviews and guidelines for critically appraising self-report measures are offered in Exercise 21. Exercise 22 suggests guidelines for estimating risk and making predictions. Suggestions are included for understanding and communicating risk. Exercise 23 provides an opportunity to review a diagnostic test and Exercise 24 provides an opportunity to review the clarity of descriptions in a widely used classification system, the *Diagnostic and Statistical Manual* of the American Psychiatric Association (DSM). Exercise 25 suggests important points to check when critically appraising research regarding causes. Considerable attention has been devoted to preparing user-friendly checklists and flow charts for appraising different kinds of research including STARD for diagnostic measures, STROBE for reporting observational studies, CONSORT guidelines for reviewing effectiveness studies, QUORUM for reviewing meta-analyses and MOOSE for reviewing observational studies.

Purpose

1. To identify the hallmarks of well-designed treatment-evaluation studies
2. To accurately evaluate practice and policy-related research
3. To estimate the magnitude of a treatment's effect

Background

Central to both critical thi nking and evidence-informed practice is weighing evidence critically and fairly when you and your clients seek answers to life-affecting questions. This exercise will help you to answer the following questions: (1) What does this study tell me about the effectiveness of this method compared with others? (2) Which treatment helps clients the most? (3) Is one study better than another? (4) What are the hallmarks of a sound study? You will be introduced to a quality-study rating form developed by Gibbs, CONSORT Guidelines (www.consort-statement.org) and a user-friendly third type of rating form. An example of a hierarchy regarding quality of evidence is

1. evidence obtained from at least one properly randomized controlled trial;
2. evidence from a systematic review (e.g., Cochrane or Campbell review)
3. evidence obtained from well-designed controlled trials without randomization;
4. evidence obtained from well-designed cohort or case-controlled analytic studies, preferably from more than one center or research group;
5. evidence obtained from multiple time series with or without the intervention; dramatic results in uncontrolled experiments (e.g., the results of the introduction of penicillin treatment in the 1940s) could also be regarded as this type of evidence;
6. opinions of respected authorities based on clinical experience, descriptive studies and case reports, or reports of expert committees (Berg, 2000, p. 25 in Geyman, Deyo, & Ramsey, 2000).

How sound are statistical tests used? (see Box 19.1).

BOX 19.1   Ten Ways to Cheat on Statistical Tests When Writing Up Results

1. Throw all your data into a computer and report as significant any relationships where $p < 0.05$.

2. If baseline differences between the groups favor the intervention group, remember not to adjust for them.

3. Do not test your data to see if they are normally distributed. If you do, you might get stuck with nonparametric tests, which aren't as much fun.

4. Ignore all withdrawals ("dropouts") and nonresponders, so the analysis only concerns subjects who fully complied with treatment.

5. Always assume that you can plot one set of data against another and calculate an 'r-value' (Pearson correlation coefficient) and that a "significant" r-value proves causation.

6. If outliers (points that lie a long way from the others on your graph) are messing up your calculations, just rub them out. But if outliers are helping your case, even if they appear to be spurious results, leave them in.

7. If the confidence intervals of your result overlap zero difference between the groups, leave them out of your report. Better still, mention them briefly in the text but don't draw them in on the graph and ignore them when drawing your conclusions.

8. If the difference between two groups becomes significant four and a half months into a six month trial, stop the trial and start writing up. Alternatively if at six months the results are 'nearly significant', extend the trial for another three weeks.

9. If your results prove uninteresting, ask the computer to go back and see if any particular subgroups behaved differently. You might find that your intervention worked after all in Chinese females aged 52 to 61.

10. If analyzing your data the way you plan to does not give the result you wanted, run the figures through a selection of other tests.

Source: Greenhalgh, T. (2006). *How to read a paper: The basic of evidence-based medicine (3rd. ed.)*. Malden, MA: Blackwell (p. 74).

Instructions

Step 1

First, review the Quality of Study Rating Form in Box 19.2. This form was developed to provide a standard for appraising the quality of studies of treatment effectiveness (Gibbs, 1991). This form contains room at the top to describe the study by noting (1) the type of client who participated (e.g., dyslexic children, older persons with Parkinson's disease), (2) the treatment method(s) evaluated, (3) the most important outcome measures, and (4) the reference for the study in APA format.

Items 1 to 16 will help you to appraise the soundness of a study and how it compares with others. Based on hundreds of studies reviewed by

Box 19.2   Quality of Study Rating Form (QSRF)*

Your Name _____ Date _____

Course _____ Instructor's Name _____

Client type(s) _____ Intervention method(s) _____

Outcome measure to compute *ES1* _____

Outcome measure to compute *ES2* _____

Outcome measure to compute *ES3* _____

Source (APA Format) _____

_____

Criteria for Rating Study

Clear Definition of Treatment							
1. Who (4 pts.)	2. What (4 pts.)	3. Where (4 pts.)	4. When (4 pts.)	5. Why (4 pts.)	6. Subjects randomly assigned to treatment or control. (10 pts.)	7. Analysis shows equal treatment and control groups before treatment. (5 pts.)	8. Subjects were blind to group assignment. (5 pts.)

9. Subjects randomly selected for inclusion in study. (4 pts.)	10. Control (nontreated) group used. (4 pts.)	11. Number of subjects in smallest treatment group exceeds 20. (4 pts.)	12. Outcome measure has face validity. (4 pts.)	13. Outcome measure was checked for reliability. (5 pts.)	14. Reliability measure greater than.70 or rater agreement greater than 70%. (5 pts.)

(continued)

Box 19.2 Continued

Criteria for Rating Effect Size

15. Those rating outcome rated it blind (10 pts.)	16. Outcome was measured after treatment was completed. (4 pts.)	17. Test of statistical significance was made and p < .05 (10 pts.)	18. Follow-up was greater than 75%. (10 pts.)	19. Total quality points (add 1-18).	20. Effect size (ES1) = (mean of treatment — mean or alternate or control ÷ (standard deviation of alternate or control group).

Criteria for Rating Effect Size

21. Effect size (ES2) = Absolute risk reduction = (Percent improved in treatment) − (percent improved in control).	22. Effect size (ES3) = Number needed to treat = 100 + ES2.

Adaptions made based on Gibbs (2003). See also "Quality of Study Rating Form: An Instrument for Synthesizing Evaluation Studies." Gibbs (1989), *Journal of Social Work Education*, 25(1), p. 67; Gibbs (1991). *Scientific Reasoning for Social Workers* (pp. 193–197). Copyright owned by L. E. Gibbs.

students, Gibbs found that studies with eighty points are very unusual; those with fifty to eighty points fall in the top third, and those with fewer than forty points are the most common. Note that being guided solely by an overall score can be highly misleading since a few minor characteristics of a study may outweigh critical deficits such as lack of a comparison or control group. This is why we include other options in this exercise. Lack of a comparison group allows the play of alternative explanations such as the following:

- *History:* Events that occur between the first and second measurement in addition to the experimental variables may account for changes (e.g., clients may get help elsewhere).
- *Maturation:* Simply growing older/living longer may be responsible especially when longtime periods are involved.

- *Instrumentation:* A change in the way something is measured (e.g., observers may change how they record).
- *Testing Effects:* Assessment may result in change.
- *Mortality:* These may be differential loss of people from different groups.
- *Regression:* Extreme scores tend to return to the mean.
- *Self-Selection Bias:* Clients are often "self-selected" rather than randomly selected. They may differ in critical ways from the population they are assumed to represent and differ from clients in a comparison group.
- *Helper Selection Bias:* Social workers may select certain kinds of clients to receive certain methods.
- *Interaction Effects:* Only certain clients may benefit from certain services, others may even be harmed (Campbell & Stanley, 1963).

Biases in both the interpretation and use of research findings are common (Mac Coun, 1998). Placebo effects may account for as much or more than may the effects of a treatment (see for example Antonuccio, Burns, & Danton, 2002). Recent research suggests that SSRIS (selective serotonin reuptake inhibitors prescribed to decrease depression) do not help most depressed people more than placebos (Kirsch, et al., 2008; Turner & Rosenthal, 2008). Thus, basing a decision regarding rigor of a study on an overall score is *not* advisable. Indeed some rating systems include the most critical features first and if the study does not meet them, you may disregard the study because of a critical flaw as shown in Box 19.3.

Explanation of Criteria in Box 19.2

In the Client Type and Treatment Methods sections, state briefly and specifically what the key identifying features are for client type (e.g., adult victims of sex abuse). Also list the principal treatment method and outcome measure. Use one form for each treatment comparison.

Give either zero points or the point value indicated if the study meets the criterion, as numbered and described subsequently:

1. The author describes *who* is treated by stating the subjects' average age, standard deviation of age and sex or proportion of males and females, and diagnostic category, for example, child abusers, schizophrenics.

BOX 19.3 Validity Screen for an Article About Therapy

1.	Is the study a randomized controlled trial? How were patients selected for the trial? Were they properly randomized into groups using concealed assignment?	Yes (go on)	No (stop)
2.	Are the people in the study similar to my clients?	Yes (go on)	No (stop)
3.	Are all participants who entered the trial properly accounted for at its conclusion? Was follow-up complete and were few lost to follow-up compared with the number of bad outcomes? Were patients analyzed in the groups to which they were initially randomized (intention-to-treat analysis)?	Yes (go on)	No (stop)
4.	Was everyone involved in the study (subjects and investigators) "blind" to treatment?	Yes	No
5.	Were the intervention and control groups similar at the start of the trial?	Yes	No
6.	Were the groups treated equally (aside from the experimental intervention)?	Yes	No
7.	Are the results clinically as well as statistically significant? Were the outcomes measured clinically important?	Yes	No
8.	If a negative trial, was a power analysis done?	Yes	No
9.	Were other factors present that might have affected the outcome?	Yes	No
10.	Are the treatment benefits worth the potential harms and costs?	Yes	No

Note: A "stop" answer to any of the questions should prompt you to seriously question whether the results of the study are valid and whether you should use this intervention.

Source: From Miser, W.F. (1999). Critical Appraisal of the Literature. *Journal of the American Board of Family Practice*, 12, 315–333. Adapted from material developed by The Department of Clinical Epidemiology and Biostatistics at McMaster University and by the Information Mastery Working Group. (See also Guyatt et al, 2008.) Reprinted by permission of the American Board of Family Medicine.

---

2. The authors tell *what* the treatment involves so specifically that you could apply the treatment with nothing more to go on than their description, or they refer you to a book, videotape, or article that describes the treatment method.

3. Authors state *where* the treatment occurred so specifically that you could contact people at that facility by phone or by letter.

4. Authors tell the *when* of the treatment by stating how long subjects participated in the treatment in days, weeks, or months or tell how many treatment sessions were attended by subjects.

5. Authors either discuss a specific theory that describes *why* they used one or more treatment methods or they cite literature related to the use of the method.

6. The author states specifically that subjects were *randomly assigned* to groups or refers to the assignment of subjects to treatment or control groups on the basis of a table of random numbers or other accepted randomization procedure. Randomization implies that each subject has an equal chance of being assigned to either a treatment or control group. If the author says subjects are randomly assigned but assigns subjects to treatments by assigning every other one or by allowing subjects to choose their groups, subjects are not randomly assigned.

7. Analysis shows these subjects were similar on key variables prior to treatment. (5 pts.)

8. Subjects were blind to being in treatment or control group. (5 pts.)

9. *Selection* of subjects is different from *random assignment*. Random selection means subjects are taken from some pool of subjects for inclusion in a study by using a table of random numbers or other random procedures; for example, if subjects are chosen randomly from among all residents in a nursing home, the results of the study can be generalized more confidently to all residents of the nursing home.

10. Members of the *nontreated control group* do not receive a different kind of treatment; they receive *no* treatment. An example of a nontreated control group would be a group of subjects who are denied group counseling while others are given group counseling. Subjects in the nontreated control group might receive treatment at a later date, but do not receive treatment while experimental group subjects are receiving their treatment.

11. Those in the treatment group or groups are those who receive some kind of special care intended to help them. It is this treatment that is being evaluated by those doing the study. The results of the study will state how effective the treatment or treatment groups have been when compared with each other or with a nontreated control group. In order to meet criterion 9, the number of subjects in the smallest treatment group should be determined by a power analysis. This should be for example at least 21. (Not everyone would agree with this number.) Here, "number of subjects" means total number of individuals, not number of couples or number of groups.

12. Validity concerns whether a measure assesses what it is designed to measure. For example, does a self-report measure of alcohol use accurately reflect alcohol use? (For further discussion of different kinds of validity see Exercise 21.) Examples of outcome measures used to assess the effectiveness of a treatment might include number of days spent in the community after release from treatment before readmission, score on a symptom rating scale, or number of days after release from treatment during which no alcohol was consumed. For this criterion, it is not enough to merely state that outcome was measured in some way; the author must describe *how* the outcome was measured. Are surrogates of important outcomes used— "stand-ins" for outcomes of concern. For example, does less plaque in arteries result in decreased mortality? Does a self-report measure accurately reflect changes in community resources? A focus on surrogate indicators that do not reflect outcomes of interest to clients such as quality and length of life is a deceptive practice. (For a discussion of ideal features of surrogate outcomes see Greenhalgh, 2006.)

13. *Reliability* refers to the consistency of measurement. Two or more people may independently rate the performance of clients in treatment or nontreated groups. (See Exercise 21 for further discussion of reliability.) The reliability criterion is satisfied only if the author of the study affirms that evaluations were made of the outcome measure's reliability and the *author gives a numerical value of some kind, for this measure of reliability.* Where multiple outcome criteria are used, reliability checks of the major outcome criteria satisfy number 10.

14. The reliability coefficient discussed in number 11 is 0.70 or greater (70% or better).

15. Raters of outcome were blind to group assessment. (10 pts.)

16. *At least one outcome measure was obtained after treatment was completed.* After release from the hospital, after drug therapy was completed, after subjects quit attending inpatient group therapy— all are posttreatment measures. For example, if subjects were released from the mental hospital on November 10, and some measure of success was obtained on November 11, then the study meets criterion 9. Outcome measured both during treatment and after treatment ended is sufficient to meet this criterion.

17. *Tests of statistical significance* are generally referred to by phrases such as "differences between treatment groups were significant at the .05 level" or "results show statistical significance." Give credit for

meeting this criterion *only* if the author identifies a test of statistical significance by name (e.g., analysis of variance, chi square, *t* test) *and* gives a *p* value, for example $P < 0.05$, and the *P* value is equal to or smaller than 0.05. Please note that statistical testing is controversial, and misunderstandings are common. Some common ways of cheating on statistical tests are described in Box 19.1.

18. The authors should include an "intention-to-treat" analysis. The proportion of subjects *successfully followed-up* refers to the number contacted to measure outcome compared with the number who began the experiment. To compute the proportion followed-up for each group studied (i.e., treatment group, control group), determine the number of subjects who initially entered the experiment in the group and determine the number successfully followed-up. (If there is more than one follow-up period, use the longest one.) Then for each group, divide the number successfully followed-up by the number who began in each group and multiply each quotient by 100. For example, if twenty entered a treatment group, but fifteen were followed-up in that group, the result would be: (15/20) 100 = 75%. Compute the proportion followed-up for all groups involved in the experiment. If the *smallest* of these percentages equals or exceeds 75%, the study meets the criterion.

19. Total quality points (TQP) is the sum of the point values for criteria 1 to 15.

20. Effect size (ES1) is a number that summarizes the strength of effect of a given treatment. Effect Size 1 (ES1) gets larger if one method has a greater effect than a second (or a control), given that larger numbers on the outcome measure mean greater effect. As a rough rule, a small ES1 is approximately .2, a medium one about .5, and a large one about .8 or greater (Cohen, 1977, p. 24). When ES1 approaches zero, there is essentially no difference in the relative effectiveness of the compared treatments. A method that produces a negative ES1 produces a harmful (iatrogenic) effect. The index can be computed as follows;

$$\text{ES1} = (x_t - x_c)/(S_c)$$
$$= \frac{(\text{Mean of treatment} - \text{Mean of control or alternate treatment group})}{\text{Standard deviation of control or alternate treatment}}$$

This formula is for computing ES1 when outcome means of treatment groups and control groups are given. To compute an effect size from information presented in an article, select two means to compare; for example, outcome might be a mean of a treatment group compared with a mean of a nontreated control group. Subtract the mean of the second group from the mean of the first group and divide this value by the standard deviation of the second group. (Standard deviations are indicated by various signs and symbols, including s.d., S; s, or SD). ES1 maybe a negative or positive number. If the number is positive, the first group may have the greater treatment effect—this assumes that positive outcome on the outcome measure implies larger numbers on that measure. If the ES1 is negative when comparing a treatment group against a control group, the treatment may produce a harmful or iatrogenic effect. If the number is negative when comparing two alternate treatments, the first treatment is less effective than the second. The larger a positive ES1, the stronger the effect of treatment.

21. We can also compute ES2 for proportions or percentages, using the formula

$$ES2 - P_t - P_c = \left(\frac{\text{Number improved in treatment}}{\text{Total number in treatment group}} \right) \times 100$$

$$- \left(\frac{\text{Number improved in alternate treatment or control}}{\text{Total number in alternate treatment or control}} \right) \times 100$$

Effect Size 2 (ES2) measures the difference between the percent of subjects improved in one group compared with the percent improved in another treatment (or control group). If 30% improve in one treatment and 20% improve in the other, then ES2 is 10% (i.e., 30% – 20% = 10%). Though ES2 is easier to interpret than ES1, many studies fail to include sufficient information to compute ES2. Assume that we are comparing the proportion in a treatment group who are improved against the proportion in a control group who are improved. Let us say that 70% of those in the treatment group are improved and 50% of those in the control group are also improved for a particular outcome measure. ES2 then equals 70% minus 50%, or 20%. Thus, the proportion of improvement attributable to the treatment may be 20%.

22. Effect size (*ES3*) = Number needed to treat = 100 ÷ *ES2*.

Step 2

After reading the Holden, Speedling, and Rosenberg (1992) study (Box 19.4) complete Practice Exercise 19.

BOX 19.4 Article for review

Reproduced with permission of authors and publishers from:
Holden, G., Speedling, E., & Rosenberg, G. Evaluation of an intervention
designed to improve patients' hospital experience. *Psychological Reports*,
1992, 71, 547–550.

EVALUATION OF AN INTERVENTION DESIGNED TO IMPROVE PATIENTS' HOSPITAL EXPERIENCE[1]

Gary Holden, Edward Speedling, Gary Rosenberg;
Mount Sinai School of Medicine
New York, New York

Summary—The influence of a videotape, shown in a hospital admitting room, on patients' state anxiety and concerns about hospitalization was assessed in a preliminary study. For both state anxiety and specific concerns regarding hospitalization the pretest scores on each variable accounted for the preponderance of the variance in the posttest scores. In both instances, the intervention and the interaction of the intervention with the pretest scores accounted for less than 1% of variance in the outcome. While finding small effects to be significant for such a small sample (N = 93) is unlikely, the sample size was adequate to detect medium to large effects. More important was the fact that 73.33% of the videotape intervention group indicated that they did not watch the video, which leads us to the conclusion that this intervention as tested is not worthwhile.

Being admitted to a hospital is an anxiety producing event. We were recently asked to do a preliminary study of the effect of a videotape shown in a hospital admitting room. The videotape included a role model who was depicted through a stay in this particular hospital. The videotape provided information about the process of hospitalization and showed the model encountering problems representative of typical patient concerns and finding solutions to those problems.

Gagliano (1988) reviewed studies using film or video in patient education published between 1975 and 1986 (cf. Nielsen & Sheppard, 1988). She noted that: "[a] strength of video is role-modeling. When applied to well defined, self-limited stressful situations, role modeling in video decreases patients' anxiety, pain, and sympathetic arousal while increasing knowledge, cooperation, and coping ability" (p. 785). More recent research supports the use of videotape interventions in health care settings (Allen, Danforth, & Drabman, 1989; Rasnake & Linscheid, 1989). The central question addressed by this study was whether experimental subjects would report significantly less anxiety than control subjects after viewing the videotape during the admission process.

[1] The authors acknowledge the ongoing support and assistance of Robert Southwick, Erica Rubin, and the Mount Sinai Medical Center admitting room staff, in the completion of this project. Requests for reprints should be addressed to G. Holden, D.S.W., Box 1252, Mount Sinai School of Medicine, 1 Gustave L. Levy Place, New York, NY 10029–6574. Reproduced with permission of the authors and publisher.

(continued)

BOX 19.4 Continued

METHOD

The State-Trait Anxiety Inventory was selected as the primary outcome measure because its psycho-metric properties are well-established and it has been used widely (Spielberger, 1983). Subjects completed the State anxiety scale at both pretest and posttest. They completed the Trait anxiety scale at pretest only. An additional scale was created to assess patients' concerns regarding specific aspects of hospitalization. Subjects completed this scale at both pretest and posttest. Subjects were English-speaking, nonemergency admissions to a large, urban, tertiary care medical center. Eligible consenting patients were enrolled in the admissions office, with group assignments being random. These patients completed the initial assessment battery shortly after arrival. Patients completed the second assessment in the admissions area following the admission process.

INTERVENTION

Initially, two versions of the intervention were employed as previous researchers found structured viewing of a videotaped intervention was superior to incidental viewing (Kleemeier & Hazzard, 1984). In the structured viewing condition subjects were taken to a quiet room and given a brief explanation of what they were about to see before actually viewing the 14-min. long videotape. In the regular viewing condition, subjects were told that this videotape about hospitalization was playing on a monitor in the corner of the room and they could watch it if they chose. This second condition represents the more pragmatic use of such an intervention given the pace in most waiting rooms.

RESULTS

The first result was that the structured viewing condition was quickly dropped because the refusal rate was very high. Patients were unwilling to leave the admitting room, despite reassurances that staff would always know where they were and they would not 'lose any time' by participating in this condition. Participation rates were virtually the same in the control condition and the regular viewing condition (54.2 % vs. 55.3%, respectively). Sufficient data were available for 93 subjects (48 control and 45 treated subjects). Statistical analyses were performed using SPSS/PC + 4.0 software.

The two groups were not significantly different (p = 0.05) in terms of gender, age, pretest trait anxiety, pretest state anxiety, pretest concerns, posttest state anxiety, or posttest concerns, although the differences in pretest state anxiety fell just short of significance (p = 0.051). To assess the effects of the videotape on posttest state anxiety, an analysis of covariance using pretest state anxiety as the covariate was performed (Pedhazur & Schmelkin, 1991). Pretest state anxiety was the only significant predictor, accounting for 78 % of the variance in posttest state anxiety. The intervention and the interaction of intervention and pretest state anxiety accounted for less than 1 % of additional unique variance in posttest state anxiety. The same analysis for the other posttest variable of interest (specific concerns regarding hospitalization) used pretest concerns as the covariate. Similarly, specific patients' concerns at pretest accounted for slightly over 75% of the variance in specific concerns at posttest. The intervention and the interaction of intervention and pretest specific concerns accounted for less than 1 % of additional unique variance in specific concerns at posttest.

(continued)

BOX 19.4 Continued

This finding should be considered in light of the fact that 33 out of 45 experimental subjects indicated that they had not watched the video. Separate analysis of covariance for the two groups (experimental subjects who did and did not watch the video) again demonstrated that virtually all of the variance in posttest state anxiety and in posttest specific concerns was explained by their respective pretest scores.

DISCUSSION

Although this was originally conceived as a randomized trial, subject self-selection into the study precludes inferences based on the assumption that randomization was achieved. There may have been differential selection into the experimental group by those initially higher in state anxiety and the change from pretest to posttest on state anxiety in the experimental group may have reflected regression towards the mean. Hypothesis guessing may also have occurred in both groups. These factors may have been operating because the institutional review board in the institution where the research was carried out required that subjects be given a full explanation of each of the experimental conditions in the informed consent. Generalization of these results is further restricted by the unique aspects of a patient sample from New York City.

Conclusions about the intervention are also affected by the fact that we found that 33 of 45 individuals in the experimental group did not watch the videotape. This might lead one to conclude that the treatment was not reliably implemented. We would disagree in that the point of this study was to evaluate the effects of a videotape intervention as it would likely be implemented in a busy admitting room. In reality, if admitting room staff tell incoming patients that a videotape is playing continuously for them, some individuals will choose to attend to it and some will not. We believe that this study did represent the treatment as it might be carried out in a nonexperimental setting.

TABLE 1   COMPARISON FO PRE- AND POSTINTERVENTION DIFFERENCES BETWEEN CONTROL AND EXPERIMENTAL GROUPS (n = 93).

Variable	Control group, n = 48		Experimental Group, n = 45	
	M	SD	M	D
Gender (% women)	41.7		51.2	
Age (years)	51.1	16.6	53.1	15.6
Pretest Trait Anxiety	36.0	8.4	35.2	11.0
Pretest State Anxiety	41.0	13.8	46.7	13.8
Posttest State Anxiety	40.0	13.9	43.3	14.3
Pretest Specific concerns	2.2	.5	2.1	.6
Posttest Specific concerns	2.2	.6	2.1	.6

Note: Higher scores on anxiety and concerns scales indicate higher anxiety or concern.

(*continued*)

BOX 19.4 Continued

The failure of the more structured viewing condition tells us that the priority for patients is getting through admissions as quickly as possible. Normally admissions requires that patients move from the waiting area to a number of offices and back again. If patients are asked if they are willing to move to yet another room, to engage in an activity that is presented as...an optional aspect of admissions, it is easy to understand (in retrospect) the decision of many to decline to participate.

It is apparent that use of a videotape playing continuously in the admitting room was not supported in this study. Such use while perhaps helpful to some patients may in fact annoy others (e.g., readmissions who may have seen it previously, those waiting for admission for long time periods who might be exposed to the videotape multiple times, etc.). Yet there may be a group of individuals who might be interested in viewing such a videotape during admission. A potential solution that merits further study would be to allow individual viewing (e.g., with earphones) of videotapes for those who desire to do so while experimentally varying the content of the videotape (e.g., male vs. female or African American vs Latin actors and actresses, amount of optimism portrayed, etc.). A videotape intervention may also be useful if employed at a different time. For instance, the patient might view the video prior to admission (e.g., in the office of the patient's private physician or in the patient's home) or once arriving in a hospital room (e.g., using a portable videotape setup on a cart or via closed circuit television). The use of informational media might also be extended to the preparation of current hospital patients for subsequent transitions to other institutions (e.g., nursing homes). Given the potential use of video tape for relatively low-cost improvement of patients' hospital experiences, these possibilities deserve further attention.

References

ALLEN, K. D., DANFORTH, J. S. & DRABMAN, R. S. (1989) Videotaped modeling and film distraction for fear reduction in adults undergoing hyperbaric oxygen therapy. Journal of Consulting and Clinical Psychology, 57, 554–558.

GAGLIANO, M. E. (1988). A literature review on the efficacy of video inpatient education. Journal of Medical Education, 63, 785–792.

KLEEMEIER, C. P., & HAZZARD, A. P. (1984) Videotaped parent education in pediatric waiting rooms. Patient Education and Counseling, 6, 122–124.

NIELSEN, E., & SHEPPARD, M. A. (1988). Television as a patient education tool: a review of its', effectiveness. Patient Education and Counseling, 11, 3–16.

PEDHAZUR, E. J., & SCHMELKIN, L. P. (1991) Measurement, design and analysis: an integrated approach. Hillsdale, NJ: Erlbaum.

RASNAKE, L. K., & LINSCHEID, T. R. (1989). Anxiety reduction in children receiving medical care: developmental considerations. Developmental and Behavioral Pediatrics, 10, 169–175.

SPIELBERGER, C. D. (1983). Manual for the State-Trait Anxiety Inventory. Palo Alto, CA: Consulting Psychologists Press.

Your Name _____ Date _____

Instructor's Name _____ Course _____

1. Assume that you work as a member of an interdisciplinary team in a hospital. You and other members of your team have observed that patients being admitted to the hospital seem anxious and bewildered by the experience. You wonder if patients would feel less anxious if they watched a brief videotape that addressed common questions during admission. One of your colleagues has done a computer search of the literature and retrieved the study described in Box 19.4. Read the article in Box 19.4.

2. After reviewing the explanation of criteria on the QSRF, rate the study in Box 19.4 on the blank form in Box 19.2.

    a. Record the total Quality Points you gave to the Holden, Speedling, and Rosenberg article (1992) on the Quality of Study Rating Form here: _____

    b. What is the Effect Size 1 for Posttest State Anxiety? _____

    c. Based on Total Quality Points and ES1, would you recommend that your hospital produce a short videotape to be shown to patients in admission? ____ Yes ____ No

        Please explain the reasons for your answer:

        _____

        _____

        _____

        _____

        _____

3. Complete Box 19.3. Validity Screen for an article about therapy.

4. Download information regarding the CONSORT guidelines and review the study using this checklist. (See also Zwarenstein et al., 2008.) (Ask your instructor for clarification as needed.)

5. How do reviews based on the form in Box 19.3 and CONSORT guidelines compare to overall score on the Quality of Study Rating Form in Box 19.2? Describe how using an overall score may be misleading.

_____

_____

_____

_____

_____

6. Based on criteria in those two other review forms, what would you recommend?

_____

_____

_____

_____

7. Please describe what have you learned in this exercise.

_____

_____

_____

_____

_____

EXERCISE 20   CRITICALLY APPRAISING RESEARCH REVIEWS: HOW GOOD IS THE EVIDENCE?

Purpose

1. To describe characteristics of rigorous research review
2. To accurately evaluate practice and policy-related research
3. To make informed decisions

Background

Research reviews have many purposes including discovering the evidentiary status of an intervention program such as multisystemic family therapy or the accuracy of a diagnostic measure (e.g., see Littell, Popa, & Forsythe, 2005). Reviews differ, not only in their purpose, but in the rigor of review and the clarity with which procedures used are described (Littell, Corcoran, & Pillai, 2008). Concerns about incomplete, unrigorous reviews resulted in the creation of the Cochrane and Campbell Collaborations which prepare, disseminate and maintain high quality reviews regarding specific questions such as "Are Scared Straight programs for preventing delinquency effective?" (Petrosino, Turpin-Petrosino, & Buehler, 2003). Characteristics of high quality systematic reviews include the following:

State objectives of the review and outline eligibility (inclusion/exclusion) for studies.

Exhaustively search for studies that seem to meet eligibility criteria.

Tabulate characteristics of each study identified and assess it's methodologic quality.

Apply eligibility criteria and justify any exclusions.

Assemble the most complete data feasible, with involvement of investigators.

Analyze results of eligible studies; use statistical synthesis of data (meta-analysis) if appropriate and possible.

Perform sensitivity analyses, if appropriate and possible (including subgroup analyses).
Prepare a structured report of the review, stating aims, describing materials and methods, and reporting results (see Chalmers, 1993).

We should not assume that a review is complete or rigorous, even Cochrane and Campbell reviews (Shea, Moher, Graham, Pham, & Tugwell, 2002). As Straus et al. (2005) caution: "Systematic reviews of inadequate quality may be worse than none, because faculty decisions may be made with unjustified confidence" (p. 138). Because reviews vary in quality and purpose, both clients and professionals should be skilled in evaluating them. The example given in this exercise concerns an effectiveness question. Your instructor may also give you practice in critically appraising a review article regarding a diagnostic test or assessment measure.

Instructions

Please complete Practice Exercise 20.

Practice Exercise 20   Critically Appraising Research Reviews: How Good Is the Evidence?

Your Name _____ Date _____

Course _____ Instructor's Name _____

INSTRUCTIONS

Step 1: Your instructor will select a review for you to evaluate. You will need to access this on the Internet or obtain a copy from your instructor. Write full reference of this review here: _____

_____

_____

Step 2: Review QUORUM (Quality of Reporting of Meta-Analyses) guidelines for appraising research reviews (www.consort-statement.org/QUORUM.pdf) as well as guidelines in Box 20.1.

Step 3: Complete the form in Box 20.1 related to the review article your instructor has selected.

Step 4: If odds ratios and confidence intervals are given, prepare a Forest Plot of all the trials regarding effects (Littell, Corcoran, &Pillai, 2008). Your instructor will give you examples of Forest Plots and discuss their value.

Step 5: Compare QUORUM guidelines with those in Box 20.1. Describe any important differences.

_____

_____

_____

_____

_____

_____

_____

Step 6:   Your overall critique of this review.

_____

_____

_____

_____

_____

_____

Step 7:   What is the clinical or policy "bottom line"?

_____

_____

_____

_____

_____

_____

BOX 20.1 Steps in Determining the Validity of a Meta-analysis

1. Was the literature search done well?

   a. Was it comprehensive? — Yes No
   b. Were the search methods systematic and clearly described? — Yes No
   c. Were the key words used in the search described? — Yes No
   d. Was the issue of publication bias addressed? — Yes No

2. Was the method for selecting articles clear, systematic, and appropriate?

   a. Were there clear, preestablished inclusion and exclusion
      criteria for evaluation? — Yes No
   b. Was selection systematic? — Yes No
      i. Was the population defined? — Yes No
      ii. Was the exposure/intervention clearly described? — Yes No
      iii. Were all outcomes described and were they compatible? — Yes No
   c. Was selection done blindly and in random order? — Yes No
   d. Was the selection process reliable? — Yes No
      i. Were at least two independent selectors used? — Yes No
      ii. Was the extent of selection disagreement evaluated? — Yes No

3. Was the quality of primary studies evaluated? — Yes No

   a. Did all studies, published or not, have the same standard applied? — Yes No
   b. Were at least two independent evaluators used and was inter-rater
      agreement assessed and was it reported and adequate? — Yes No
   c. Were the evaluators blinded to authors, institutions, and
      results of the primary studies? — Yes No

4. Were results from the studies combined appropriately? — Yes No

   a. Were the studies similar enough to combine results? — Yes No
      i. Were the study designs, populations, exposures, outcomes,
         and direction of effect similar in the combined studies? — Yes No
   b. Was a test for heterogeneity done and was its *p* value
      nonsignificant? — Yes No

5. Was a statistical combination (meta-analysis) done properly? — Yes No

   a. Were the methods of the studies similar? — Yes No
   b. Was the possibility of chance differences statistically addressed? — Yes No
      i. Was a test for homogeneity done? — Yes No
   c. Were appropriate statistical analyses performed? — Yes No
   d. Were sensitivity analyses used? — Yes No

6. Are the results important? — Yes No

   a. Was the effect strong? — Yes No
      i. Was the odds ratio large? — Yes No
      ii. Were the results reported in a clinically meaningful manner,
          such as the absolute difference or the number needed to treat? — Yes No
   b. Are the results likely to be reproducible and generalizable? — Yes No
   c. Were all clinically important consequences considered? — Yes No
   d. Are the benefits worth the harm and costs? — Yes No

Source: From "Applying a Meta-analysis to Daily Clinical Practice," by W. F. Miser, 2000, in *Evidence-based Clinical Practice: Concepts and Approaches* (p. 60), edited by J. P. Geyman, R. A. Deyo, and S. D. Ramsey, Boston: Butterworth Heinemann. Reprinted with permission.

Purpose

To provide an opportunity to enhance skills in critically appraising self-report measures

Background

Hundreds of self-report measures are described in the professional literature. Are these valid? Do they measure what they claim to measure? (e.g., see Aiken & Groth-Marnat, 2006). Assessment provides a foundation for intervention (whether working with individuals, groups, or communities) and involves "looking before leaping" (describing client concerns and hoped-for outcomes and discovering related factors). A key part of assessment is clearly describing client concerns and related client characteristics and circumstances. Examples of vague descriptions include "anti-social behavior," "poor parenting skills." Invalid self-report measures may give an incorrect view of a client's concerns, repertoires, and life circumstances. You may be influenced by initial impressions and not change your views in light of new evidence. (See discussion of anchoring and insufficient adjustment in Exercise 8.) Misleading data can waste time, effort, and resources and result in selection of ineffective or harmful interventions. Biases that interfere with accurately describing concerns are more likely to remain unrecognized when descriptions are vague. We may be mislead by the vividness of behaviors such as extreme temper tantrums and overlook alternative positive behaviors that are less vivid and rarely reinforced so rarely occur (e.g., Crone & Horner, 2003; Pryor, 2002).

Some Useful Concepts

A measure is reliable when different observers arrive at very similar ratings using that measure; it is valid when it measures what it is designed to measure. Assuming that standardized measures are valid would be a mistake.

Reliability refers to the consistency of results provided by the same person at different times (time-based reliability), by two different raters of the same events (inter-rater reliability), or by parallel forms or split-halfs of a measure (item-bound reliability). The first kind is known as test-retest reliability or stability. Reliability places an upward boundary on validity. Unreliable measures cannot be valid. For example, if responses on a questionnaire vary from time to time in the absence of real change, you cannot use it to predict what a person will do in the future. Reliability can be assessed in a number of ways, all of which yield some measure of consistency.

In *test-retest reliability*, the scores of the same individuals at different times are correlated with each other. We might administer the Beck Depression Inventory to several persons whom we think might be "depressed," then administer it again with the same instructions a few days or weeks later to see if the scores are similar over time. Correlations may range from +1 to −1. The size of the correlation coefficient indicates the degree of association. A zero correlation indicates a complete absence of consistency. A correlation of +1 indicates a perfect positive correlation. The stability (reliability of a measure at different times in the absence of related events that may influence scores), of some measures is high. That is, you can ask a client to complete a questionnaire this week and five weeks from now and obtain similar results (in the absence of real change). Other measures have low stability. Coefficients of reliability are usually sufficient if they are. 70 or better. However, the higher the better.

Homogeneity is a measure of internal consistency. It assesses the degree to which all the items on a test measure the same characteristics. The homogeneity of a test (as measured, for example, by "coefficient alpha") is important if all the items on it are assumed to measure the same characteristics. If a scale is multidimensional (e.g., many dimensions are assumed to be involved in a construct such as "loneliness" or "social support"), then correlation among all items would not be expected. We could calculate the *internal consistency* by computing the correlations of each item with the total score of a measure and averaging these correlations. We could compute a measure's split-half reliability by dividing the items randomly into two groups of ten items each, administering both halves to a group of subjects, then seeing if the halves correlate well with each other.

Validity concerns the question, Does the measure reflect the characteristics it is supposed to measure? For example, does a client's behavior in a role play correspond to what the client does in similar real-life situations? Direct measures are typically more valid than indirect measures. For instance, observing teacher-student interaction will probably offer more accurate data than asking a student to complete a questionnaire assumed to offer information about classroom. There are many kinds of validity.

Predictive validity refers to the extent to which a measure accurately predicts behavior at a later time. For example, how accurately does a measure of suicidal potential predict suicide attempts? Can you accurately predict what a person will do in the future from his or her score on the measure? (For a valuable discussion of challenges in predicting future behavior and the importance of considering baserate data, see Faust, 2007.)

Concurrent validity refers to the extent to which a measure correlates with a valid measure gathered at the same time; for example, do responses on a questionnaire concerning social behavior correspond to behavior in real-life settings?

Criterion validity is used to refer to predictive and concurrent validity.

Content validity refers to the degree to which a measure adequately samples the domain being assessed. For example, does an inventory used to assess parenting skills include an adequate sample of such skills?

Face validity refers to the extent to which items included on a measure make sense "on the face of it." Given the intent of the instrument, would you expect the included items to be there? For example, drinking behavior has face validity as an outcome measure for decreasing alcohol use.

Construct validity refers to the degree to which a measure successfully measures a theoretical construct-the degree to which results correspond to assumptions about the measure. For example a finding that depressed people report more negative thoughts compared with nondepressed people adds an increment of construct validity to a measure designed to tap such thoughts. In a measure that has construct validity, different methods of assessing a construct (e.g., direct observation and self-report) yield similar results, and similar methods of measuring *different* constructs (e.g., aggression and altruism) yield different results. That is, evidence should be available that a construct can be distinguished from different constructs. For a description of different ways construct validity can be established, see for example, Aiken & Groth-Marnat (2006). Do scores on a measure correlate in predicted ways with other measures? They should have a positive correlation with other measures of the same construct (e.g, depression) and a negative correlation with measures that tap opposite constructs (e.g., happiness, and glee).

Instructions

1. Your instructor will select an assessment measure for you to review or select one that is used in your agency and complete Practice Exercise 21.

Your Name _____ Date _____

Instructor's Name _____ Course _____

1.   Measure to be reviewed:

_____

_____

_____

_____

_____

2.   Describe the purpose of this measure:

_____

_____

_____

_____

_____

3.   Describe the reliability of this measure. What kind of reliability was evaluated? What were the results? Give facts and figures, for example, size of correlations. Was the reliability reported the most important?

_____

_____

_____

_____

_____

4. Describe the kind of validity evaluated. What were the results? Give facts and figures, for example, size of correlations found. Was this the most important kind of validity to report?

_____

_____

_____

_____

_____

5. Are claims made regarding the reliability and validity of this self-report measure accurate based on your review? _____ Yes _____ No. Please discuss.

_____

_____

_____

_____

_____

6. Describe ethical problems in using self-report measures of unknown or low reliability and validity.

_____

_____

_____

_____

_____

Purpose

To introduce you to concepts basic to risk assessment and decision making, such as sensitivity, specificity, positive predictive value, and base rate. This exercise introduces you to different ways to estimate risk. Some are easier than others.

Background

Risk assessment is integral to helping clients and is common in all helping professions. Actuarial methods of prediction rely on known associations between certain variables and an outcome such as future child abuse. Such methods have been found to be more accurate compared to relying on consensus among experts or clinical judgment (e.g., see Grove & Meehl, 1996; Houts, 2002). Decisions made can affect client well-being and survival. Mental-health staff asses the risk of harm to clients (suicide) and others (homicide). Child-welfare workers make judgments about the potential risk of child abuse. Teachers screen children for learning and interpersonal problems and refer children for intervention. Helpers usually base decisions about clients on their *implicit* estimation of the likelihood of certain events. They usually do not describe estimates in terms of specific probabilities, but use vague words such as *probably*, *likely*, or *high risk*.

Assessing risk and communicating this accurately to clients is an important skill. Research shows that we often neither calculate risk accurately nor communicate it clearly to clients (Paling, 2006). Let's take an example of just how inaccurate counselors may be in describing risk. This example from Gigerenzer (2002) concerns reporting of HIV test results.

Session 1: The Counselor Was a Female Social Worker

Sensitivity? [See Glossary]
- **False-negatives really never occur. Although, if I think about the literature, there were reports of such cases.**

- I don't know exactly how many.
- It happened only once or twice.

False positives? [See Glossary]
- No, because the test is repeated; it is absolutely certain.
- If there are antibodies, the test identifies them unambiguously and with absolute certainty.
- No, it is absolutely impossible that there are false positives; because it is repeated, the test if absolutely certain.

Prevalence? [See Glossary]
- I can't tell you this exactly.
- Between about 1 in 500 and 1 in 1000.
- Positive predictive value?
- As I have now told you repeatedly, the test is absolutely certain.

The counselor was aware that HIV tests can lead to a few false negatives [see glossary] but incorrectly informed Ebert that there are no false positives. Ebert asked for clarification twice, in order to make sure that he correctly understood that a false positive is impossible. The counselor asserted that a positive test result means, with absolute certainty, that the client has the virus; this conclusion follows logically from her (incorrect) assertion that false positives cannot occur (pp. 129–230).

Part 1: The Importance of Providing Absolute As Well as Relative Risk and Using a Common Reference Number

Key concepts in understanding risk are illustrated by a study by Skolbekken (1998) described in Gigerenzer (2002) entitled "Reduction in total mortality for people who take a cholesterol lowering drug (provastatin)." Those enrolled in the study had high-risk levels of cholesterol and took part in the study for 5 years (see also Box 22.1).

Absolute risk reduction: The absolute risk reduction is the proportion of patients who die without treatment (placebo) minus those who die with treatment. [For example] Pravastatin reduces the number of people who die from 41 to 32 in 1000. That is, the absolute risk reduction is 9 in 1000, which is 0.9%.

Relative risk reduction: The relative risk reduction is the absolute risk reduction divided by the proportion of patients who die without treatment. [For example] For the present data, the relative risk reduction is 9 divided by 41, which is 22%. Thus, pravastatin reduces the risk of dying by 22%

Number needed to treat: The number of people who must participate in the treatment to save one life is the number needed to treat (NNT). This number can be easily derived from the absolute risk reduction. [See Box 22.1.] The number of people who needed to be treated to save one life is 111, because 9 in 1000 deaths (which his about 1 in 111) are prevented by the drug (Gigerenzer, 2002, p. 35).

Notice that relative risk reduction seems much more important than does absolute risk reduction. Because of this, the former is misleading.

BOX 22.1   The 2 × 2 Table

	Outcome	
	Yes	No
Exposed	a	b
Not exposed	c	d

Relative risk (RR)
$$\frac{a/(a + b)}{c/(c + b)}$$

Relative risk reduction (RRR) is
$$\frac{c/(c + b) - a/(a + b)}{c/(c + b)}$$

Absolute risk reduction (ARR)
$$\frac{c}{c + b} - \frac{c}{c + b}$$

Number needed to treat (NNT)
$$\frac{1}{ARR}$$

Odds ratio (OR)
$$\frac{a/b}{c/d} = \frac{ad}{cb}$$

Source: Adapted from Guyatt, G., Rennie, D., Meade, M. O., & Cook, D. J. (2008). *Users' guides to the medical literature: A manual for evidence-based clinical practice. (2nd Ed.)*, p. 88. Chicago: American Medical Association.

For over a decade, experts in risk communication have been pointing out that statements of relative risks totally fail to provide "information" to patients because they have no context to know that, say a "50% increased risk" is measured in relation to. In view of this universal condemnation of the practice, it is shameful when health care agencies, pharmaceutical companies and the media persist in making public pronouncements about risks or benefits solely in this manner. It is well known that if patients only hear data expressed as relative risks, they take away deceptively exaggerated impressions of the differences (Paling, 2006, p. 14).

Indeed presenting only relative risk is a key propaganda method designed to raise alarm and sell alleged remedies. As Gigerenzer (2002) notes, relative risk reduction suggests "higher benefits than really exist" (p. 35). Number needed to treat provides further information when making decisions. Consider the provastatin example. We can see "that of 111 people who swallow the tablets for 5 years, 1 had the benefit, whereas the other 110 did not" (p. 36). Note that presenting risk reduction in relation to a common number (1 out of 1000) contributes to under-standing. Paling (2006) urges professionals (and researchers) to provide absolute risk and to use easy-to-understand visual aids such as those he illustrates in his user-friendly book.

An example when talking about risks of disease.

Say the absolute risk of developing a disease is 4 in 100 in nonsmokers. Say the relative risk of the disease is increased by 50% in smokers. The 50% relates to the "4"—so the absolute increase in the risk is 50% of 4, which is 2. So, the absolute risk of developing this disease in smokers is 6 in 100.

An example when talking about treatments.

Say men have a 2 in 20 risk of developing a certain disease by the time they reach the age of 60. Then, say research shows that a new treatment reduces the relative risk of getting this disease by 50%. The 50% is the relative risk reduction, and refers to the effect on the "2". 50% of 2 is 1. This means that the absolute risk is reduced from 2 in 20, to 1 in 20. http://www/patient.co.uk/showdoc/27000849/ (Accessed 10/19/07, pp. 1–2).

Say that the records show that for a defined population of people, about 2 out of 100 are at risk of having a heart attack over the next year. Then imagine that a new study comes out reporting that if such patients take an aspirin daily, their risks of a heart attack will be lowered. Instead of 2 out of 100 suffering a heart attack, only 1 person out of 100 would be expected to do so (Paling, 2006, p. 15).

Let us say that you fall into this defined population. What is your risk? Be on your guard for those who present only relative risk reduction. Encourage clients to consider their absolute risk. (See also Welsch, 2004.)

Part 2: Using Probabilities

We may be asked to estimate the likelihood of events in terms of *explicit* (specific) probabilities, from 0% (certain not to happen), to 50% (as likely to happen as not), to 100% (certain to happen). Let's say that you are asked to estimate the likelihood that we will all die someday. You might say that this event is "certain" (100% probability). If a doctor is asked, "What is the probability that an eighty-year-old white male patient will die within the next five years?" he might say, "Very likely" and translate this estimate to a 44% probability based on a life expectancy table. A member of a parole board might be asked about the likelihood that a given inmate will be charged for and be convicted of another criminal offense within the first eighteen months after the inmate's release from prison. If pressed to be explicit, the parole-board member might say that the chance of this is "fairly low," meaning 20%.

We make judgments and decisions based on both prior and new information. For example, you may have prior information about clients before you see them. When you interview clients, you gather new information. A parole-board member in Nevada may know that thirty of the last hundred inmates released from prison committed a new offence within eighteen months of their release. Knowing this, and nothing more about an inmate about to be released, the parole-board member may estimate that there is a 30% chance (prior baserate-probability) that the inmate will commit more crimes. To increase accuracy, the parole-board member may gather additional information about the client by completing a risk-assessment scale based on the inmate's prior history.

This part of Exercise 22 introduces Bayes's Theorem as a way to integrate prior and new information about a client to help you judge the likelihood of a behavior.

Instructions

Follow the next four steps.

Step 1

Read the description of each situation that follows and give the requested probability estimates. We will give you information about the following:

1. *Prior probability*—the likelihood that the client has a particular problem, given only the information that you have before you do further assessment.
2. *Sensitivity*—among those known to have a problem, the proportion whom a test or measure said had the problem.
3. *Specificity*—among those known not to have the problem, the proportion whom the test or measure has said did not have the problem.

Based on the prior probability, sensitivity, and specificity given in Situations 1–4 below, estimate the probability requested and record your answer.

SITUATION 1

Imagine that you are an administrator in a community correction agency that serves criminal offenders on probation. From agency records you know that 3% of your clients committed a new offense during the past year and were sent to prison. Thus, 3% is the prior probability (baserate or prevalence rate), and your best estimate, that a new client who is referred to your agency will commit further crimes in the next year, knowing nothing more about a client.

Now, let's say that you have a new assessment tool called the Probation Risk Assessment Measure (PRAM). PRAM's sensitivity is 95%, that is, you know from experience with the measure last year that 95% of those who failed on probation had tested positively—the test had said they would fail. PRAM's specificity is 93%, that is, you know from experience with the measure last year that 93% of those who had tested negatively—the test had said they would not fail—did not commit more crimes. Given these three values-3% prior probability, 95% sensitivity, and 93% specificity-and that PRAM indicates that client X will commit further crimes within the next year, what is your estimate that the client will?

Your estimate: _____

Estimate based on Bayes's Theorem

(calculate this later): _____

SITUATION 2

Imagine again that you are an administrator in a community correction agency that serves criminal offenders on probation. From agency records you know that 35% of your clients committed a new offense during the past year and were sent to prison. Thus, 35 % is the prior probability (and your best estimate) that a new client whom you know nothing else about will commit further crimes in the next year.

Imagine you have used the Probation Risk Assessment Measure (PRAM), which has a sensitivity of 95% and a specificity of 93%. Given these three values-35% prior probability (baserate), 95% sensitivity, and 93% specificity-and that PRAM indicates that client X will recidivate within the next year, what is your estimate that the client will?

Your estimate: _____

Estimate based on Bayes's Theorem

(calculate this later): _____

SITUATION 3

You are an administrator who heads the Medically Fragile Special Education Needs Program in Midwestern School District. Your agency receives 300 referrals from teachers, parents, and physicians each year, which must be evaluated to see which children in the district should get special services. Your records show that, during the past year, 50% of those referred needed services, according to a three-hour Battelle Developmental Inventory followed by interviews and a multidisciplinary team evaluation.

You are thinking of using the Denver Developmental Screening Test (DST), which takes less time to complete. This has a sensitivity of 94% (i.e., you know from experience that 94% of those who were said to need services by the DST, did need services) and a specificity of 97% (i.e., you know from experience that 97% of those indicated as not needing services did not need services). What is the probability that clients referred this year who are tested with DST and found by DST to need services in fact will need services?

Your estimate: _____

Estimate based on Bayes's Theorem

(calculate this later): _____

SITUATION 4

Again, you are an administrator who heads the Medically Fragile Special Education Needs Program in Midwestern School District. You are considering administering the Denver Developmental Screening Test (DST) to all preschool and grade-school children in your district to determine which children should receive agency services. Your records show that during the past year, 150 (1%) of 15,000 children in your school district needed services. The DST has a 94% sensitivity and a 97% specificity.

If 15,000 children are screened with DST, what is the probability that they will in fact need services if the DST indicated they do?

Your estimate: _____

Estimate based on Bayes's Theorem

(calculate this later): _____

Step 2

Insert the values for prevalence rate, sensitivity, and specificity in the formula for Bayes's Theorem (given here) to find the predictive value of a positive test result for Situation 1.

Bayes's Theorem

$$PPV = \frac{(\text{Prevalence})(\text{Sensitivity})}{(\text{Prevalence})(\text{Sensitivity}) + (1 - \text{Prevalence})(1 - \text{Specificity})}$$

Step 3

Compare your answer with the one below. We have worked out Bayes's Theorem for Situation 1 to provide a model for solving Situations 2 to 4.

$$\text{PPV} = \frac{(.03)\,(.95)}{(.03)\,(.95) + (1 - 0.03)(1 - 0.93)} = .30 \text{ or } 30\%$$

Step 4

Compute the predictive value of a positive test for Situations 2 to 4 and record your answers next to your estimates in Situations 1 to 4.

FOLLOW-UP ACTIVITIES AND QUESTIONS

1. Is the predictive value of a positive test greater when the baserate is relatively high or when it is relatively low? (Hint: Compare Situation 1 with Situation 2, Situation 3 with Situation 4).

    _____

    _____

    _____

    _____

    _____

2. Compare all four values of your estimated probabilities with those computed with Bayes's Theorem. Did you tend to overestimate or underestimate probabilities compared with those found by using Bayes's Theorem?

    _____

    _____

    _____

    _____

3. Complete Practice Exercise 22.1.

Part 3: Using Frequencies to Understand and Communicate Risk

It is much easer to calculate risk using frequencies (see Box 22.2). Consider an example from Gigerenzer (2002) regarding an HIV test he was required to take at the United States. Consulate in Germany to comply with

---

Box 22.2   How Natural Frequencies Facilitate Bayesian Computations

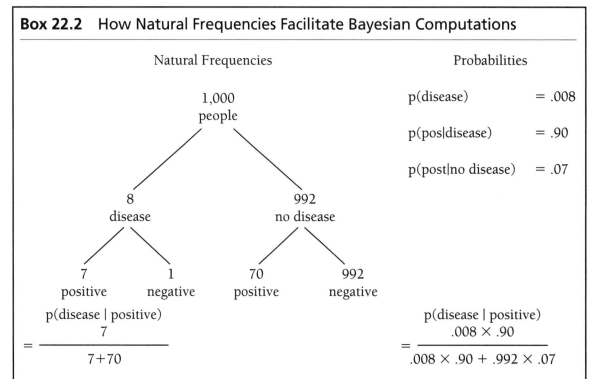

Using the figures on the left it is easy to estimate the chances of disease given a positive test (or symptom). We have to pay attention to only two numbers, the number of patients with a positive test and the disease (a = 7) and the number of patients with a positive test and no disease (b = 70). The person on the right has received the same information in probabilities making this estimation more difficult. The structure of this equation is the same as the one on the left—a/(a + b)—but the natural frequencies *a* and *b* have been transformed into conditional probabilities, making the formula for probabilities much more complex. Source: Reprinted with the permission of Simon & Schuster, Inc., from *Calculated Risks: How to Know When Numbers Deceive You* by Gerd Gigerenzer. Copyright @ 2002 by Gerd Gigerenzer. All rights reserved.

---

immigration requirements to travel to the United States. He had the following information at that time:

> *About 0.01 percent of men with no known risk behavior are infected with HIV (base rate). If such a man has the virus, there is a 99.9 percent chance that the test result will be positive (sensitivity). If a man is not infected, there is a 99.99 percent chance that the test result will be negative (specificity).*

What is the chance that a man who tests positive actually has the virus? Most people think it is 99% or higher (p.124). Let's convert this to frequencies:

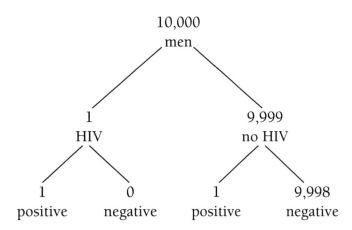

Thus two men out of 10,000 men with no known risk behavior will test positive.

Let's take another example:

> **...over a 5-year period, 15 out of 1000 post menopausal women are predicted to get breast cancer—even if they don't take hormone therapy. If they do take hormone therapy over that period, 19 out of 1000 can be expected to get the disease. It is immediately evident that this strategy for communicating likelihoods is far easier for patients to understand than comparing odds of 1 in 67 with the odds of 1 in 53. Frequencies immediately show we are dealing with a difference of 4 extra people out of 1000 over a 5-year period (Paling, 2006, p. 13).**

Complete Practice Exercise 22.2. Practice Exercise 22.3 provides an opportunity to critique an article regarding risk.

Practice Exercise 22.1   Critically Appraising a Prediction/Risk Instrument*

Your Name _____ Date _____

Course _____ Instructor's Name _____

Source in APA Format _____

_____

_____

_____

CRITERION	EXPLANATION	VALUE (Insert Value Reported in Source or Zero if Not Reported)
Sensitivity	a/(a + c)	
Specificity	d/(b + d)	
Positive Predictive Value	a/(a + b)	
Negative Predictive Value	d/(d + c)	
Prevalence Rate	(a + c)/(a + b + c + d)	
Blinded Prediction	Were those who judged the gold standard blind to the prediction scale's score?	Yes _____ No _____
Follow-up	Were clients followed up long enough to test predictive accuracy?	Yes _____ No _____
Follow-up Rate	Were greater than 80% followed up in the prediction instrument's evaluation?	List percent followed up (0–100): _____%
Reliability Checked by Independent Raters	Were ratings of the client's risk level checked by independent raters and compared?	Yes _____ No _____
Reliability Coefficient	Ideally with reliability coefficient greater than .70	Enter reliability coefficient: _____
Representativeness	Were subjects in the study sufficiently like your clients that results apply to your clients?	Yes _____ No _____
Validation Study	Was the measure tested in a setting other than the one in which it was developed and found to have predictive value?	Yes _____ No _____
Benefit to Client and Significant Others	Are the benefits of using the measure worth the harms and costs?	Yes _____ No _____

Note: See contingency table in Box 22.1.
*Use one form per source.

Your Name _____ Date _____

Instructor's Name _____ Course _____

INSTRUCTIONS

First, read the example below and calculate risk using probabilities. Then calculate risk using frequencies.

SITUATION 1

Sally, a medical social worker, is employed in a hospital. Her client, Mrs. Sabins age 45, said that her doctor recommends that she get a mammogram to screen for breast cancer. She is asymptomatic. She asked about possible risks but she said that the doctor brushed aside her questions. She would like to know more about the accuracy of this test and asks for your help. Let's say that "The following information is available about asymptomatic women aged 40 to 50 in such as region who participate in mammography screening":

> The probability that one of these women has breast cancer is 0.8 percent. If a woman has breast cancer, the probability is 90 percent that she will have a positive mammogram. If a woman does not have breast cancer, the probability is 7 percent that she will still have a positive mammogram. Imagine a woman who has a positive mammogram. What is the probability that she actually has breast cancer? (Gigerenzer, 2002, p. 41).

Your answer: _____

Translate probabilities into frequencies and illustrate these in a diagram below:

SITUATION 2

Another patient approaches Sally (in Situation 1) regarding how to interpret risk—in this case a symptom free 50-year-old man. His physician recommended that he get a hemoccult test to detect occult blood in the stool. This test is used in routine screening for early detection of colon cancer. He wants more information about the accuracy of the test. Imagine that, based on information from screening symptom free people over 50 years of age, we have the following data:

> The probability that one of these people has colorectal cancer is 0.3 percent [baserate]. If a person has colorectal cancer, the probability is 50 percent that he will have a positive hemoccult test. If a person does not have colorectal cancer, the probability is 3 percent that he will still have a positive hemoccult test. Imagine a person (over age 50, no symptoms) who has a positive hemoccult test in your screening. What is the probability that this person actually has colorectal cancer? (Gigerenzer, 2002, pp. 104–105).

Your answer: _____

Translate probabilities into frequencies and illustrate these in a diagram below.

SITUATION 3

> About 0.01 percent of men with no known risk behavior are infected with HIV (base rate). If such a man has the virus, there is a 99.9 percent chance that the test result will be positive (sensitivity). If a man is not infected, there is a 99.99 percent chance that the test will be negative (specificity)." (Gigerenzer, 2002, p. 124).

What is the chance that a man who tests positive actually has the virus?

Your answer: _____

Translate probabilities into frequencies and illustrate these in a diagram below.

Practice Exercise 22.3 Reviewing an Aritcle Concerning Risk

Your Name _____ Date _____

Instructor's Name _____ Course _____

1. Select an article describing a risk assessment measure and critique this using
    information in Box 22.1 and Practice Exercise 22.1.

2. Give complete sentence:

    _____

    _____

    _____

    _____

3. Your critique: _____

    _____

    _____

    _____

    _____

    _____

    _____

    _____

    _____

Purpose

To enhance your skill in critically appraising assessment measures and highlight the harms of using tests that do not measure what they claim to measure

Background

Professionals often use tests to make decisions about clients. These tests may either provide helpful guidelines or offer misleading data that appear to inform but do the opposite—misinform. Consider the reflex dilation test. In Britain, Hobbs and Wynne (1986) (two pediatricians) suggested that a simple medical test could be used to demonstrate that buggery or other forms of anal penetration had occurred. Here is their description

> **Reflex dilation, well described in forensic texts...usually occurs within about 30 seconds of separating the buttocks. Recent controversy has helped our understanding of what is now seen as an important sign of traumatic penetration of the anus as occurs in abuse, but also following medical and surgical manipulation.... The diameter of the symmetrical relaxation of the anal sphincter is variable and should be estimated. This is a dramatic sign which once seen is easily recognized.... The sign is not always easily reproducible on second and third examinations and there appear to be factors, at present, which may modify the eliciting of this physical sign. The sign in most cases gradually disappears when abuse stops (Hanks, Hobbs, & Wynne, 1988, p. 153).**

News of this test spread quickly, and because of this test many children were removed from their homes on the grounds that they were being sexually abused. (For a critique see Harvey, & Nowlan, 1989.)

Instructions

1. Review Box 23.1 as well as relevant terms in Glossary and complete Practice Exercise 23 (see also Box 22.1).
2. Check your answers against those provided by your instructor.

Your Name _____ Date _____

Course _____ Instructor's Name _____

1.   Review Box 23.1 as well as relevant terms in the Glossary.

2.   Identify diagnostic test to be reviewed and give most relevant citation:

   _____

   _____

   _____

3.   Describe the purpose of this test: _____

   _____

   _____

   _____

4.   What questions should be raised about this test? List each separately and describe why you would ask this question. Review material on reliability and validity in Exercise 22 as needed as well as concepts such as false positive and false-negative rates. Consult STARD guidelines for reviewing diagnostic measures and consider these in your review (Bossuyt, et al., 2003).

   _____

   _____

   _____

   _____

   _____

5.   Would you use this test?   Yes _____   No _____

Please explain your answer:

_____

_____

_____

_____

_____

_____

_____

_____

_____

_____

_____

_____

_____

BOX 23.1 Definitions and Calculations for a Perfect ("Gold Standard") Diagnostic Test

Definitions

Sensitivity: A/(A + C)
Specificity: D/(D + B)
False-negative rate: C/(C + A)
False-positive rate: B/(B + D)
Positive predictive value: A (A + B)
Negative predictive value: D/(C + D)
Pretest disease probability: (A + C)/(A + B + C + D)
Posttest disease probability, positive result: A/(A + C)

Posttest disease probability, negative result: C/(C + D)

Test	Disorder Present	Disorder Absent	Total
Test Positive	A	B	A + B
Test Negative	C	D	C + D
Total	A + C	B + D	N = (A + B + C + D)

Calculations:

Sensitivity: 100 (100 + 0) = 100%
Specificity: 100 (100 + 0) = 100%
Positive predictive value: 100%
Posttest disease probability negative test: 0%

Test	Disorder Present	Disorder Absent	Total
Test Positive	100	0	100
Test Negative	0	100	100
Total	100	100	200

Source: "Assessing accuracy of diagnostic and screening tests," by J. G. Elmore & E. J. Boyko (2000), in *Evidence-based clinical practice: Concepts and approaches* (p. 85) edited by J. P. Geyman, R. A. Deyo, & S. D. Ramsey. Boston: Butterworth Heinemann. Reprinted with permission.

Purpose

To increase your skill in critically appraising classification systems such as the *Diagnostic and Statistical Manual of Psychiatric Disorder*

Background Information

Labels are used to categorize people (e.g., alcoholic, hyperactive, sexually abused, autistic, sexually dysfunctional). The DSM (2002) is in widespread use. The Mental Health Parity Act requires all health insurers to provide equivalent benefits for mental disorders (described in the DSM) as they do for physical illnesses (*New York Times*, 3/5/08). Many people have questioned the reliability and validity of categories used in the DSM (Kutchins & Kirk, 1997; Houts, 2002). This exercise gives you an opportunity to explore the clarity of descriptions in the DSM.

Instructions

1. Review the diagnostic criteria for Attention Deficit/Hyperactivity Disorder used in the DSM (see Box 24.1). Circle each word that you think is vague and describe what you think it means on a list using Practice Exercise 24. Do not compare notes or discuss your impressions with other students while doing this.

2. When everyone has completed Step 1, your instructor will guide you in a review of results and their implications, considering the following questions:

   a. Did students note different words as vague? What was the range of number of words circled? _____ to _____.

   b. Were different meanings attributed to different words?
      ___ Yes ___ No

If Yes, please give some examples:

_____

_____

_____

_____

    c. Were cultural differences raised?

_____

_____

_____

_____

FOLLOW-UP QUESTIONS

1. What do the results imply for clients? Hundreds of diagnostic labels are included in the DSM-IV (American Psychiatric Association, 2000). Does use of such labels do more good than harm? (See, for example, Boyle, 2002; Houts, 2002; Kirk & Kutchins, 1992; Kutchins & Kirk, 1997.)

_____

_____

_____

_____

_____

_____

2. What does this exercise imply for practitioners?

_____

_____

_____

3. How does this exercise illustrate the difference between diagnosis and assessment? (See e.g., Gambrill, 2006.)

4. Describe how you could gather information that would help you to clarify vague terms.

BOX 24.1   Diagnostic Criteria for Attention-Deficit/Hyperactivity Disorder

A.   Either (1) or (2):

    (1)   six (or more) of the following symptoms of inattention have persisted for at least 6 months to a degree that is maladaptive and inconsistent with developmental level:

Inattention

    (a)   often fails to give close attention to details or makes careless mistakes in schoolwork, work, or other activities.

    (b)   often has difficulty sustaining attention to tasks or play activities.

    (c)   often does not seem to listen when spoken to directly.

    (d)   often does not follow through on instructions and fails to finish schoolwork, chores, or duties in the workplace (not due to oppositional behavior or failure to understand instructions).

    (e)   often has difficulty organizing tasks and activities.

    (f)   often avoid, dislikes, or is reluctant to engage in tasks that require sustained mental effort (such as schoolwork or homework).

    (g)   often loses things necessary for tasks or activities (e.g., toys, school assignments, pencils, books, or tools).

    (h)   is often easily distracted by extraneous stimuli.

    (i)   is often forgetful in daily activities.

    (2)   six (or more) of the following symptoms of hyperactivity-impulsivity have persisted for at least 6 months to a degree that is maladaptive and inconsistent with developmental level:

Hyperactivity

    (a)   often fidgets with hands or feet or squirms in seat.

    (b)   often leaves seat in classroom or in other situations in which remaining seated is expected.

    (c)   often runs about or climbs excessively in situations in which it is inappropriate (in adolescents or adults, may be limited to subjective feelings of restlessness).

    (d)   often has difficult playing or engaging in leisure activities quietly.

    (e)   is often "on the go" or often acts as if "drive by a motor."

    (f)   often talks excessively.

Impulsivity

    (g)   often blurts out answers before questions have been completed.

    (h)   often has difficulty awaiting turn.

    (i)   often interrupts or intrudes on others (e.g., butts in to conversations or games).

B.   Some hyperactive-impulsive or inattentive symptoms that cause impairment were present before age 7 years.

C.   Some impairment from the symptoms is present in two or more settings (e.g., at school [or work] or at home).

Source: American Psychiatric Association (2000). *Diagnostic and statistical manual of mentaldisorders.* (revised 4th ed.). Washington, DC: Author. pp. 92–93. Reprinted with permission.

Practice Exercise 24   Vague Words and Examples of What You Think These Mean

Your Name _____ Date _____

Course _____ Instructor's Name _____

Item No. (e.g., 1a/2b)	Word	What you think this means

EXERCISE 25   EVALUATING RESEARCH REGARDING CAUSES

Purpose

To highlight important questions to raise regarding research about causes

Background

Professionals make decisions about the causes of client concerns. For example, is depression a brain disease? Is it related to the environmental factors, such as loss of a significant other? Is it caused by negative thoughts? Does medication cure or cause abnormal brain states? (see Moncrieff, 2008; Moncrieff & Cohen, 2006). Is it in the genes? (e.g., see Joseph, 2004). Some examples of proposed causes follow (Haynes, 1992, p. 74).

Proposed Cause	Concern
Beliefs	Health care noncompliance
Biochemical variables	Schizophrenia
Childhood obesity	Adult obesity
Classical conditioning	General behavior disorders
	Chemotherapy side effects
Cognitive schemas	Depression
Cognitive interference	Sexual dysfunction
Contingency management	Antisocial boys
Cultural norms	Bulimia

Many different kinds of causes are possible

- *Sufficient causes*: Y occurs whenever X occurs: therefore, X is sufficient to cause Y; X must precede Y if X is a cause of Y.
- *Insufficient cause*: That cause that, *by itself*, is insufficient to produce the effect, but can function as a causal variable in combination with other variables.
- *Necessary cause*: Y never occur without X.

- *Necessary and sufficient cause*: Y occurs whenever X occurs, and Y never occurs without X.
- *First cause*: That cause upon which all others depend—the earliest event in a causal chain.
- *Principal cause*: That cause upon which the effect *primarily* depends.
- *Immediate cause:* That cause that produces the effect without any intervening events.
- *Mediating cause*: A cause that produces its effect only through another cause (Byerly, 1973; Mc Cormick, 1937; Haynes, 1992, p. 26).

Causal factors differ in how long it takes for a cause to affect behavior (latency) and the time required to stabilize an effect (equilibrium). Clues to causality include temporal order, contiguity in time and space, covariation and availability of alternative possibilities (Einhorn & Hogarth, 1986). Causal effects may depend on critical periods such as developmental stage. Kuhn (1992) examined the kind of evidence used to support theories about alleged causes of a problem. She divided this into three kinds. One is *genuine evidence.* Criteria here are (1) it is distinguishable from description of the causal inference itself; and (2) it bears on its correctness (p. 45). Kinds of covariation evidence include (1) correspondence (evidence that does no more than note a co-occurrence of antecedent and outcome); (2) covariation (there is a comparison or quantification); and (3) correlated change (does b change after a?). In appealing to evidence external to the causal sequence, we go "beyond the antecedent and outcome themselves to invoke some additional, external factor" (p. 55) such as appealing to counterfactual arguments. Kinds of indirect evidence include (1) analogy (particular to particular); (2) assumption (general to particular), (3) discounting (elimination of alternatives); and (4) partial discounting.

Another major category included pseudoevidence. Kuhn describes *pseudoevidence* as taking the form of scenario or general script depicting how the phenomena might occur (p. 65). They are usually expressed in general terms. Defining characteristics that distinguish pseudoevidence from genuine evidence is that, in contrast to the latter, pseudoevidence cannot be sharply distinguished from description of the causal sequence itself (pp. 65–66). There are generalized scripts and scripts as unfalsifiable illustrations. Here subjects "equate evidence with examples" (p. 79). A scenario (example) is viewed as "sufficient to account for the phenomenon." Counter examples are dismissed as exceptions' (p. 80). "Because the examples are proved, the theory is proved" (p. 80). A request for evidence may be followed by a restating of or elaboration of the original theory; there is no distinction between (decoupling of) theory and evidence (see also Introduction and Exercise 28). Lastly, Kuhn used a category of *no evidence* (either genuine or pseudo) offered in relation to the theory proposed. Included here are (a) implications that evidence is unnecessary or irrelevant; (b) assertions not connected to a causal theory; or (c) citing the phenomena itself as evidence regarding its cause.

Questions suggested by Greenhalgh (2006) regarding quality include the following:

- Is there evidence from true experiments in humans?
- Is the association strong?
- Is the association consistent from study to study?
- Is the temporal relationship appropriate (i.e., did the postulated cause precede the postulated effect)?
- Is there a dose-response gradient (i.e., does more of the postulated effect follow more of the postulated cause)?
- Does the association make epidemiological sense?
- Does the association make biological sense?
- Is the association specific?
- Is the association analogous to a previously proven causal association? (p. 83).

The disadvantages of accepting limited causal models include inaccurate predictions and in effective intervention (see Haynes, 1992, p. 68). Misleading oversimplifications may occur (see Exercise 7). This brief overview should alert you to the challenges in identifying causes, especially via studies that explore correlations among variables.

Instructions

1. Read the article assigned by your instructor.
2. Complete Practice Exercise 25.

Your Name _____ Date _____

Instructor's Name _____ Course _____

1. Name and source of article: _____

_____

_____

2. Describe (using quotes) claims regarding causality (give page numbers).

_____

_____

_____

_____

_____

3. Describe research method used (e.g., correlational design, RCT, etc.).

_____

_____

_____

_____

_____

4. Describe below any problems regarding claims about causality.

_____

_____

_____

5. Has correlation been distinguished from regression and has the correlation coefficient been calculated and interpreted correctly? (Greenhalgh, 2006).

6. Describe the implications for clients of false claims regarding causality (e.g., inflated).

PART 6
Reviewing Decisions

This section includes a number of exercises related to making decisions. Exercise 26 provides a checklist to rate plans for helping clients relative to twenty-two criteria. Exercise 27 provides an opportunity to consider ethical issues that arise in everyday practice based on the vignettes in Exercises 6 to 8. Critical thinkers raise questions about commonly accepted practices, and, because they value seeking the truth over following authority and dogma, they may find themselves in ethical binds. Deciding what is most ethical will often require careful consideration of the implications of different options. Exercise 28 is designed to enhance your skill in clarifying and critically examining arguments related to claims made that affect client's lives. Exercise 29 highlights harms that may occur because of a lack of critical thinking. Exercise 30 suggests questions for thinking critically about case records and Exercise 31 identifies important ingredients of clear service agreements. Lastly Exercise 32 offers opportunities to spot, describe, and evaluate claims.

Purpose

To enhance critical appraisal of intervention plans

Background

Professionals make decisions about what intervention methods may result in hoped-for outcomes. The checklist included in this exercise describes points to check when deciding on plans. For example, are negative effects likely, are cultural differences considered, are plans acceptable to clients and significant others, and does related research suggest that plans selected will be effective?

Instructions

1. Choose a client with whom you are working, or, your instructor may provide a case example.
2. Complete the Checklist for Reviewing Intervention Plans in this exercise.
3. Add up the circled numbers to determine an overall score.

Your Name _____ Date _____

Course _____ Instructor's Name _____

N = Not at all satisfactory; L = A little satisfactory; S = Satisfactory; I = Ideal

	No.	Item	N	L	S	I
	1.	Assessment data support the plan's selection.	0	1	2	3
	2.	The plan addresses problem-related circumstances.	0	1	2	3
	3.	The plan offers the greatest likelihood of success as shown by critical tests.[a]	0	1	2	3
	4.	There are empirically based principles that suggest that the plan will be effective with this client.[b]	0	1	2	3
	5.	The plan is feasible.	0	1	2	3
	6.	The plan and rationales for it are acceptable to participants.	0	1	2	3
	7.	The plan, including intermediate steps, is clearly described.	0	1	2	3
	8.	The least intrusive methods are used.	0	1	2	3
	9.	The plan builds on available client skills.	0	1	2	3
	10.	Significant others (those who interact with clients such as family members) are involved as appropriate.	0	1	2	3
	11.	The plan selected is the most efficient in cost, time, and effort.	0	1	2	3
	12.	Positive side effects are likely.	0	1	2	3
	13.	Negative side effects are unlikely.	0	1	2	3
	14.	Cues and reinforcers for desired behaviors are arranged.	0	1	2	3
	15.	Cues and reinforcers for undesired behaviors are removed.	0	1	2	3

No.	Item	N	L	S	I
16.	Arrangements are made for generalization and maintenance of valued outcomes.	0	1	2	3
17.	Chosen settings maximize the likelihood of success.	0	1	2	3
18.	Cultural differences are considered as necessary.	0	1	2	3
19.	Multiple services are well integrated.	0	1	2	3
20.	Participants are given a clear written description of the plan.	0	1	2	3
21.	The plan meets legal and ethical requirements.	0	1	2	3
22.	The probability that the plan will be successful in achieving desired outcomes is high ($P > 0.80$).	0	1	2	3

a. There is scientific evidence that your plan is most likely (compared to other plans) to result in hoped-for outcomes with this client. Give complete citation for most rigorous test/review article here.

_____

_____

_____

_____

_____

b. Please describe related principles.

_____

_____

_____

_____

_____

FOLLOW-UP QUESTIONS

1.   Is there any way you could increase the likelihood of success given available resources?

_____ Yes _____ No

If *No*, this is because

____ I have selected the plan most likely to be successful. (Describe criteria you used to make this selection.)

____ I don't know how to offer other plans more likely to succeed.

____ I know how to offer more effective services but don't have the time.

____ I don't have the resources needed to offer a more effective plan. (Please clearly describe what you need).

____ The client is not willing to participate.

____ Other (please describe). _____

_____

Please explain your answer more fully here.

_____

_____

_____

_____

If *Yes*, please describe how.

_____

_____

_____

_____

2.   Are there items on the checklist that you do not think are important? If so, please identify which ones and explain why you selected them.

_____

_____

_____

_____

3. What items do you think are especially important from the client's point of view? Please identify the items and explain why you selected them.

_____

_____

_____

4. Do you think the "illusion of knowledge" (see discussion in Part 1) affected your decision? _____ Yes _____ No. Please give reasons for your answer below.

_____

_____

_____

_____

_____

_____

_____

EXERCISE 27   CRITICAL THINKING AS A GUIDE TO MAKING ETHICAL DECISIONS

Purpose

To illustrate the value of critical thinking as a guide to making ethical decisions in professional contexts.

Background

Baron (1985) suggests that the very purpose of critical thinking is to arrive at moral or ethical decisions. Professional codes of ethics describe ethical obligations of professionals, for example, the code of ethics of the American Psychological Association, The National Association of Social Workers, and the American Medical Association . Ethical obligations described in these codes are illustrated in this exercise. The ethical obligations described illustrate the call for transparency and for accountability in codes of ethics—our obligation to be honest with clients, for example, concerning our competence to provide the services we offer or recommend and to accurately describe the risks and benefits of recommended practices and policies as well as the risks and benefits of alternatives (including doing nothing). Honoring these obligations is more the exception that the rule (e.g., see Braddock, Edwards, Hasenberg, Laidley, & Levinson, 1999).

Ethical dilemmas (e.g., situations in which there are competing interests) require careful consideration from multiple points of view to be resolved in the best way.

Instructions

1. Review the Checklist of Ethical Concerns in Box 27.1.
2. Select vignettes in Exercises 6 to 8 to review. Your instructor may help you choose them.
3. Note the game and vignette number and ethical issue that you think arises in that vignette on the Practice Exercise 27.
4. For each ethical issue selected, please describe how it pertains to the vignette selected.

BOX 27.1 Ethical Concerns

A.   *Keeping Confidentiality*
- _____ 1. Limits on confidentiality are described.
- _____ 2. Confidentiality is maintained unless there are concerns about harm to others.

B.   *Selecting Objectives*
- _____ 3. Objectives focused on result in real-life gains for clients.
- _____ 4. Objectives pursued are related to key concerns of clients.

C.   *Selecting Practices and Policies*
- _____ 5. Assessment methods used provide accurate, relevant information.
- _____ 6. Assessment, intervention, and evaluation methods are acceptable to clients and to significant others.
- _____ 7. Intervention methods selected are those most likely to help clients attain outcomes they value.
- _____ 8. Evaluation methods used are most likely to reveal degree of progress or harm.

D.   *Involving Clients as Informed Participants*
- _____ 9. The accuracy of assessment methods used is clearly described to clients.
- _____ 10. Risks and benefits of recommended services are clearly described including possible side effects.
- _____ 11. Risks and benefits of alternative options are described (including the option of doing nothing).
- _____ 12. Clear descriptions of the cost, time, and effort involved in suggested methods are given in language intelligible to clients.
- _____ 13. Competence to offer needed services is accurately described to clients.
- _____ 14. Appropriate arrangements are made to involve others in decisions when clients cannot give informed consent.

E.   *Being Competent*
- _____ 15. Valid assessment methods are used with a high level of fidelity.
- _____ 16. Intervention methods used are provided with a high level of fidelity.
- _____ 17. Effective communication and supportive skills are used including empathic response.

F.   *Being Accountable*
- _____ 18. Arrangements are made for ongoing feedback about progress using valid progress indicators. Data concerning prevention is shared with clients in a timely manner.

G.   *Encouraging a Culture of Thoughtfulness*
- _____ 19. Positive feedback is provided to colleagues for the critical evaluation of claims and arguments.
- _____ 20. Efforts are made to change agency procedures and policies that decrease the likelihood of offering clients evidence-informed practices and policies.

Your Name _____ Date _____

Course _____ Instructor's Name _____

REASONING-IN PRACTICE VIGNETTES	*Game*	*Number*	*Ethical Issue*
	_____	_____	_____
	_____	_____	_____
	_____	_____	_____
	_____	_____	_____
	_____	_____	_____
	_____	_____	_____
	_____	_____	_____
	_____	_____	_____
	_____	_____	_____
	_____	_____	_____
	_____	_____	_____
	_____	_____	_____
	_____	_____	_____
	_____	_____	_____
	_____	_____	_____
	_____	_____	_____
	_____	_____	_____
	_____	_____	_____
	_____	_____	_____

FOLLOW-UP QUESTIONS

1. Please identify any particular game, vignette, or ethical issue that you think particularly important or have a question that you would like to discuss.

_____

_____

_____

_____

_____

_____

2. Do you believe that you are ethically bound to think critically about your practice?
   _____ Yes _____ No

   Please describe reasons for your answer.

   _____

   _____

   _____

   _____

3. Why do you think ethical issues are often overlooked or ignored in everyday practice?

   _____

   _____

   _____

   _____

Purpose

To increase skill in critically appraising arguments related to practice and policy-related claims

Background

Argument analysis is a vital practice skill (see, e.g., Kuhn, 1991; Tindale, 2007). Practitioners hear and offer arguments daily for and against life-affecting decisions. Reading research reports is a form of argument analysis (Jenicek & Hitchcock, 2005). Here, we define an argument not as a conflict, but as a group of statements, one or more of which (the premises) are offered in support of another (the conclusion). An argument is used to suggest the truth or demonstrate the falsity of a claim. "A good argument... offers reasons and evidence so that other people can make up their minds for themselves" (Weston, 1992, p. xi). (See Walton, 1995 for discussion of the importance of context in detecting inappropriate blocks to critical appraisal of claims.) A key part of an argument is the claim, conclusion, or position put forward. Excessive wordiness may make a conclusion difficult to identify. A second consists of reasons or premises offered to support the claim. These will differ in their relevance to a claim, their acceptability, and in their sufficiency to support a claim. (See later section describing guidelines for evaluating arguments.) A third component consists of the reasons given for assuming that the premises are relevant to the conclusion. These are called warrants. Jenicek and Hitchcock (2005) suggest that to arrive at a conclusion based on the best relevant obtainable evidence:

- we must be *justified in accepting the premises;* that is, they must be evidence [informed]. Further,
- our premises *must include [key] relevant justified available information.*

the conclusion must follow in virtue of a *justified general warrant*. And,

- if the warrant is not universal, we must be justified in assuming that in the particular case there are *no known contradictions (rebuttals) that rule out application of the warrant* (p. 41).

Let's say a teacher consults the school psychologist about James (age 10), who is a hard-to-manage student and doing poorly in his school work. The psychologist tells the teacher that the student has ADHD (Attention-Deficit Hyperactive Disorder) and should be placed on Ritalin because hyperactivity is caused by a brain disease. What are the premises here? What warrants are appealed to? Are they sound? Has Ritalin been found to decrease hyperactivity? Is this mode of intervention more effective than rearranging environmental contingencies such as the behaviors of teachers, parents, and peers? Are there alternative accounts (rival hypotheses) that point to a different conclusion? (For practice in identifying rival hypotheses, see Huck & Sandler, 1979.)

If a claim is made with no reason, piece of evidence, or statement of support provided, then there is no argument. Many editorials and letters to the editor make a point but provide no argument. They give no reasons for the position taken. As Weston (1992) notes, it is not a mistake to have strong views. The mistake is to have nothing else. Many propaganda strategies give an illusion of argument. General rules for composing arguments include the following:

1. Distinguish between premises and conclusion
2. Present your ideas in a natural order
3. Start from accurate premises
4. Use clear language
5. Avoid fallacies including loaded language (see Exercises 6 to 8)
6. Use consistent terms
7. Stick to one meaning for each term (based on Weston, 1992, p. v).

An argument may be unsound because there is something wrong with its logical structure, because it contains false premises, or because it is irrelevant to the claim or is circular. Weston suggests that the two greatest lacks are basing conclusions on too little evidence (e.g., generalizing from incomplete information) and overlooking alternatives.

A first step in evaluating arguments suggested by Damer (1995) is to identify which of several statements in a piece of writing or discourse is the conclusion. The conclusion of an argument should be the statement or claim that has at least one other statement in support of it. In a long argument, there may be more than one conclusion. More than one argument may be presented. If so, treat each argument separately. Remember, opinions are not arguments.

There are four general criteria of a good argument: (1) the premises are relevant to the truth of the conclusion; (2) they are acceptable; (3) when viewed together the premises constitute sufficient grounds for the truth of the conclusion; and (4) the premises provide an effective rebuttal to all reasonable challenges to the argument. An argument that violates anyone of these criteria is flawed. Criteria suggested by Damer (1995) follows:

1. *The Relevance Criterion:* The premises must be *relevant* to the conclusion. A premise is relevant if it makes a difference to the truth or falsity of the conclusion. A premise is irrelevant if its acceptance has no bearing on the truth or falsity of the conclusion. In most cases, the relevance of a premise is also determined by its relation to other premises. In some cases, additional premises may be needed to make the relevance of another premise apparent.

2. *The Acceptability Criterion:* The premises must be acceptable. Acceptability means that which a reasonable person should accept. A premise is *acceptable* if it reflects any of the following:

   • A claim that is a matter of undisputed common knowledge. A claim that is adequately defended in the same discussion or at least capable of being adequately defended on request or with further inquiry.
   • a conclusion of another good argument
   • an uncontroverted eyewitness testimony
   • an uncontroverted report from an expert in the field

A premise is *unacceptable* if it reflects any of the following:

   • A claim that contradicts any of the following: the evidence, a well-established claim, a reliable source, or other premises in the same argument

- A questionable claim that is not adequately defended in the context of the discussion or in some other accessible source
- A claim that is self-contradictory, linguistically confusing, or otherwise unintelligible
- A claim that is no different from, or that is as questionable as, the conclusion that it is supposed to support
- A claim that is based on a usually unstated but highly questionable assumption or an unacceptable premise

The premises of an argument should be regarded as acceptable if each meets at least one of the conditions of acceptability and if none meet a condition of unacceptability.

3. *The Sufficient Grounds Criterion:* The premises of a good argument must provide sufficient grounds for the truth of its conclusion. If the premises are not sufficient in number, kind, and weight, they may not be strong enough to establish the conclusion, even though they may be both relevant and acceptable. Additional relevant and acceptable premises may be needed to make the case. This is perhaps the most difficult criterion to apply, because there are not clear guidelines to help us determine what constitutes sufficient grounds for the truth of a claim or the rightness of an action. Argumentative contexts differ and thus create different sufficiency demands. There are many ways that arguments may fail to satisfy the sufficiency criterion:

- A premise may be based on a small or unrepresentative sample. For example, a premise may rely on anecdotal data (e.g., the personal experience of the arguer or of a few people of his or her acquaintance).
- A premise might be based on a faulty causal analysis.
- Crucial evidence may be missing.

4. *The Rebuttal Criterion:* A good argument should provide an *effective rebuttal* to the strongest arguments against your conclusion and the strongest arguments in support of alternative positions. A good argument, usually presented in relation to another side to the issue, must meet that other side head-on. Most people can devise what *appears* to be a good argument for whatever it is that they want to believe or want others to believe. There cannot be good arguments in support of both sides of opposing or contradictory positions,

because at least half the arguments presented will not be able to satisfy the rebuttal criterion. (See other sources for further detail such as Walton, 1992a; 1996.)

The ultimate key to distinguishing between a good and a mediocre argument is how well the rebuttal criterion has been met. Rebuttal is frequently neglected for several reasons. First, people may not discover any good answers to challenges to their position, so they just keep quiet about them. Second, they may not want to mention the contrary evidence for fear that their position will be weakened by bringing it to the attention of opponents. Finally, they may be so convinced by their own position that they don't believe that there is another side to the issue. They may be "true believers" and no amount of evidence could change their minds. Good arguers examine counterexamples as well as examples compatible with their claim. They look at *all* the evidence. As a critical thinker, you cannot discount information simply because it conflicts with your opinions.

Instructions

1. Review the guidelines for evaluating arguments.
2. Locate a practice or policy claim and related argument. Make a copy of this so it is readily available.
3. Review the argument and complete the Practice Exercise 28.
4. Exchange your argument analysis with another student for review.

FOLLOW-UP QUESTIONS

1. What was the most difficult part of completing your argument analysis?

   _____

   _____

   _____

   _____

   _____

2. Did you come up with effective rebuttals to your argument?

_____

_____

_____

_____

_____

3. Access austhink advanced mapping program (www.austhink.com). Do you think this would be useful in enhancing your argument analysis skills?

_____

_____

_____

_____

_____

4. Would you be willing to have your arguments regarding your decisions critiqued on a routine basis? ____ Yes ____ No. Identify a computer-based program that offers feedback about practice decisions and related arguments. Can you use this to gain corrective feedback? ____ Yes ____ No. Please describe reasons for your answer. Send an argument to the Argument Clinic for review. http://vos.ucsb.edu/browse.asp

_____

_____

_____

_____

_____

Your Name _____ Date _____

Course _____ Instructor's Name _____

Select a practice or policy claim and related argument. We recommend a short one made up of just a few sentences. Longer statements quickly become complex. It is often easiest to identify the conclusion (claim) first. Longer arguments often have more than one claim or conclusion. Attach a copy to this form.

1.   What is the claim (conclusion)? _____

   Premise 1:

   _____

   _____

   Warrant(s): _____

   _____

   _____

   Premise 2:

   _____

   _____

   Warrant(s): _____

   _____

   _____

   Premise 3:

   _____

   _____

*Warrant(s):*_____

_____

_____

2. Examine each premise and warrant using the following criteria and write your answers below, including your reasons for them.

    • Is it relevant? (Does it have a bearing on whether the conclusion is true?) If so, explain how.

    _____

    _____

    _____

    _____

    • Is it acceptable? (Would a reasonable person accept it?)

    _____

    _____

    • Does it provide sufficient grounds? If so, explain how.

    _____

    _____

    _____

    • Were there logical or informal fallacies? If so, describe. See for example Internet sources such as Stephen Downes' *Guide to Logical Fallacies* and *Twenty-Five Ways to Suppress the Truth: The Rules of Disinformation* by H. M. Sweeney or *Fallacy Files* by Caroll (Internet) as well as description of fallacies in Exercises 6 to 8.

    Fallacy (name):_____

        How it appears: _____

    _____

    _____

    Fallacy (name):_____

        How it appears:_____

    Fallacy (name):_____

How it appears:_____

_____

_____

• Can you provide an effective rebuttal to counterarguments? If yes, describe the strongest counterargument as well as your rebuttal.

_____

_____

_____

_____

_____

_____

Purpose

This exercise introduces three sources of error highlighted by Howitt (1992) that may result in faulty decisions: templating, justification, and ratcheting. Each is explained and an opportunity is provided to practice identifying them.

Background

Templating involves checking the individual against a "social template" to see whether he or she fits a particular pattern. An instigating event, such as a bruise or scratch detected on a child by a health visitor, leads to the "suspect" person being compared with the template. Howitt (1992) believes that templating differs from stereotyping because the latter involves attributing characteristics to individuals not because of a specific event, but because they belong to a broad category of people (e.g., she is a "bad driver" because she is a "woman," not because she has gotten into three accidents in the last month). Such stereotyping is often obvious and likely to be rejected.

Justification refers to using theory to "justify" decisions rather than critically examining the beliefs and evidence that have influenced the decisions. For example, some child protection errors result from views that justify contradictory courses of action. Consider the assumption that a family or family member is only "treatable" if they understand the implications of and admit responsibility for what has happened. If they say they did abuse the child, the child is removed; if they say they did not, they are assumed to be lying, and the child is removed. Thus, for the family in which abuse has not occurred, a truthful denial is no different in its outcome from false denial in families with abuse. The family is damned if it does and damned if it doesn't. The view justifies all possible explanations and increases the risk that a child will be or remain separated from his or her family. Focusing on justification rather than on critically examining your beliefs may result in errors based on "pseudodiagnosticity," where some assumption that may be true in relation to some cases is overgeneralized to many cases.

Ratcheting refers to a tendency for the child-protection processes to move in a single direction. Changing a decision or undoing its effects seems infrequent, even in circumstances where these are appropriate. Consider the difference between *taking-into-care* and *coming-out-of-care* decisions. Criteria governing the former may differ from those of the latter. A troublesome child may enter care to provide respite for his or her parents. However, when the parents feel able to cope, child-protection workers may not return the child home. Ratcheting has a "never going back" quality that may appear to protect the helper by reducing the chances of a "risky" decision resulting in problems and criticism.

Instructions

1. Read the Background information.
2. Read the Case Example that follows.
3. Complete Practice Exercise 29.
4. Discuss your answers with your instructor and other students.

Case Example

The key events began shortly after the family had moved into a new home. The family consisted of Mr. and Mrs. Fletcher and Stuart (age 3), who was from a previous relationship of Mrs. Fletcher's. Mrs. Fletcher was 27 and the husband was 30 years old. The couple were married about five weeks before the precipitating incident took place. Stuart was in bed, and it was about 10:30 P.M. According to his mother, he got up to go to the toilet. Climbing over a safety gate at the top of the stairs, he caught his foot in it and fell down the steps. Alerted by his call, the parents picked him up. They found a carpet burn on the side of his knee. However, the next morning he complained of a "headache." Concerned about the possibility of a concussion, Mrs. Fletcher examined him further but could find additionally only "two tiny little bruises on his rib cage." She telephoned her doctor, who suggested that she should visit his surgery. Coincidentally, the health visitor arrived (Mrs. Fletcher was pregnant) and drove them there. Mrs. Fletcher described what happened.

So we got there and he examined Stuart....He said to Stuart how have you done this? And Stuart said I fell down the stairs last night because I climbed over the safety gate and I was naughty, you know...and then the doctor said to him has your mummy hit you? And Stuart said no. And he said has your daddy hit you? And Stuart said no...and he said I'm very sorry to say this but I think either you or your husband has abused your son, in other words you've hit him: what have you got to say? And I said well that's just ridiculous. I mean this was my family doctor, who'd known me since I was born myself.

Her doctor asked her to take Stuart to see a hospital pediatrician, whose views were that "this is just a waste of time" since the injuries and the story were perfectly consistent and that "there is no evidence in my opinion that this child has been abused at all." Mrs. Fletcher was told to go home,

at which point there was a knock at the door and a nurse said could she have a word with the pediatrician....So he went out, he was gone for 5 minutes, and he came back in. And he said I'm very sorry Mrs. Fletcher, but your doctor has rung the social services and informed them that he thinks that the child is at risk, and a social worker was there at the hospital....In the space of two hours, this was, social services have been to a magistrate and they've taken a place of safety order, just on the say-so of my doctor.

In the meantime, the police arrived at the hospital. Mrs. Fletcher's parents also got there after being telephoned. Eventually her husband also reached the hospital. He was immediately arrested by two police officers in spite of the fact that the idea that he abused Stuart was ridiculous-Stuart had fallen down the stairs.

They said your wife doesn't want anything to do with you so you might as well tell us the truth, because she knows you've been hitting your son and she's just totally disgusted with you, in fact you're probably never going to see her again...
...this policeman sat by him and gave him a cigarette, and he said I can't say as I blame you because after all he's not yours is he. Somebody's been with your wife before you, how does that make you feel? I bet you hate that child. The husband said well he's not mine but, you know, I think of him as my son.

The father was not prosecuted. Within a few days, Mrs. Fletcher miscarried and she attributes this to the child-abuse allegations. She claims no prior or later miscarriages. Within four weeks of the intervention, a court application for an interim-care order failed because of a lack of evidence, but a two-week adjournment was granted. In the end, no substantial evidence was provided.

> **All they said was we've visited Mr. and Mrs. Fletcher in their home and we feel because the father is not the natural father, we believe that he, the son, is at risk from the stepfather, because he isn't the natural father.... They're a new family, they've only just been married, they've only just moved into this house, and we feel that the son is at risk and should remain on the at risk register. .. and that they should have this care order.**

Eventually, the boy's name was removed from the at-risk register. This Mrs. Fletcher saw as being the consequence of the threat of a judicial review of the case. All through the period of being on the at-risk register, Mr. Fletcher's children from a previous marriage had visited for overnight stays. After the removal from the at-risk register,

> **my husband's ex-wife was contacted by the social services where she lives.... She had this note saying would she please telephone this particular social worker... So she went alone and the social worker told her that her ex-husband had been accused of child abuse, and that in his opinion he didn't think that the children should be allowed to come down here and see their father unless it was in the presence of their grandmother, like my husband's mother.**

Your Name _____ Date _____

Course _____ Instructor's Name _____

Give an example of each source of error from the case example.

1.   Templating:

_____

_____

_____

_____

_____

2.   Justification:

_____

_____

_____

_____

_____

3.   Ratcheting:

_____

_____

_____

_____

_____

FOLLOW-UP QUESTIONS

1. How do your answers compare with those of other students?

    _____

    _____

    _____

    _____

    _____

2. Have you observed any of these three dysfunctional patterns of thinking? If so, please
    describe what you observed and the consequences of such thinking.

    _____

    _____

    _____

    _____

    _____

    _____

    _____

    _____

    _____

Purpose

To increase your skills in preparing and critiquing case records

Background

Professional practice requires preparing and reviewing case records. Recording should contribute to effective service (e.g., see Griffin & Classen, 2008). Records help to avoid mistakes based on faulty recollections and are useful in planning service and reviewing progress. Reviews of case records reveal many deficiencies that and have long been of concern (Tallant, 1988). These include unnecessary repetition, missing data, and poor organization. Computerized case records are replacing written ones. (See literature describing results of moving to computerized records and how to maximize accuracy and timeliness.) Case records are most likely to be useful if they have certain characteristics such as clearly describing important client characteristics and circumstances and hoped-for outcomes. Vague words include "aggressive," "anti-social," "is likely," "rarely." (See also Exercise 24.) Common problems with case records include the following:

- Emphasizing assumed pathology of clients and overlooking assets
- Vague descriptions of client concerns and related circumstances
- Vague description of hoped-for outcomes
- Incomplete assessment, for example, environmental circumstances are overlooked
- Alternative views of problems are not explored
- Client assets are overlooked
- Evidence against favored views is not included
- Important information is missing
- Inclusion of irrelevant content
- Unsupported speculation
- Use of jargon, biobabble, psychobabble (vague, ambiguous terms)
- Use of uninformative negative labels

- Conclusions made are based on small, biased samples
- Descriptive terms are used as explanations
- Description of assessment methods used is vague.
- Description of intervention methods used is vague.
- Vague or missing information about progress
- Reasons for inferences are not clearly described.
- Inferences made are not compatible with the empirical literature (e.g., the assumption that self-report accurately describes interaction patterns in real life) (Tallent, 1988).

Rules of thumb such as asking, "Is this material useful?" can help you to decide what to record. Well-designed forms will facilitate recording and review of material. Increasingly, case recording is computerized removing problems of unreadable handwriting and hopefully encouraging completeness, timeliness, and helpfulness (such as sharing records with all involved professionals).

Instructions

1. Select a detailed case study presented in the professional literature (or use a record given to you by your instructor). Review this using the guidelines in Practice Exercise 30. You could also note fallacies and their frequency such as ad hominem arguments and appeals to unfounded authority.
2. Determine your overall score: _____. (Scores range from 0 to 69.)
3. Be prepared to describe the reasons for your ratings.

Practice Exercise 30   Guidelines for Reviewing Case Records

Your Name _____ Date _____

Course _____ Instructor's Name _____

Key: 0 = (Not at all);   1 = (Somewhat);   2 = (Mostly);   3 = (Complete).

1.	Important demographic data are included.	0 1 2 3
2.	Relevant historical information is included.	0 1 2 3
3.	Client concerns are clearly described.[a]	0 1 2 3
4.	An overview of concerns is included.	0 1 2 3
5.	Hoped-for outcomes related to each concern as well as intermediate steps are clearly described.[b]	0 1 2 3
6.	Sources of assessment data are noted.	0 1 2 3
7.	Outcomes focused on are directly related to presenting concerns.	0 1 2 3
8.	Client characteristics and circumstances related to hoped-for outcomes are clearly described.[c]	0 1 2 3
9.	Baseline (preintervention) levels of relevant behaviors, thoughts or feelings are described.	0 1 2 3
10.	Uninformative labels are avoided.	0 1 2 3
11.	Self-report is complemented by observational data when relevant and feasible.	0 1 2 3

12.	Data collected are clearly summarized.	0 1 2 3
13.	Relevant client assets are clearly described.	0 1 2 3
14.	Environmental resources are clearly described.	0 1 2 3
15.	Grounds for inferences about causes of concerns are clearly described and support the conclusions.	0 1 2 3
16.	Content is up-to-date.	0 1 2 3
17.	Grounds for inferences regarding causes are well reasoned (both logically and empirically) and support inferences.	0 1 2 3
18.	There is little irrelevant material (content with no intervention guidelines).	0 1 2 3
19.	Intervention methods are clearly described.	0 1 2 3
20.	Degree of progress is clearly described, based on ongoing monitoring of specific, relevant progress indicators.	0 1 2 3
21.	A log of contacts is included.	0 1 2 3
22.	Handwriting is easy to read.	0 1 2 3
23.	The report is well organized.	0 1 2 3

[a] This includes a clear description of related behaviors, feelings, and thoughts as well as their duration, frequency, or rate (as relevant), and the situations in which they occur.

[b] A clear description includes what is to be done, when, where, by whom, and how often.

[c] These include relevant antecedents, consequences, and setting events.

1. Describe concerns regarding your agency's records.

_____

_____

_____

_____

2. How could these concerns be remedied?

_____

_____

_____

_____

_____

_____

3. Seek a description of the latest developments in critiquing practice decisions using computerized case records and describe how related information could be used in your setting

_____

_____

_____

_____

_____

_____

EXERCISE 31   CRITICALLY APRAISING SERVICE AGREEMENTS

Purpose

To enhance skills in preparing service agreements

Background

Professionals often see clients under coercive circumstances. That is, clients are not voluntary participants. They may have been reported to the Department of Children and Family Services for neglect or abuse of their children. They may be confined against their will in psychiatric centers or required to comply with medication regimes in outpatient community treatment. It is especially important in such circumstances to have clear agreements with clients both for ethical and practical reasons. Service agreements are often vague which is unfair to clients who do not know what they must do for example, to regain custody of their children. An example of a vague outcome is "increase parenting skills." Questions here are: What skills? When? How long?, and so on. This exercise provides an opportunity to critically appraise the clarity and completeness of service agreements. For example, is the overall goal clear (e.g., to regain custody of a child)? Are objectives that must be attained to achieve this goal clearly described? Are consequences of degree of participation clearly noted?

Instruction

Use one of your written service agreements or one provided by your instructor. Review this using practice exercises and prepare a written critique.

Practice Exercise 31 Critically Appraising Service Agreements

Your Name _____ Date _____

Course _____ Instructor's Name _____

Key: 0 (Not at all);   1 (Somewhat);   2 (Mostly);   3 (Complete)

1.	An overall goal is noted (e.g., decrease alcohol use).	0 1 2 3
2.	Objectives related to the goal are clearly described.	0 1 2 3
3.	Objectives are directly related to the goal.	0 1 2 3
4.	Required intermediate steps are clearly described.	0 1 2 3
5.	Criteria for meeting objectives are clearly described and directly related to objectives. That is, degree of progress will be easy to determine.	0 1 2 3
6.	Participants are noted.	0 1 2 3
7.	The consequences of meeting (or not meeting) objectives are clearly described.	0 1 2 3
8.	The form is signed by all participants.	0 1 2 3

Overall critique*

_____

_____

_____

_____

*Attach a copy of service agreement (as relevant).

Purpose

To increase your skills in evaluating claims that affect the well-being of clients

Background

Many kinds of claims are made in the helping professions. These include claims about causes, the effectiveness of interventions, the accuracy of risk measures and prognoses, and the validity of diagnostic classification systems. Consider the following claims:

- Genograms are valuable in understanding clients.
- Multisystemic Family Therapy is more effective compared to other programs for youth.
- Brief psychological debriefing is helpful in decreasing post-traumatic stress disorder.
- Brief programs for the depressed elderly are helpful.
- Decreasing plaque decreases mortality.
- Suicide in adolescents can be prevented.
- Drinking causes domestic violence.
- The DSM is a valid classification system.

Bogus claims, both in the media and in the professional literature abound. It is vital for professionals to have skill and knowledge in spotting claims, identifying what kind they are, and what kind of evidence is needed to explore their accuracy (e.g., see Littell, 2008; Montori, et al., 2004). These include

1. claims about problems (Is X a problem? Who says so? Who stands to benefit?);
2. claims about risks (e.g., Is X a risk?);
3. claims about prevalence (e.g., Stranger abduction is common.);
4. claims about the accuracy of descriptions (e.g., She is depressed.);
5. claims about causes (e.g., Alcohol use increases domestic abuse);

6. claims about assessment measures (e.g., How valid is _____?);
7. claims about the accuracy of predictions including prognoses;
8. claims about the effectiveness of interventions;
9. claims about prevention (e.g., Can we prevent _____?);
10. claims about ethical obligations (e.g., regarding informed consent).

Instructions: Complete Practice Exercise 32

Step 1	Describe a claim of interest to you that affect the lives of clients.
Step 2	Give source.
Step 3	Describe the kind of claim.
Step 4	Describe evidence offered in support of claim.
Step 5	Describe the kind of evidence needed to critically evaluate the claim.
Step 6	Describe best evidence found for the claim after a search for relevant literature.
Step 7	Describe relevance in gaps between 4 and 6 for client.

Your Name _____ Date _____

Course _____ Instructor's Name _____

1.   Claim (Describe here). Give *exact* quote.

_____

_____

_____

2.   Source: _____

_____

3.   Kind of claim: _____

4.   Evidence offered in support of claim: _____

_____

_____

_____

5.   Evidence needed to support claim: _____

_____

_____

_____

6.   Best evidence found for claim after search: _____

_____

_____

_____

7. Describe relevance of gaps between 4 and 6 for client:

_____

_____

_____

_____

_____

_____

PART 7
Improving Educational and Practice Environments

The four exercises included in Part 7 are designed to help you to apply critical thinking in your work and educational environments. Exercise 34 contains a checklist for reviewing the extent to which there is a culture of thoughtfulness. Exercise 35 suggests a measure of teaching critical thinking. Exercise 36 describes how you can set up a journal club and Exercise 37 offers guidelines for encouraging continued self-development regarding the process of evidence-informed practice. Exercise 38 offers an opportunity to increase self-awareness of personal obstacles to critical thinking. Formidable obstacles lie ahead for those who resolve to critically appraise judgments and decisions. Our students, who confront these obstacles for the first time in their work and professional practice, often report a mixture of amazement, discomfort, aloneness, and feeling out of step. The examples that follow may help you to prepare for reactions to raising questions.

A master's degree student in one of my classes at the University of California at Berkeley had her field work placement in a hospital. During a team meeting, a psychiatrist used a vague diagnostic category. The student asked "Could you please clarify how you are using this term?" He replied "I always wondered what they taught you at Berkeley and how I know that it is not much."

Students in my research class at Berkeley are asked to seek an answerable question regarding agency services from their field work supervisor and to advise them that they will seek out related research regarding effectiveness. One student who worked at an agency which offered play therapy to all clients for all problems said to the student seemingly quite annoyed, "I really am not interested in what the research says. I do play therapy because I enjoy it."

Polly Doud, who graduated from the University of Wisconsin-Eau Claire, described events during a hospital case conference involving social workers, nurses, and a physician. She identified the problem as "appeal to authority." The nurses and social workers had carefully examined the evidence about a patient's care and had arrived at a consensus. The doctor entered the room and, after a superficial examination of the patient's situation, decided on a course of action. Polly said, "If the nurses and social workers, myself included, had spoken up about the things that we had brought up before he walked in the room, I think things would have been different." Polly was concerned because accepting the doctor's conclusion, without counterargument, may have jeopardized patient care.

Sandra Willoughby, another University of Wisconsin-Eau Claire student described events during an inservice training for professionals conducted by a woman advocating "alternative therapies" including "feeling/touch" and "art therapy" as treatments for women in a refuge house for battered women. Sandra entered the conference room "planning to question her methods." The presenter never referred to data regarding effectiveness, nor to studies evaluating it; she advocated for her methods based on "her personal experience with suffering and long depression, having lived through pain so that she can identify with clients, and therefore, help them." Sandra felt uncomfortable asking for evidence about the method's effectiveness because

> **We had all gone around and introduced ourselves before the speaker began talking, and they were all therapists and professionals in the field, and I introduced myself as a "student," so I also felt, "Who am I to say anything?"**

Sandra also felt uncomfortable asking about effectiveness because "I'm looking around the room at the other professionals and I'm noticing a lot of 'nodding' and nonverbals that say, 'That's great.'"

Sandra also "sensed from her [the presenter] a lot of vulnerability, and she even almost teared up a couple of times." When the presentation was over, Sandra's colleagues did not ask a single question about effectiveness, but asked only "supportive" questions like, "How do we refer clients to you?" Sandra said,

> How can I ask the questions that I want to ask but in a safe way? Feeling very uncomfortable, I did end up asking her. She talked [in response to Sandra's question about effectiveness]—a lot about spiritual emergence as a phenomenon that people go through and how she helps them through this...She kept using "spiritual emergence" over and over without defining it....She just described why she does it [the treatment] as far as energy fields in the body.

Sandra concluded from this experience that asking whether a method works and how this is known "is not commonplace." We think that Sandra's experience may be typical across the helping professions. She was one of the first students who attended a professional conference, often attended by hundreds, who asked "Is your method effective? How do you know?"

Here is the lesson from all this: Expect to be out of step. Expect to feel uncomfortable as a critical thinker and "question raiser." Expect to encounter the view that you are odd, insensitive, even cynical if you ask questions about a method's effectiveness. But take heart in knowing that raising "hard" questions regarding the evidentiary status of practices and policies is integral to helping clients and avoiding harming them or offering ineffective services. Raising such questions is vital to the process and philosophy of evidence-based practice which is valued by many professionals and clients.

EXERCISE 33 ENCOURAGING A CULTURE OF THOUGHTFULNESS

Purpose

This exercise provides an opportunity to review the extent to which your work setting encourages critical appraisal of decisions that affect the lives of clients. This review should help you to identify changes you and your colleagues could pursue to enhance a culture of thoughtfulness in which critical appraisal of judgments and decisions is the norm and in which all involved parties including clients are involved as informed participants.

Background

The environments in which we work influence our behavior. These environments may encourage or discourage critical thinking which, in turn, will influence the quality of decisions.

Instructions

1. Complete Practice Exercise 33.
2. Give your total score. (The range is 44 to 220.) Score = _____.
3. Complete following questions.

Your Name _____ Date _____

Setting (e.g., agency) _____

Please circle the numbers to the right that best describe your views.

SD = Strongly Disagree;   **D** = Disagree;   **N** = Neither;   **A** = Agree;   **SA** = Strongly Agree

No.	Characteristics of Your Work Environment	SD	D	N	A	SA
1.	Evidence against as well as in support of favored views is sought.	1	2	3	4	5
2.	Critical appraisal of claims that affect clients' lives is the norm; related questions are welcomed.	1	2	3	4	5
3.	Getting at the "truth" is valued over "winning" an argument.	1	2	3	4	5
4.	Criteria used to select practices and policies are clearly described.	1	2	3	4	5
5.	The buddy-buddy syndrome is common (agreement based on friendship rather than cogency of argument).	1	2	3	4	5
6.	Clients are involved as informed participants (clearly appraised of the risks and benefits of recommended services as well as alternatives).	1	2	3	4	5
7.	Testimonials and case examples are often used to promote practices.	1	2	3	4	5
8.	Disagreements are viewed as learning opportunities.	1	2	3	4	5
9.	Staff prepare and share relevant CATS (Critically Appraised Topics).	1	2	3	4	5
10.	The agency has a website clearly and accurately showing the evidentiary status of practices and policies used.	1	2	3	4	5
11.	Staff are blamed for errors.	1	2	3	4	5
12.	Services and practices used have been critically tested and found to do more good than harm.	1	2	3	4	5

No.	Characteristics of Your Work Environment	SD	D	N	A	SA
13.	Staff have ready access to up-to-date relevant databases.	1	2	3	4	5
14.	Fear of retribution for disagreeing with "higher ups" is common.	1	2	3	4	5
15.	Client progress is evaluated based on clear relevant outcomes and is regularly shared with clients.	1	2	3	4	5
16.	ParticParticipants honor the same standards of evidence for claims they make as those they hold for others.	1	2	3	4	5
17.	InflatInflated claims are rarely made.	1	2	3	4	5
18.	ProceProcess measures are used to assess the effectiveness of services (e.g., number sessions attended).	1	2	3	4	5
19.	Staff are encouraged by administrators to consider the evidentiary status of practices and policies.	1	2	3	4	5
20.	Participants accept the burden of proof principle—our obligation to provide reasons for our views.	1	2	3	4	5
21.	Administrators model key behaviors involved in evidence-informed practice such as posing well-structured questions regarding agency services.	1	2	3	4	5
22.	Participants thank others who point out errors in their thinking.	1	2	3	4	5
23.	Agency reports clearly describe outcomes sought and results attained; "palaver" is minimal (see Altheide, & Johnson, 1980).	1	2	3	4	5
24.	Alternative views are sought.	1	2	3	4	5
25.	Administrators encourage staff to hide mistakes and errors.	1	2	3	4	5
26.	Reliance on questionable criteria is avoided (e.g., unfounded authority, tradition).*	1	2	3	4	5
27.	Diversionary tactics are avoided (e.g., red herring, angering an opponent).*	1	2	3	4	5
28.	Ad hominems are common.	1	2	3	4	5
29.	Inferences regarding the causes of client concerns are compatible with empirical research findings.	1	2	3	4	5
30.	Disagreements focus on important points and are made without sarcasm or put-downs or signs of contempt (e.g., rolling the eyes).	1	2	3	4	5

No.	Characteristics of Your Work Environment	SD	D	N	A	SA
31.	Staff are blamed for errors they make.	1	2	3	4	5
32.	Administrators avoid behaviors that encourage group think.	1	2	3	4	5
33.	People change their mind when there is good reason to do so.	1	2	3	4	5
34.	Well-argued alternative views are rarely considered carefully.	1	2	3	4	5
35.	Implications of proposed options are clearly described.	1	2	3	4	5
36.	Participants are encouraged to blow the whistle on practices/lapses that affect client's well being.	1	2	3	4	5
37.	It is common to hear phrases such as "I don't know."	1	2	3	4	5
38.	Unjustified excuses for poor quality services are common.	1	2	3	4	5
39.	A system is in place to identify errors and to plan how to decrease them	1	2	3	4	5
40.	Staff gain client feedback regarding the helpfulness of each meeting.**	1	2	3	4	5
41.	Errors and mistakes are viewed as learning opportunities.	1	2	3	4	5
42.	Most services used are of unknown effectiveness.	1	2	3	4	5
43.	Staff work well together in teams.	1	2	3	4	5
44.	There are a number of taboo topics.	1	2	3	4	5

*Rate per minute of specific fallacies during meetings could be noted.

**See Client Feedback Form used by David Burns.

Scoring: Add the weights for items 1, 2, 3, 4, 6, 8, 9, 10, 12, 13, 15, 16, 17, 19–24, 26, 27, 29, 30, 32–37, 39–41, 43.

        Subtotal: _____

Reverse the weights for the following items and add them: 5, 7, 11, 14, 18, 25, 28, 31, 34, 38, 42, 44.

        Subtotal: _____   Total = _____

1. Which three items are your workplace's greatest strengths?

    a. _____

    b. _____

    c. _____

2. Which three items are your workplace's greatest weaknesses?

a. _____

b. _____

c. _____

FOLLOW-UP QUESTIONS

1. Suggest a plan for increasing one characteristic of a culture of thoughtfulness and describe this below.

_____

_____

_____

_____

2. Implement the plan and describe results.

_____

_____

_____

_____

3. What is the fallacy rate in case conferences? (See also Exercise 11.) Identify key fallacies of interest, drawing on fallacies described in Exercises 6 to 8. Keep track of how often each occurs during case conferences. Divide each by the number of minutes observed to determine rate per minute.

_____

_____

_____

_____

Fallacies selected   *Rate*

1. _____   _____

2. _____   _____

3. _____   _____

EXERCISE 34   EVALUATING THE TEACHING OF CRITICAL THINKING SKILLS

Purpose

This exercise provides an opportunity to assess the extent to which an instructor models critical-thinking skills.

Background

Classrooms vary in the extent to which critical-thinking values, knowledge, and skills are taught. The Teaching Evaluation Form in this exercise describes characteristics of teaching style related to critical thinking. We thank the late Professor-Emeritus Michael Hakeem of the University of Wisconsin-Madison for his contributions to this list. The list of statements have not been subjected to any item analysis, nor have reliability or validity checks been done, so we know little of the instrument's measurement properties. For example, a question to be pursued is, Do students who rate their instructors high on teaching critical thinking learn more related values, knowledge, and skills compared with students who rate their instructors low?

Instructions

1. On Practice Exercise 34 please circle each answer that most accurately describes the extent to which you agree or disagree with the statement. Leave none blank. Do not put your name on the form.
2. Determine your score using the instructions given and note this at the end of the form.

Practice Exercise 34   Teaching Evaluation Form

Date: _____ Course: _____ Instructor's Name: _____

Please circle the numbers in the columns that best describe your views.

SD = Strongly Disagree;   **D** = Disagree;   **N** = Neutral;   **SA** = Strongly Agree;   **A** = Agree

No.	Characteristics of Instructor's Teaching Style	SD	D	N	A	SA
1.	Presents arguments for as well as against different positions on controversial issues.	1	2	3	4	5
2.	Describes key controversies concerning topics discussed.	1	2	3	4	5
3.	Encourages students to critically appraise claims.	1	2	3	4	5
4.	Thanks students who bring in research studies that argue against her/his views.	1	2	3	4	5
5.	Relies on case examples to support claims and arguments.	1	2	3	4	5
6.	Describes the evidentiary status of claims.*	1	2	3	4	5
7.	Finds out where students stand on an issue before presenting related arguments and counterarguments.	1	2	3	4	5
8.	Teaches students how to find and critically appraise evidence for themselves about topics discussed.	1	2	3	4	5
9.	Relies on personal experience to support claims.	1	2	3	4	5
10.	Encourages students to base conclusions on sound documentation such as high-quality research studies.	1	2	3	4	5
11.	Gives assignments that emphasize how rather than what to think.	1	2	3	4	5
12.	Clearly defines major terms used in the class.	1	2	3	4	5
13.	Accurately presents disliked perspectives.	1	2	3	4	5
14.	Rewards students for coming to their own well-reasoned conclusions rather than for simply agreeing with him/her.	1	2	3	4	5
15.	Teaches students how to pose clear questions.	1	2	3	4	5
16.	Helps students generalize important principles to other situations.	1	2	3	4	5

No.	Characteristics of Instructor's Teaching Style	D	D	N	A	SA
17.	"Sells" a particular point of view.	1	2	3	4	5
18.	Gives examinations that require applications of course content.	1	2	3	4	5
19.	Describes how conclusions were reached.	1	2	3	4	5
20.	Gives specific examples to illustrate and explain content.	1	2	3	4	5
21.	Would not change his or her mind no matter what evidence a student presented.	1	2	3	4	5
22.	Encourages students to think for themselves.	1	2	3	4	5
23.	Makes fun of those who disagree with her or her position.	1	2	3	4	5
24.	Presents conclusions tentatively, noting that they may be found to be false or a better theory may be found to account for them.	1	2	3	4	5
25.	Identifies assumptions related to conclusions.	1	2	3	4	5
26.	Assigns readings that generally support one particular point of view.	1	2	3	4	5
27.	Emphasizes that finding out what is true is more important than "winning" an argument.	1	2	3	4	5
28.	Teaches students that all ways of knowing are equally valid.	1	2	3	4	5
29.	Shows students the specific steps followed in drawing conclusions.	1	2	3	4	5
30.	Teaches students how to search for accurate answers for themselves (e.g., pose well-structured questions).	1	2	3	4	5
31.	Encourages students to locate research that contradicts her or his preferred views.	1	2	3	4	5
32.	Assigns readings that argue for and against views.	1	2	3	4	5

*This refers to whether a claim has been critically tested, with what rigor and with what outcome.

Scoring: Add the weights for items 1, 2, 3, 4, 6, 7, 8, 10, 11, 12, 13   **Score** *(Range: 31–155)*
14, 15, 16, 18, 19, 20, 22, 24, 26, 28–31.   Subtotal: _____

Reverse the weights for the following items and add them: 5, 9, 17, 21, 23, 25, and 27.
   Subtotal: _____   Total = _____

1.   Which item(s) seem most important as characteristics for an instructor who encourages critical thinking?

_____

_____

_____

_____

_____

Purpose

To describe how to set up a journal club to encourage continued learning over your career and to work with others to locate practice and policy-related research vital to decisions that affect clients' lives

Background

The purpose of a journal club may be (1) to acquire the best evidence to inform decisions about a client (need driven), (2) to learn about new evidence related to your practice (evidence-driven), or (3) to learn evidence-informed practice skills (skill driven) (Straus, Richardson, Glasziou, & Haynes, 2005) (p. 227). Activities may include the following (e.g., see Straus, et al., 2005):

1. Identify learning needs, for example, start with a client where there is uncertainty about what to do. Pose a well-structured question.
2. Share related reports (the best available literature) located between meetings—distribute photocopies of abstracts, original articles, abstracts of Cochrane or Campbell reviews. Decide which item(s) everyone will read before the next session.
3. Critically appraise evidence located using appropriate criteria (see e.g., Greenhalgh, 2006 as well as Exercises 19 to 25) at the next session and apply information to the decision that must be made—apply this information to the client.

Suggestions these authors offer for setting up a journal club include the following:

1. Identify other interested parties who are interested in one or more of the aims described above
2. Agree on goals of the club, for example, to acquire EBP skills
3. Identify group learning techniques that will contribute to success and describe norms for creating a facilitating task environment

4. Arrange tools needed "to learn, practice, and teach in evidence-based ways, including quick access to evidence resources" (Straus, et al., 2005, p. 229)
5. Share examples of critically appraisal topics (CATs) (see Exercise 15)
6. Acquire skills in facilitating group discussions and teaching the process of EBP

   Recommendations for making your presentation include the following: (www.med.umich.edu/pediatrics/ebm/jcguide.htm)

   a. The clinical question, How it was formed, Explain the thought process (5 minutes),
   b. HOW you found what you found (2 minutes);
   c. WHAT you found (3 minutes);
   d. the VALIDITY & APPLICABILITY of what you found (7 minutes);
   e. how what you found will ALTER your work with the client (8 minutes);
   f. self-assessment of how you did with the process (1 minutes).

7. Complete Practice Exercise 35

Practice Exercise 35   Forming A Journal Club

Your Name _____ Date _____

Course _____ Instructor's Name _____

INSTRUCTIONS

First, review the instructions for setting up a journal club. Your instructor may model a journal club session "in action" using the fish bowl technique in which you watch a session. Select four other classmates or four other staff employed by your agency and set up a journal club drawing on the background information in this exercise.

1.   Location of journal club: _____

2.   Participants' names: _____

   _____

   _____

   _____

   _____

3.   Goal of journal club: _____

   _____

   _____

   _____

4.   Learning techniques that will be used. _____

   a. _____

   b. _____

   c. _____

   d. _____

5. Describe tools needed and indicate whether you have access to them.

    a. _____   _____ Yes _____ No

    b. _____   _____ Yes _____ No

    c. _____   _____ Yes _____ No

6. Describe progress in achieving goal.

    Were you successful? _____ Yes _____ No

    If yes, please describe your reasons.

    _____

    _____

    _____

    _____

    If no, please describe obstacles.

    _____

    _____

    _____

    _____

7. Attach related documentation such as your CAT and best research report.

EXERCISE 36   ENCOURAGING CONTINUED SELF-DEVELOPMENT REGARDING THE PROCESS OF EVIDENCE-INFORMED PRACTICE

Purpose

Encourage continue learning over your career

Background

One advantage of being a professional is continued learning over your career. Self-development questions pertain to life-long learning (Straus, et al., 2005). (See Box 36.1.) Examples include:

Am I posing any well-structured questions regarding vital decisions my clients and I must make? Am I searching for research related to any vital questions? Can I accurately appraise the quality of an effectiveness study? Am I getting more efficient in searching for research related to my information needs? (See list in Exercise 36.) Am I decreasing instances of the "illusion of knowledge" (accurately recognizing areas of ignorance)? Am I getting better in avoiding jargon, oversimplifications, and palaver? Are my empathy scores from clients improving? Am I giving fewer unjustified excuses for poor quality service? Am I increasing my effectiveness in encouraging fellow staff to consider the evidentiary status of services?

Instructions

Complete Practice Exercise 36.

Box 36.1   Self-Evaluation Questions Regarding the Process of Evidence-Based Practice

A.   Asking Well-Structured Questions

   1.   Am I asking any practice questions at all?
   2.   Am I asking well-formed (3–4 part) questions?
   3.   Am I using a "map" to locate my knowledge gaps and articulate questions?
   4.   Can I get myself "unstuck" when asking questions?
   5.   Do I have a working method to save my questions for later answering?
   6.   Is my success rate of posing well-structured questions rising?
   7.   Am I modeling asking well-structured questions for others?

B.   Finding the Best External Evidence

   1.   Am I searching at all?
   2.   Do I know the best sources of current evidence for decisions I make?
   3.   Do I have ready access to searching resources needed to locate the best evidence for questions that arise?
   4.   Am I finding useful external evidence from a widening array of sources?
   5.   Am I becoming more efficient in my searching?
   6.   How do my searches compare with those of research librarians or colleagues who have a passion for providing best current care?

C.   Critically Appraising Evidence for its Validity and Usefulness

   1.   Am I critically appraising external evidence at all?
   2.   Are critical appraisal guides becoming easier for me to apply?
   3.   Am I becoming more accurate and efficient in applying critical appraisal measures such as pretest probabilities, number needed to treat (NNTs)?
   4.   Am I creating any CATS (critically appraised topics)?

D.   Integrating Critical Appraisal With Clinical Expertise and Applying the Results

   1.   Am I integrating my critical appraisals in my practice at all? Could I do better?
   2.   Am I becoming more accurate and efficient in clearly and accurately sharing vital information (such as NNT) with my clients?
   3.   Am I involving clients as informed participants in shared decision making based on clear description of benefits and cots of both recommended and alternative options?
   4.   Can I explain (and resolve) disagreements about management decisions in terms of this integration?

(continued)

Box 36.1 Continued

E. Relationship Skills

1. Am I seeking feedback after each meeting from clients regarding their perceptions of my empathy and helpfulness of sessions? (See feedback scale developed by David Burns.)
2. Are my empathy ratings from clients improving?

F. Self-Evaluation and Helping Others Learn Evidence-Based Practice

1. Am I helping others learn how to ask well-structured questions?
2. Am I raising more questions regarding claims made that affect services clients receive and receiving more positive responses?
3. Am I teaching and modeling searching skills?
4. Am I teaching and modeling critical appraisal skills?
5. Am I teaching and modeling the integration of best evidence with my clinical expertise and my clients' preferences?
6. Am I helping others enhance their skills in offering empathic and disarming responses.
7. Am I using fewer unjustifiable excuses? (See McDowell, 2000; Pope & Vasquez, 2007).
8. Do I admit more often that "I was wrong"?

Source: Parts A, B, C, D, & F adapted from *Evidence-Based Medicine: How to Practice and Teach EBM* (pp. 220–228), by Sackett, D. L., Straus, S. E., Richardson, W. S., Rosenberg, W., & Haynes, R. B. 1997, New York: Churchill Livingstone. Reprinted with permission. See also Straus et al. (2005).

Practice Exercise 36 Encouraging Continued Self-Development Regarding the Process of Evidence-Informed Practice

Your Name _____ Date _____

Course _____ Instructor's Name _____

1. Select a self-development goal from Box 36.1 and describe this here.

   _____

   _____

   _____

2. Describe your baseline. (How often you now engage in this step.)

   _____

3. Describe a plan for achieving your goal here. (See for example Watson and Tharp, 2007.) If you select the goal of enhancing client empathy ratings, use the client feedback form designed by David Burns (2008) so you can gain feedback from clients after every meeting.

   _____

   _____

   _____

   _____

   _____

   _____

4. Describe how you will evaluate your success.

   _____

   _____

   _____

5. Carry out your plan and describe exactly what you did here.

_____

_____

_____

_____

_____

6. Describe results of carrying out your plan. Where results what you hoped for? If Yes, describe why you think you were successful. If No, describe why you think you were unsuccessful. What obstacles got in your way?

_____

_____

_____

_____

_____

7. Critique your plan based on relevant self-management literature (e.g., see Watson & Tharp, 2007).

_____

_____

_____

_____

_____

8. Describe what you learned from this process.

_____

_____

_____

_____

_____

EXERCISE 37 INCREASING SELF-AWARENESS OF PERSONAL OBSTACLES TO CRITICAL THINKING

Background

There are many obstacles to thinking critically about decisions that affect the lives of clients and patients. Some are personal such as arrogance which encourages the illusion of knowledge. Others are environmental.. This exercise provides an opportunity to examine personal obstacles and to take steps to overcome them. There are different kinds of personal obstacles. Some are motivational such as not caring about clients. Some are related to a lack of self-management skills such as poor time management (see Watson & Tharp, 2007). Some are due to a lack of knowledge concerning your particular learning style and how it may contribute to or detract from acquiring knowledge and skills that can help you to help your clients. Personal obstacles include misleading views of knowledge and how it can be gained (Best, 2006; Hoffer & Pintrich, 2002). Some are related to a lack of interpersonal skills for raising questions in diplomatic ways (see Exercise 17). Some are due to unrealistic expectations, for example, that you can help everyone (when this is not possible). Self-deception involves misleading ourselves to accept as true which is not true. You may for example accept unjustifiable excuses for lack of success (see McDowell, 2000; Pope & Vasquez, 2007; Tavris & Aronson, 2007). You may have to increase your skills in suspending judgement (Pettit, 1993) and avoiding cognitive biases (Ariely, 2008) and arrange more effective supports for causal reasoning (Jonassen & Ionas, 2006). You may have to increase your willingness to recognize errors and to learn from them (Bosk, 1979). "Self-deception is a way to justify false beliefs to ourselves" (*Skeptics Dictionary*).

Instructions

Step 1   Review the list of barriers described in Box 37.1 and check those that apply to you.

Step 2   Complete Practice Exercise 37.1.

Step 3   Complete Practice Exercise 37.2.

BOX 37.1 Personal Barriers to Critical Thinking

1. *Motivational Blocks*
    ___ Valuing winning over discovering approximations to the truth
    ___ Vested interest in an outcome
    ___ Cynicism
    ___ Unrealistic expectations
    ___ Lack of curiosity
    ___ Arrogance
    ___ Lack of zeal

2. *Emotional Blocks*
    ___ Fatigue
    ___ Anger
    ___ Anxiety (e.g., regarding social disapproval)
    ___ Low tolerance for ambiguity/uncertainty
    ___ Inability to "incubate"
    ___ Appeal of vivid material

3. *Perceptual Blocks*
    ___ Defining problem too narrowly (e.g., overlooking environmental causes)
    ___ Overlooking alternative views
    ___ Stereotyping
    ___ Judging rather than generating ideas
    ___ Seeing what you expect to see.

4. *Intellectual Blocks*
    ___ Relying on questionable criteria to evaluate claims
    ___ Failing to critically evaluate beliefs
    ___ Using inflexible problem-solving strategies
    ___ Failing to get accurate information concerning decisions
    ___ Using a limited variety of problem-solving languages (e.g., words, illustrations, models)
    ___ Disdain for intellectual rigor

5. *Cultural Blocks*
    ___ Valuing John Wayne thinking (strong pro/con positions with little reflection)
    ___ Fear that the competition of ideas would harm the social bonding functions of false beliefs

6. *Expressive Blocks*
    ___ Inadequate skill in writing and speaking clearly
    ___ Social anxiety

7. *Excuses Used* (See Practice Exercise 37.2)

Source: Adapted from Adams, J. L. (1986). *Conceptual blockbusting: A guide to better ideas (3rd ed.).* Reading, MA: Addison-Wesley (see also Gambrill, 2005, 2006).

Your Name _____ Date _____

Course _____ Instructor's Name _____

1.   Describe a personal obstacle you would like to work on. (See Box 37.1.)

    _____

    _____

2.   What kind of an obstacles is this? _____

    _____

3.   Describe how this affects your work with clients.

    _____

    _____

    _____

    _____

4.   Describe a plan for decreasing this barrier, drawing on empirical literature.

    _____

    _____

    _____

5.   Carry our your plan. (Describe what you did.)

    _____

    _____

    _____

6. Describe your results.

_____

_____

_____

_____

7. Discuss reasons for less success than you expected.

_____

_____

_____

_____

_____

Practice Exercise 37.2   Excuses Used For Poor Quality Service: Justifiable Or Not?

Your Name _____ Date _____

Course _____ Instructor's Name _____

Consider excuses you have heard others use as well as excuses you have used. Which ones do you think are justified? Here are some examples (e.g., see McDowell, 2000; Pope & Vasquez, 2007).

1. My supervisor (administrator) told me to do it.
2. Other people do it.
3. That's the way it's been done in the past.
4. I didn't have time; I was busy.
5. We care about our clients.
6. This is the standard of practice.
7. I was under a lot of stress.
8. My client was difficult.
9. I did not know about the ethical guidelines.
10. Something is better than nothing.
11. No one will find out.
12. My consultant said it is ok.
13. I didn't mean it.
14. No one complained about it.
15. I didn't have the resources needed.
16. Everything is relative.
17. If it sounds good, it is good.
18. If most people believe it, it's true.
19. Other schools do it.
20. We can't measure outcomes.
21. My professional organization says it is ok.
22. No law was broken.

1. Note here the numbers above referring to excuses you think are justified.

2. Select one that you think is unjustified and describe a related real-life situation. Describe your reasons and discuss with other students.

_____

_____

_____

_____

3. Select an excuse you have used that you think is justified and describe this here.

_____

_____

Please describe the exact situation in which you used this and why you think it is justified.

_____

_____

_____

_____

_____

Glossary

Absolute risk	Difference in risk between the control group and the treated group. (See Practice Exercise 22.1.)
Absolute risk reduction	The absolute arithmetic difference in rates of bad outcomes between experimental and control participants in a trial, calculated as the experimental event rate (EER) and the control event rate (CER), and accompanied by a 95% CI (Bandolier Glossary, accessed 10/20/07).
Critical discussion	"Essentially a comparison of the merits and demerits of two or more theories... The merits discussed are mainly the *explanatory power* of the theories... the way in which they are able to solve our problems and explain things, the way in which the theories cohere with certain other heavily valued theories, their power to shed new light on old problems and to suggest new problems. The chief demerit is inconsistency, including inconsistency with the results of experiments that a competing theory can explain" (Popper, 1994, pp. 160–161).
Cynicism	A negative view of the world and what can be learned about it.
Eclecticism	The view that people should adopt whatever theories or methodologies are useful in inquiry, no matter their source, and without undue worry about their consistency
Empiricism	"The position that all knowledge (usually, but not always, excluding that which is logico-mathematical) is in some way 'based upon' experience. Adherents of empiricism differ markedly over what the 'based upon' amounts to—'starts from' and 'warranted in terms of' are, roughly, at the two ends of the spectrum of opinion" (Phillips, 1987, p. 203). Uncritical empiricism takes for granted that our knowledge is justified by empirical facts (Notturno, 2000, p. xxi).
False negative rate	Percentage of persons incorrectly identified as not having a characteristic.
False positive rate	Percentage of individuals inaccurately identified as having a characteristic.

Hermeneutics	"The discipline of interpretation of textual or literary material, or of meaningful human actions" (Phillips, 1987, p. 203).
Knowledge	Problematic and tentative guesses about what may be true (Popper, 1992, 1994).
Likelihood ratio	Measure of a test result's ability to modify pretest probabilities. Likelihood ratios indicate how many times more likely a test result is in a client with a disorder compared with a person free of the disorder. A likelihood ration of 1 indicates that a test is totally uninformative. "A likelihood ratio of greater than 1 indicates that the test is associated with the presence of the disease whereas a likelihood ratio less than 1 indicates that the test result is associated with the absence of disease. The further likelihood ratios are from 1 the stronger the evidence for the presence or absence of disease. Likelihood ratios above 10 and below 0.1 are considered to provide strong evidence to rule in or rule out diagnosis respectively in most circumstances" (Deeks & Altman, 2004, p. 168).
Likelihood ratio of a positive test result (LR +)	The ratio of the true positive rate to the false positive rate: sensitivity/(1−specificity).
Likelihood of a negative test result (LR −)	The ratio of the false negative to the true negative rate: (1−sensitivity)/specificity (adapted from Pewsner, et al., 2004).
Logical positivism	The main tenet is the verifiability principle of meaning: "Something is meaningful only if it is verifiable empirically (i.e., directly, or indirectly, via sense experiences) or if it is a truth of logic or mathematics" (Phillips, 1987, p.204). The reality of purely theoretical entities is denied.
Nonjustificationist epistemology	The view that knowledge is not certain. It is assumed that although some knowledge claims may be warranted, there is no warrant so firm that it is not open to question (see Karl Popper's writings).
Negative predictive value (NPV)	The proportion of individuals with negative test results who do not have the target condition. This equals 1 minus the posttest probability, given a negative test result.
Number Needed to treat (NNT)	The number of clients who need to be treated to achieve one additional favorable outcome, calculated as 1/ARR and accompanied by 95% CI (confidence interval).
Paradigm	A theoretical framework that influences "the problems that are regarded as crucial, the ways these problems are conceptualized, the appropriate methods of inquiry, the relevant standards of judgment, etc." (Phillips, 1987, p. 205).
Phenomenology	"The study, in depth, of how things appear in human experience" (Phillips, 1987, p. 205).
Positive predictive value (PPV)	The proportion of individuals with positive test results who have the target condition. This equals the posttest probability, given a positive test result.

Post positivism	The approach to science that replaced logical positivism decades ago (see for example Phillips, 1987, 1992).
Post-test odds	The odds that a patient has the disorder after being tested (pretest odds X LR [likelihood ratio]).
Posttest probability	The probability that an individual with a specific test result has the target conditions (posttest odds/[1 + posttest odds]).
Pretest odds	The odds that an individual has the disorder before the test is carried out (pretest probability/[1−pretest probability]).
Pretest probability (prevalence)	The probability that an individual has the disorder before the test is carried out.
Pseudoscience	Material that makes science like claims but provides no evidence for these claims.
Predictive accuracy	The probability of a condition given a positive test result.
Prevalence rate (base rate, prior probability)	The frequency of a problem among a group of people. The best estimate of the probability of a problem before carrying out a test.
Quackery	Commercialization of unproven, often worthless and sometimes dangerous products and procedures either by professionals or others (Jarvis, 1990; Young, 1992).
Relative risk	The ratio of risk in the treated group (EER) to risk in the control group (CER). RR = ERR/CER
Relative risk reduction (RRR)	The relative risk reduction is the difference between the EER and CER (EER−CER) divided by the CER, and usually expressed as a percentage. Relative risk reduction can lead to overestimation of treatment effect. (Bandolier Glossary, accessed 10/20/07.)
Relativism	The belief that a proposition can be true for individuals in one framework of belief but false for individuals in a different framework. Relativists "insist that judgments of truth are always relative to a particular framework or point of view" (Phillips, 1987, p. 206).
Retrospective accuracy	The probability of a positive test given that a person has a condition.
Science	A process designed to develop knowledge through critical discussion and testing of theories.
Scientific objectivity	This "consists solely in the critical approach" (Popper, 1994, p. 93). It is based on mutual rational criticism in which high standards of clarity and rational criticism are valued (Popper, 1994; p. 70). (See also *Critical discussion*, mentioned earlier.)
Scientism	This term is used "to indicate slavish adherence to the methods of science even in a context where they are inappropriate" and "to indicate a false or mistaken claim to be scientific" (Phillips, 1987, p. 206).
Sensitivity	Among those known to have a problem, the proportion whom a test or measure said had the problem.

Skepticism	The belief that all claims should be carefully examined for invalid arguments and errors of fact.
Specificity	Among those known not to have a problem, the proportion whom the test or measure has said did not have the problem.
Theory	Myths, expectations, guesses, conjectures about what may be true. A theory always remains hypothetical or conjectural. "It always remains guesswork. And there is no theory that is not beset with problems" (Popper, 1994, p. 157).
Theory-ladenness (of perception)	"The thesis that the process of perception is theory-laden in that the observer's background knowledge (including theories, factual information, hypotheses, and so forth) acts as a 'lens' helping to 'shape' the nature of what is observed" (Phillips, 1987, p. 206).
True negative rate	Percentage of individuals accurately identified as not having a characteristic.
True positive rate	Percentage of individuals accurately identified as having a characteristic.
Truth	An assertion is true if it corresponds to, or agrees with, the facts" (Popper, 1994, p. 174). People can never be sure that their guesses are true. "Though we can never justify the claim to have reached truth, we can often give some very good reasons, or justifications, why one theory should be judged as nearer to it than another" (Popper, 1994, p. 161).

References

AIKEN, L. R. & GROTH-MARNAT, G. (2006). *Psychological testing and assessment* (12th Ed.). Boston, MA: Allyn & Bacon.

AKOBENG, A. K. (2005). Evidence in + practice. *Archives of Disease in Childhood*, 90(8), 849–852.

ALTHEIDE, D. L. & JOHNSON, J. M. (1980). *Bureaucratic propaganda.* Boston, MA: Allyn & Bacon.

ALTMAN, D. G. (2002). Poor-quality medical research: What can journals do? *Journal of the American Medical Association*, 287, 2765–2767.

AMBADY, N. & ROSENTHAL, R. (1993). Half a minute: Predicting teacher evaluations from thin slices of nonverbal behavior and physical attractiveness. *Journal of Personality and Social Psychology*, 64, 431–441.

AMERICAN PSYCHIATRIC ASSOCIATION. (2000). *Diagnostic and statistical manual of mental disorders* (4th Ed.). Washington, DC: American Psychiatric Association.

ANGELL, M. (2005). *The truth about the drug companies: How they deceive us and what to do about it.* New York: Random House.

ANTONUCCIO, D. O., BURNS, D. D., & DANTON, W. G. (2002). Antidepressants: A triumph of marketing over science. *Prevention & Treatment*, 5(article 25) posted 7/15/02, pages 1–17.

APFEL, R. J. & FISHER, S. M. (1984). *Do no harm: DES and the dilemmas of modern medicine.* New Haven, CT: Yale University Press.

ARIELY, D. (2008). *Predictably irrational: The hidden forces that shape our decisions.* New York: Harper.

ARKES, H. R. (1981). Impediments to accurate clinical judgment and possible way to minimize their impact. *Journal of Consulting and Clinical Psychology*, 49(3), 323–330.

ASCH, S. E. (1956). Studies of independence and conformity: Minority of one against a unanimous majority. *Psychological Monographs*, 70(9) (Whole No. 416).

ASIMOV, I. (1989). The relativity of wrong. *Skeptical Inquirer*, 14, 35–44.

ASPDEN, P., WOLCOTT, J. A., BOOTMAN, J. L., & CRONENWETT, L. R. (Eds.) (2007). *Preventing medication errors.* Washington, DC: The National Academics Press.

BAER, D. M. (2003). *Program evaluation: Arduous, impossible, or political?* In H. E. Briggs & T. L. Rzepnicki (Eds.), *Using evidence in social work practice: Behavioral perspectives* (pp. 310–322). Chicago: Lyceum.

BALONEY DETECTION KIT. Carol Sagan. Available on Internet.

BARON, J. (1985). *Rationality and intelligence.* New York: Cambridge University Press.

BARON, J. (1994). *Thinking and deciding.* New York: Cambridge University Press.

BARON, J. (2000). *Thinking and deciding* (3rd Ed.). Cambridge, England: Cambridge University Press.

BARON, R. F. (2005). So right it's wrong: Groupthink and the ubiquitous nature of polarized group decision making. In M. T. Zanna (Ed.), *Advances in experimental social psychology, Vol. 37* (pp. 219–253). San Diego: Elsevier.

BAUER, H. H. (2001). *Fatal attractions: The troubles with science.* New York: Paraview Press.

BAUER, H. H. (2004). *Science or pseudoscience: Magnetic healing, psychic phenomena, and the other heterodoxies.* University of Illinois Press. Champaign, IL.

BAUER, H. H. (2007). *The origin, persistence and failings of HIV/AIDS theory.* Jefferson, NC: McFarland & Co.

BAUSELL, R. B. (2007). *Snake oil science: The truth about complementary and alternative medicine.* New York: Oxford.

BELL, T. & LINN, M. C. (2002). Beliefs about science: How does science instruction contribute? In B. K. Hoffer & P. R. Intrich (Eds.), *Personal Epistemology: The psychology of beliefs about knowledge and learning* (pp. 321–346). Mahwah NJ: Erlbaum.

BENNETT, B. S. & O'ROURKE, S. P. (2006). A prolegomenon to the future study of rhetoric and propaganda: Critical foundations. In G. S. Jowett & V. O'Donnell (Eds.), *Readings in propaganda and persuasion: New and Classic Essays* (pp. 51–71). Thousand Oaks, CA: Sage.

BERENDES, H. W. & LEE, Y. H. (1993). The 1953 clinical trial of diethylstilbestrol during pregnancy: Could it have stopped DES use? *Controlled Clinical Trials, 14,* 179–182.

BERG. A. O. (2000). Dimensions of evidence. In J. P. Geyman, R. A. Deyo, & S. D. Ramsey (Eds.), *Evidence-based clinical practice: Concepts and approaches* (pp. 21–28). Boston, MA: Butterworths-Heineman.

BERGER, R. & PLLIAVIN, I. (1976). The effect of casework: A research note. *Social Work, 21,* 205–208.

BEST, J. (2004). *More dammed lies and statistics: How numbers confuse public issues*. Berkeley, CA: University of California Press.

BEST, J. (2006). *Flavor of the month: Why smart people fall for fads*. Berkeley, CA: University of California Press.

BLENKNER, M., BLOOM, M., & NIELSEN, M. (1971). A research and demonstration project of protective services. *Social Casework*, 52 (8), 483–499.

BLOOM, M. J., FISCHER, J., & ORME, J. G. (2005). *Evaluating practice: Guidelines for the accountable professional* (5th Ed.). Boston, MA: Allyn & Bacon.

BOSK, C. L. (1979). *Forgive and remember: Managing medical failure*. Chicago: University of Chicago Press.

BOSSUYT, P. M., REITSMA, J. B., BRUNS, D. E., GATSONIS, C. A., GLASZIOU, P. P., IRWIG, L. M., et al. (2003). The STARD statement for reporting studies of diagnostic accuracy: Explanation and elaboration. *Clinical Chemistry*, 49, 7–18.

BOYLE, M. (2002). *Schizophrenia: A scientific delusion?* (2nd Ed.). London: Routledge

BRADDOCK, C. H., EDWARDS, K. A., HASENBERG, N. M., LAIDLEY, T. L., & LEVINSON, W. (1999). Informed decision making in outpatient practice. Time to get back to basics. *Journal of the American Medical Association*, 282(24), 2313–2320.

BREGGIN, P. R. (1991). *Toxic psychiatry*. New York: St. Martin's Press.

BROCK, T. C. & GREEN, M. C. (Eds.) (2005). *Persuasion: Psychological insights and perceptions* (2nd Ed.). Thousand Oaks, CA: Sage.

BRODY, H. (2007). *Hooked: Ethics, the medical profession, and the pharmaceutical industry*. New York: Rowman & Littlefield.

BROMLEY, H., DOCKERY, G., FENTON, C., NHLEMA, B., SMITH, H., & TOLHURST, R., et al. (2002). *Criteria for evaluating qualitative studies*. Retrieved June 12, 2007, from www.liv.ac.uk/lstm/learning_teaching/masters/masters_docs/criteira_eval_qual.studies.pdf.

BROOKFIELD, S. D. (1987). *Developing critical thinkers*. San Francisco, CA: Jossey-Bass.

BROWNE, M. N. & KEELEY, S. M. (2006). *Asking the right questions: A guide to critical thinking* (5th Ed.). Upper Saddle River, NJ: Pearson.

BUNGE, M. (1984). What is pseudoscience? *The Skeptical Inquirer*, 9(1), 36–47.

BUNGE, M. (2003). The pseudoscience concept, dispensable in professional practice, is required to evaluate research projects: A reply to Richard J. McNally. *Scientific Review of Mental Health Practice*, 2, 111–114.

BURNHAM, J. C. (1987). *How superstition won and science lost: Popularizing science and health in the United States.* New Brunswick, NJ: Rutgers University Press.

BURNS, D. (2008). Workshop on feeling good now: New rapid recovery techniques for depression & low-self esteem. Concord, CA.

BYERLY, H. C. (1973). *A primer of logic.* New York: Harper & Row.

CAMPBELL, D. T. & STANLEY, J. C. (1963). *Experimental and quasi-experimental design for research.* Chicago, IL: Rand McNally.

CAROLL, R. T. (2003). *The skeptic's dictionary: A collection of strange beliefs, amusing deceptions and dangerous delusions.* Hobokan, NJ: Wiley.

CECI, S. J. & BRUCK, M. (1993). Suggestibility of the child witness: A historical review and synthesis. *Psychological Bulletin*, 113(3), 403–439.

CHAFFEE, J. (2006). *Thinking critically.* Boston, MA: Houghton Miftlin.

CHALMERS, I. (1993). The Cochrane Collaboration: Preparing, maintaining, and disseminating systematic reviews of the effects of health care [review]. *Annual New York Academy of Science*, 703, 156–163.

CHALMERS, I. (2003). Trying to do more good than harm in policy and practice: The role of rigorous, transparent, up-to-date evaluations *Annals of the American Academy of Political and Social Science*, 589, 22–40.

CHALMERS, I. (2004). Well-informed uncertainties about the effects of treatments. *British Medical Journal*, 328, 475–476.

CHAPMAN, G. B. (2005). The psychology of medical decision making. In D. J. Koehler & N. Harvey (Eds.), *The Blackwell handbook of judgment and decision making* (pp. 585–603). Malden, MA: Blackwell Pub.

CHAPMAN, G. B. & ELSTEIN, A. S. (2000). Cognitive processes and biases in medical decision making. In G. B. Chapman & S. A. Sonnenberg (Eds.), *Decision making in health care: Theory, psychology, and applications* (pp. 183–210). New York: Cambridge University Press.

CHENG, K. K., CHALMERS, I., & SHELDON, T. A. (2007). Adding fluoride to water supplies. *British Medical Journal*, 335, 699–702.

CIALDINI, R. B. (2001). *Influence: The new psychology of modern persuasion* (4th Ed.). New York: Quill.

CILISKA, D., THOMAS, H., & BUFFETT, C. (2008). An introduction to evidence-informed public health and a compendium of critical appraisal tools for public health practice. National Collaborating Centre for Methods and Tools.

COOKE, N. J., GORMAN, J. C., & WINNER, J. L. (2007). Team cognition. In F. T. Durso (Ed.), *Handbook of applied cognition* (pp. 239–268). Hoboken, NJ: John Wiley & Sons.

COMBS, J. E. & NIMMO, D. (1993). *The new propaganda: The dictatorship of Palaver in contemporary politics*. New York: Longman.

COULTER, A. (2002). *The autonomous patient: Ending paternalism in medical care*. London: Nuffield Trust.

COULTER, A. & ELLINS, J. (2007). Effectiveness of strategies for informing, educating, and involving patients. *British Medical Journal*, 335, 24–27.

CRONE, D. A. & HORNER, R. H. (2003). *Building positive behavior support systems in schools: Functional behavioral assessment*. New York: Guilford.

CRUMB, F. W. (1973). Boos and bouquets for Fischer [letter to the editor]. *Social Work*, 18(2), 124–126.

DAMER, T. E. (1995). *Attacking faulty reasoning: A practical guide to fallacy free argument* (3rd Ed.). Belmont, CA: Wadsworth.

DAWES, R. M. (1988). *Rational choice in an uncertain world*. San Diego, CA: Harcourt Brace Jovanovich.

DAWES, R. M. (1994). *House of cards: Psychology and psychotherapy built on myth*. New York: Free Press.

DAWES, R. M. (2001). *Everyday irrationality: How pseudo-scientists, lunatics and the rest of us systematically fail to think rationally*. Boulder, CO: Westview Press.

DEAN, G. (1987). Does astrology need to be true? Part 2: The answer is no. *The Skeptical Inquirer*, 11(3), 257–273.

DEAN, G. (Retrieved February 13, 2008). Meta-analysis of nearly 300 empirical studies: Putting astrology and astrologers to the test. From Astrology and Science website, www.astrology-and-science.com, article located at: http://www.rudolfhsmit.nl/d-meta2.htm.

DEATH OF GENERAL GEORGE WASHINGTON (1799). *The Monthly Magazine and American Review*, 1(6), 475–477.

Deeks, J. J. & Altman, D. J. (2004). Diagnostic tests for: Likelihood ratios. *British Medical Journal*, 329, 168–169.

DES JARLAIS, D. C., LYLES, C., CREPAZ, N., & THE TREND GROUP. (2004). Improving the reporting quality of nonrandomized evaluations of behavioral and public health interventions: The TREND statement. *American Journal of Public Health*, 94, 361–366.

DEYO, R. A. & PATRICK, D. L. (2006). *Hope or hype: The obsession with medical advances and the high cost of false promise.* New York: Amacom.

DINGWALL, R., EEKELAAR, J., & MURRAY, T. (1983). *The protection of children: State intervention and family life.* Oxford, England: Basil Blackwell.

DOWNES, S. Guide to Logical Fallacies. Internet.

DUNNING, D., HEATH, C., & SULS, J. M. (2004). Flawed self-assessment: Implications for health, education, and the work place. *Psychological Science in the Public Interest, 5,* 69–106.

DUTTON, D. B. (1988). *Worse than the disease: Pitfalls of medical progress.* New York: Cambridge University Press.

EDDY, D. M. (1982). Probabalistic reasoning in clinical medicine: Problems and opportunities. D. Kahneman, P. Slovic, & A. Tversky (Eds.), *Judgment under uncertainty: Heuristics and biases* (pp. 249–267). Cambridge, England: Cambridge University Press.

EINHORN, H. J. & HOGARTH, R. M. (1986). Judging probable cause. *Psychological Bulletin, 99*(1), 3–19.

EISENBERG, T. & WELLS, M. T. (2008). Statins and adverse cardio-vascular events in moderate risk females: A statistical and legal analysis with implications for FDA preemption claims. *Journal of Empirical Legal Studies, 5,* 507–550.

ELLUL, J. (1965). *Propaganda: The formation of men's attitudes.* New York: Vintage.

ELMORE, J. G. & BOYKO, E. J. (2000). Assessing accuracy of diagnostic and screening tests. J. P. Geyman, R. A. Deyo, & S. D. Ramsey (Eds.), *Evidence-based clinical practice: Concepts and approaches* (p. 85). Boston, MA: Butterworth Heinemann.

ELSTEIN, A. S., SCHULMAN, L. W., SPRAFKA, S. A., ALLAL, L., GORDON, M., JASON, H., et al. (1978). *Medical problem solving: An analysis of clinical reasoning.* Cambridge, MA: Harvard University Press.

ENGEL, S. M. (1994). *With good reason: An introduction to informal fallacies* (5th Ed.). New York: St. Martin's Press.

ENNIS, R. H. (1987). A taxonomy of critical thinking dispositions and abilities. In B. Baron & R. J. Sternberg (Eds.), *Teaching thinking skills: Theory and practice* (pp. 9–26). New York: W. H. Freeman.

ENTWISTLE, V. A., SHELDON, T. A., SOWDEN, A. J., & WATT, I. A. (1998). Evidence-informed patient choice. *International Journal of Technology Assessment in Health Care, 14,* 212–215.

EVANS, I., THORNTON, H., & CHALMERS, I. (2006). *Testing treatments: Better research for better healthcare.* London: The British Library.

FallacyFiles. www.fallacyfiles.org

FAUST, D. (2007). Decisions research can increase the accuracy of clinical judgment and thereby improve patient care. In S. O. Lilienfeld & W. T. O'Donohue (Eds.), *The great ideas of clinical science: 17 principles that every mental health professional should understand* (pp. 49–76). New York: Routledge.

FISCHER, J. (1973). Is casework effective: A review. *Social Work* 18(1), 5–20.

FISCHER, J. & HUDSON, J. W. (1976). An effect of casework? Back to the drawing board. *Social Work*, 21, 347–349.

FISCHHOFF, B. (1975). Hindsight does not equal foresight: The effect of outcome knowledge on judgment under uncertainty. *Journal of Experimental Psychology*, 1(3), 288–299.

FISCHHOFF, B. & BEYTH, R. (1975). "I knew it would happen." Remembered probabilities of once-future things. *Organizational Behavior and Human Performance*, 13, 1–16.

FRAZER, J. G. (1925). *The golden bough: A study in magic and religion.* London: Macmillan.

FREEMAN, B. (1993). *Thinking logically* (2nd Ed.). Englewood Cliffs, NJ: Prentice-Hall.

FROSCH, D. L., KRUEGER, P. M., HORNIK, R. C., CRONHOLM, P. F., & BARG, F. K. (2007). Creating demand for prescription drugs: A content analysis of television direct-to-consumer advertising. *Annals of Family Medicine*, 5, 6–13.

GAMBRILL, E. (2005). *Critical thinking in clinical practice: Improving the quality of judgments and decisions about clients* (2nd Ed.). New York: Wiley.

GAMBRILL, E. (2006). *Social work practice: A critical thinker's guide* (2nd Ed.). New York: Oxford University Press.

GAMBRILL, E. & GIBBS, L. (2002). Making practice decisions: Is what's good for the goose good for the gander? *Ethical Human Sciences & Services*, 4(1), 31–46.

GARB, H. N. (1998). *Studying the clinician: Judgment research and psychological assessment.* Washington, DC: American Psychological Association.

GELLES, R. J. (1982). Applying research on family violence to clinical practice. *Journal of Marriage and the Family*, Feb. 44, 9–20.

GELLES, R. J. & CAVANAUGH, M. (2005). Association is not causation. In. D. R. Loeske, R. J. Gelles, & M. M. Cavanaugh (Eds.) (2005).

Current controversies on family violence (2nd Ed.) (pp. 175–189). Thousand Oaks, CA: Sage.

GELLNER, E. (1992). *Postmodernism, reason, and religion.* New York: Routledge.

GEYMAN, J. P., DEYO, R. A., & RAMSEY, S. D. (2000). *Evidence-based clinical practice: Concepts and approaches.* Boston, MA: Butterworths/Heinemann.

GIBBS, L. E. (1989). The Quality of Study Rating Form: An instrument for synthesizing evaluation studies. *Journal of Social Work Education,* 25(1), 55–67.

GIBBS, L. E. (1991). *Scientific reasoning for social workers.* New York: Macmillan (Allyn & Bacon).

GIBBS, L. (2003). *Evidence-based practice for the helping professions.* Pacific Grove, CA: Thomson Learning, Brooks/Cole.

GIBBS, L. & GAMBRILL, E. (2002). Evidence–based practice: Counterarguments to objections. *Research on Social Work Practice,* 12, 452–476.

GIBBS, L., GAMBRILL, E., BLAKEMORE, J., BEGUN, A., KENISTON, A., PEDEN, B., et al. (1995). A measure of critical thinking for practice. *Research on Social Work Practice,* 5, 193–204.

GIGERENZER, G. (2002). *Calculated risks: How to know when numbers deceive you.* New York: Simon & Schuster.

GIGERENZER, G. (2007). Gut feelings. *The intelligence of the unconscious.* New York: Viking.

GIGERENZER, G. (2008). Why heuristics work. *Perspectives on Psychological Science,* 3(1), 20–29.

GOWLAND, A. (2006). The problem of early modern melancholy. *Past & Present,* 191, 77–120.

GRAY, J. A. M. (2001a). *Evidence-based health care: How to make health policy and management decisions* (2nd Ed.). New York: Churchill-Livingstone.

GRAY, J. A. M. (2001b). Evidence-based medicine for professionals. In A. Edwards & G. Elwyn (Eds.), *Evidence-based patient choice: Inevitable or impossible?* (pp. 19–33). New York: Oxford University Press.

GRAY, W. D. (1991). *Thinking critically about New Age ideas.* Belmont, CA: Wadsworth.

GRAY-LITTLE. B. & KAPLAN. D. (2000). Race and ethnicity in psychotherapy research. In C. R. Snyder & R. E. Ingram (Eds.), *Handbook of psychological change* (pp. 591–613). New York: John Wiley & Sons.

GREENHALGH, T. (2006). *How to read a paper: The basics of evidence-based medicine* (3rd Ed.). Malden, MA: Blackwell.

GREENHALGH, T., ROBERT, G., MACFARLANE, F., BATE, P., & KYRIAKIDOU, O. (2004). Diffusion of innovations in service organizations: Systematic review and recommendations. *The Milbank Quarterly*, 82, 581–629.

GRIFFIN, F. A. & CLASSEN, D. C. (2008). Detection of adverse events in surgical patients using the Trigger Tool approach. *Quality and Safety in Health Care*, 17, 253–258.

GROSS, P. R. & LEVITT, N. (1994). *Higher superstition: The academic left and its quarrels with science*. Baltimore, MD: Johns Hopkins University Press.

GROVE, W. M. & MEEHL, P. E. (1996). Comparative efficiency of informal (subjective, impressionistic) and formal (mechanical, algorithmic) prediction procedures: The clinical-statistical controversy. *Psychology, Public Policy & Law*, 2, 293–323.

GUYATT, G., RENNIE, D., Meade, M. O., & Cook, D. J. (2008). *User's guide to the medical literature: A manual for evidence-based clinical practice* (2nd Ed.). JAMA & Archives. American Medical Association.

HADLER, N. M. (2008). *Worried sick: A prescription for health in an overtreated America*. Chapel Hill, NC: University of North Carolina Press.

HAINES, A. & DONALD, A. (2002). *Getting research findings into practice* (2nd Ed.). London: BMJ Pub Group.

HALEY, J. (1980). *Leaving home*. New York: McGraw-Hill.

HALL, C. C., ARISS, L., & TODOROV, A. (2007). The illusion of knowledge: When more information reduces accuracy and increases confidence. *Organizational Behavior and Human Decision Processes*, 103, 277–290.

HALPERN, D. F. (2003). *Thought & knowledge: An introduction to critical thinking* (4th Ed.). Mahwah, NJ: Laurence Erlbaum.

HANKS, H., HOBBS, C., & WYNNE, J. (1988). Early signs and recognition of sexual abuse in the pre-school child. In K. Browne, C. Davies, & P. Stratton (Eds.), *Early prediction and prevention of child abuse*. Chichester, England: John Wiley.

HARVEY, I. M. & NOWLAN, W. A. (1989). Reflex anal dilatation: A clinical epidemiological evaluation. *Paediatric Perinatal Epidemiology*, 3, 294–301.

HASTIE, R. & DAWES, R. (2001). *Rational choice in an uncertain world: The psychology of judgment and decision making*. Thousand Oaks, CA: Sage.

HAYNES, S. N. (1992). *Models of causality in psychopathology:Toward dynamic, synthetic and nonlinear models of behavior disorders.* New York: Macmillan.

HAYNES, R. B., DEVEREAUX, P. J., & GUYATT, G. H. (2002). Editorial. Clinical expertise in the era of evidence-based medicine and patient choice [Editorial]. *ACP Journal Club*, 136: A11, pp. 1–7.

HEALTH LETTER (1992). Only 750 restrictions on doctors' hospital privileges reported in the first year of data bank operation. *Health Letter*, 8(3), Published by Public Citizen Research Group, Washington, DC.

HELLMAN, H. (2001). *Great feuds in medicine: Ten of the liveliest disputes ever.* New York: John Wiley & Sons.

HENEGAN, C. & BADENOCH, D. (2006). *Evidence-based medicine toolkit* (2nd Ed.). Malden, MA: Blackwell.

HERBERT, V. (1983). Special report on quackery: Nine ways to spot a quack! *Health*, 15(10), 39–41.

HOBBS, C. J. & WYNNE, J. M. (1986, October 4). Buggery in childhood: A common syndrome of child abuse. *The Lancet*, Oct. 4:2 (8510) 792–796.

HOCHMAN, M., HOCHMAN, S., BOR, D., & McCORMICK, D. (2008). News media coverage of medication research: Reporting pharmaceutical company funding and use of generic medication names. *Journal of the American Medical Association*, 300, 1544–1550.

HOFFER, B. K. & PINTRICH, P. R. (2002). *Personal epistemology. The Psychology of beliefs about knowledge and knowing.* Mahwah, NJ: Erlbaum.

HOFFRAGE, U. & POHL, R. (2003). (Eds.). Memories. Special Issue. *Psychology Press.*

HOGARTH, R. M. (2001). *Educating intuition.* Chicago: University of Chicago Press.

HOLDEN, G., SPEEDLING, E., & ROSENBERG, G. (1992). Evaluation of an intervention designed to improve patients' hospital experience. *Psychological Reports*, 71, 547–550.

HORWITZ, V. A. & WAKEFIELD, J. C. (2007). *The loss of sadness: How psychiatry transformed normal sorrow into depressive disorder.* New York: Oxford.

HOUTS, A. (1998). Fifteen arguments against actuarial risk appraisal. In V. L. Quinsey, G. T. Harris, M. E. Rice, & C. A. Cormier. *Violent offenders. Appraising and managing risk.* Washington, DC: American Psychological Association.

HOUTS, A. C. (2002). Discovery, invention, and the expansion of the modern diagnostic and statistical manuals of mental disorders.

In L. E. Beutler & M. L. Malik (Eds.), *Rethinking the DSM: A psychological perspective* (pp. 17–65). Washington, DC: American Psychological Association.

HOWITT, D. (1992). *Child abuse errors: When good intentions go wrong.* New York: Harvester/Wheatsheaf.

HUCK, S. W. & SANDLER, H. M. (1979). *Rival hypotheses: Alternative interpretations of data based conclusions.* New York: Harper & Row.

ISSACS, D. & FITZGERALD, D. (1999). Seven alternatives to evidence based medicine. *British Medical Journal*, 319, 1618.

JACOBSON, J. W., FOXX, R. M., & MULICK, J. A. (Eds.). (2005). *Controversial therapies for developmental disabilities: Fad, fashion, and science in professional practice.* Mahwah, NJ: Erlbaum.

JANIS, I. L. (1971; November). Groupthink. *Psychology Today*, 5, 43–46, 74–76.

JANIS, I. L. (1982). *Groupthink: Psychological studies of policy decisions and fiascoes* (2nd Ed.). Boston, MA: Houghton Mifflin.

JANIS, I. L. & MANN, L. (1977). *Decision making: A psychological analysis of conflict, choice and commitment.* New York: Free Press.

JARVIS, W. (1987). Chiropractic skeptical view. *The Skeptical Inquirer*, 12(1), 47–55.

JARVIS, W. T. (1990). *Dubious dentistry.* Loma Linda, CA: Loma Linda University School of Medicine, Department of Public Health and Preventive Medicine.

JENICEK, M. (2006). *A physician's self-paced guide to critical thinking.* American Medical Association Press.

JENICEK, M. & HITCHCOCK, D. L. (2005). *Evidence based practice: Logic and critical thinking in medicine.* American Medical Association Press.

JOHNSON, H. M. (2006). Alas for Tiny Tim, he became a Christmas cliché. *New York Times*, Op.Ed., 12, 25.

JONASSEN, D. H. & IONAS, I. G. (2006). Designing effective supports for causal reasoning. *Educational Technology Research and Development.* Boston, MA: Springer.

JOSEPH, J. (2004). *The gene illusion: Genetic research in psychiatry and psychology under the microscope.* New York: Algora Pub.

JOWETT, G. S. & O'DONNELL, V. (2006). *Propaganda and persuasion* (4th Ed.). Newbury Park, CA: Sage.

KAHANE, H. & CAVENDER, N. (1998). *Logic and contemporary rhetoric: The use of reason in everyday life* (8th Ed.). Belmont, CA: Wadsworth.

KAHNEMAN, D. (2003). A perspective on judgment and choice: Mapping bounded rationality. *American Psychologist*, 58(9), 697–720.

KAHNEMAN, D., SLOVIC, P., & TVERSKY, A. (1982). *Judgment under uncertainty: Heuristics and biases.* Cambridge, England: Cambridge University' Press.

KASSIRER, J, P. & KOPELMAN, R. I. (1991). *Learning clinical reasoning.* Baltimore, MD: Williams & Wilkins.

KATZ, J. (2002). *The silent world of doctor and patient.* Baltimore, MD: John Hopkins University Press.

KAUFMAN, J. C. & STERNBERG, R. J. (2006). *The International handbook of creativity.* New York: Cambridge University Press.

KIRCH, I., DEACON, B. J., HUEDO-MEDINA, T. B., SCOBORIA, A., MOORE, T. J., & JOHNSON, B. T. (2008). Initial severity and antidepressant benefits: A meta-analysis of data submitted to the Food and Drug Administration. *PLoS Medicine,* 5, e45.

KIRK, S. & KUTCHINS, H. (1992). *The selling of DSM: The rhetoric of science in psychiatry.* New York: Aldine de Gruyter.

KLEIN, G. (1998). *Sources of Power: How people make decisions.* Cambridge, MA: MIT Press.

KOEHLER, D. J. & HARVEY, N. (Eds.). (2005). *The Blackwell handbook of judgment and decision making.* Malden, MA: Blackwell Publishing.

KOHN, L. T., CORRIGAN, J. M., & DONALDSON, M. S. (Eds.). (2000). *To err is human: Building a safer health system.* Washington, DC: National Academy Press.

KOZLOWSKI, S. W. J. & ILGEN, D. R. (2006). Enhancing the effectiveness of work groups and teams. *Psychological Science in the Public Interest* 7(3), 77–124.

KUHN, D. (1991). *The skills of argument.* Cambridge: Cambridge University Press.

KUHN, D. (1992). Thinking as argument. *Harvard Educational Review,* 62, 155–178.

KUHN, D. & Perasall, S. (2000). Developmental origins of scientific thinking. *Journal of Cognition and Development,* 1, 113–129.

KUHN, T. S. (1970). *The structure of scientific revolutions* (2nd Ed.). Chicago: University of Chicago Press.

KUTCHINS, H. & KIRK, S. A. (1997). *Making us crazy: DSM: The psychiatric bible and the creation of mental disorders.* New York: Free Press.

LAMBERT, M. J. (Ed.). (2004). *Bergin & Garfield's handbook of psychotherapy and behavior change.* New York: John Wiley & Sons.

LAMBERT, M. J. & BERGIN, A. E. (1994). The effectiveness of psychotherapy. In A. E. Bergin & S. L. Garfield (Eds.), *Handbook of psychotherapy and behavior change* (pp. 143–189). New York: John Wiley.

LANE, H. (1991). *The mask of benevolence: Disabling the deaf community.* New York: Random House.

LANG, S. (1998). *Challenges.* New York: Springer-Verlag.

LEAPE, L. L. & BERWICK, D. M. (2005). Five years after "To Err Is Human," What have we learned? *Journal of the American Medical Association, 293,* 2384–2390.

LEWANDOWSKY, S., LITTLE, D. R., & KALISH, M. (2007). Knowledge and expertise. In F. T. Durso, R. Nickerson, S. Dumais, S. Lewandowsky, & T. Perfect (Eds.), *Handbook of applied cognition* (2nd Ed.). Chichester: Wiley.

LEWONTIN, R. C. (1991). *Biology as ideology: The doctrine of DNA.* New York: Harper Collins.

LEWONTIN, R. C. (1994). *Inside and outside: Gene, environment, and organism.* Worcester, MA: Clark University Press.

LILIENFELD, S. O. (2002). When worlds collide: Social science, politics, and the Rind et al. (1998) child sexual abuse meta-analysis. *American Psychologist, 57,* 176–188.

LILIENFELD, S. O., LYNN, S. J., & LOHR, J. M. (2003). *Science and pseudoscience in clinical psychology.* New York: Guilford.

LIPMAN, M. (1991). *Thinking in education.* Cambridge, England: Cambridge University Press. Local lady took Natex year ago-had good health ever since. (1935, May 27). Morning Call Allentown, PA, p. 7.

LITTELL, J. H. (2005). Lessons from a systematic review of effects of multisystemic therapy. *Children and Youth Services Review, 4,* 445–463.

LITTELL, J. H. (2006). The case for multisystemic therapy: Evidence or orthodoxy? *Children and Youth Services Review, 28,* 458–472.

LITTELL, J. H. (2008). Evidence-based or biased? The quality of published reviews of evidence-based practices. *Children and Youth Services Review, 30,* 1299–1317.

LITTELL, J. H., CORCORAN, J., & PILLAI, V. (2008). *Systematic Reviews and Meta-Analysis.* New York: Oxford.

LITTELL, J. H., POPA, M., & FORSYTHE, B. (2005). Multisystemic therapy for social, emotional, and behavioral problems in youth aged 10–17. *Cochrane Database of Systematic Reviews,* Issue 3.

MAC COUN, R. (1998). Biases in the interpretation and use of research results. *Annual Review of Psychology, 49,* 259–387.

MAC LEAN, E. (1981). *Between the lines: How to detect bias and propaganda in the news and everyday life.* Montreal: Black Rose Books.

MALLE, B. F. (2006). The actor-observer asymmetry in attribution: A (surprising) meta-analysis. *Psychological Bulletin,* 132(6), 895–919.

MARSHALL, B. J., WARREN, J. R. (1984). Unidentified curved bacilli in the stomach of patients with gastritis and peptic ulceration. *Lancet,* No. 1, 8390:1311-5.

MATSUOKA, J. (2007). *Social Work,* Editorial. Vol. 52 (p. 198).

MC CORD, J. (2003). Cures that harm: Unanticipated outcomes of crime prevention programs. *The Annals of the American Academy of Political and Social Science,* 587, 16–30.

MC DOWELL, B. (2000). *Ethics and excuses: The crisis in professional responsibility.* Westport, CT: Praeger.

MEDAWAR, P. B. (1967). *The art of the soluble.* London: Methuen.

MEEHL, P. E. (1973). Why I do not attend case conferences. In P. E. Meehl (Ed.), *Psychodiagnosis: Selected papers* (pp. 225–323), Minneapolis, MN: University of Minnesota Press.

MICHAEL, M., BOYCE, W. T., & WILCOX, A. J. (1984). *Biomedical bestiary: An epidemiologic guide to flaws and fallacies in the medical literature.* Boston, MA: Little, Brown.

MILLER, A., ROBSON, D., & BUSHELL, R. (1986). Parental participation in paired reading: A controlled study. *Educational Psychology,* 6(3), 77–284.

MILLER, D. (1994). *Critical rationalism: A restatement and defense.* Chicago: Open Court.

MILLER, D. J. & HERSEN, M. (Eds.) (1992). *Research fraud in the behavioral and biomedical sciences.* New York: Wiley.

MIROWSKY, J. & ROSS, C. E. (2003). *Social causes of psychological distress* (2nd Ed.). New York: Aldine de Gruyter.

MISER, W. F. (1999). Critical appraisal of the literature. *Journal of the American Board of Family Practice,* 12, 315–333.

MISER, W. F. (2000a). Applying a meta-analysis to daily clinical practice. In J. P. Geyman, R. A. Deyo, & S. D. Ramsey (Eds.), *Evidence-based clinical practice: Concepts and approaches* (pp. 57–64). Boston, MA: Butterworth & Heinemann.

MISER, W. F. (2000b). Applying a meta-analysis to daily clinical practice. In J. P. Geyman, R. A Deyo, & S. D. Ramsey (Eds.), *Evidence-based clinical practice: Concepts and approaches* (pp. 57–64). Boston, MA: Butterworth & Heinemann.

MOHER, D., COOK, D. J., EASTWOOD, S., OLKIN, I., RENNIE, D., & STROUP, D. F. for the QUORUM group (1999). Improving the quality of reports of meta-analyses of randomized controlled trials: The QUOROM statement. *Lancet*, 354, 1896–1900.

MOHER, D., SCHULZ, K. F. & ALTMAN, D. G. (2001). The CONSORT statement: Revised recommendations for improving the quality of reports of parallel group randomized trials. *Lancet*, 357, 1191–1194.

MONCRIEFF, J. (2008). *The myth of the chemical cure: A critique of psychiatry drug treatment*, PALGRAVE MACMILLAN.

MONCRIEFF, J. & COHEN, D. (2006). Do antidepressants cure or create abnormal brain states? *PLoS Medicine*, 3(7), e240.

MONCRIEFF, J. & KIRSCH, I. (2005). Efficacy of antidepressants in adults. *British Medical Journal*, 321, 155–157.

MONTE, C. F. (1975). *Psychology's scientific endeavor*. New York: Praeger.

MONTORI, V. M., JAESCHKE, R., SCHUNEMANN, H. J., BHANDARI, M., BROZEK, J. L., DEVEREAUX, P. J., & GUYATT, G. H. (2004). Users' guide to detecting misleading claims in clinical research reports. *British Medical Journal*, 329, 1093–1096.

MOORE, B. N. & PARKER, R. (1986). *Critical thinking: Evaluating claims and arguments in everyday life.* Palo Alto, CA: Mayfield.

MOORE, A. & MC QUAY, H. (2006). *Bandolier's Little Book of Making sense of the medical evidence.* New York: Oxford University Press.

MOYNIHAN, R. & CASSELS, A. (2005). *Selling sickness: How the world's biggest pharmaceutical companies are turning us into patients.* New York: Nation.

MYERS, D. G. (2002). *Social psychology.* New York: McGraw-Hill.

NAFTULIN, D. H., WARE, J. E., & DONNELLY, F. A. (1973). The Doctor Fox lecture: A paradigm of educational seduction. *Journal of Medical Education*, 48, 630–635.

NAPHY, W. G. & ROBERTS, P. (Eds.) (1997). *Fear in early modern society.* Manchester, UK: Manchester University Press.

NATIONAL ASSOCIATION OF SOCIAL WORKERS. (1999). *Code of ethics.* Silver Spring, MD: NASW.

NATIONAL SCIENCE FOUNDATION (2006). *Science and engineering Indicators (2006).* www.nsf.gov/statstics/seind06 (downloaded 10/10/08).

NEMETH, C. J. & GONCALO, J. A. (2005). Inference and persuasion in small groups. In T. C. Brock & M. C. Green (Eds.), *Persuasion: Psychological insights and perspectives* (2nd Ed.) (pp. 171–194). Thousand Oaks, CA: Sage.

NICKERSON, R. S. (1986). *Reflections on reasoning.* Hillsdale, NJ: Erlbaum.

NICKERSON, R. S. (1998). Confirmation bias: A ubiquitous phenomena in many guises. *Review of General Psychology, 2,* 175–220.

NISBETT, R. & ROSS, L. (1980). *Human inference: Strategies and shortcomings in social judgment.* Englewood Cliffs, NJ: Prentice-Hall.

NORCROSS, J. C., BEUTLER, L. E., & LEVANT, R. F. (Eds.). (2006). *Evidence-based practices in mental health: Debate and dialogue on the fundamental questions.* Washington, DC: American psychological Association.

NOTTURNO, M. A. (2000). *Science and the open society: The future of Karl Popper's philosophy.* New York: Central European University Press.

O'CONNOR, A. M., STACEY, D., ENTWISTLE, V., LLEWELLYN-THOMAS, H., ROVNER, D., HOLMES-ROVNER, M., et al. (2003). Decision aids for people facing health treatment or screening decisions. In *Cochrane Database of Systematic Reviews,* Issue 1.

O'CONNOR, A. M., WENNBERG, J. E., LEGARE, F., LLEWELLYN-THOMAS, H. A., MOULTON, B. W., SEPUCHA, K. R., et al. (2007). Toward the "tipping point": Decision aids and informed patient choice. *Health Affairs,* 26(3), 716–725.

OFSHE, R. & WATTERS, E. (1994). *Making monsters: False memories, psychotherapy, and sexual hysteria.* New York: Charles Scribners.

OLIVER, J. E. (2006). *Fat politics: The real story behind America's obesity epidemic.* New York: Oxford.

ORTIZ DE MONTELLANO, B. (1991). Multicultural pseudoscience: Spreading scientific illiteracy among minorities-Part 1. *Skeptical Inquirer,* 16, 46–50.

PALING, J. (2006). *Helping patients understand risks: 7 simple strategies for successful communication.* Gainesville, FL: the Risk Communication Institute.

PATAI, D., & KOERTGE, N. (2003). *Professing feminism: Education and indoctrination in women's studies (New Ed.).* Lanham, MD: Lexington Books.

PAUL, R. (1993). *Critical thinking: What every person needs to survive in a rapidly changing world (Rev. 3rd Ed.).* Santa Rosa, CA: Foundation for Critical Thinking.

PAUL, R. W. & ELDER, L. (2004). *Critical thinking: Tools for taking charge of your professional life.* Upper Saddle River, NJ: Prentice Hall.

PERKINS, D. (1992). *Smart schools: From training memories to educating minds.* New York: Free Press.

PERKINSON, H. (1993). *Teachers without goals, students without purpose.* New York: McGraw-Hill.

PETROSINO, A., TURPIN-PETROSINO, C., & BUEHLER, J. (2003). Scared straight and other juvenile awareness programs for preventing juvenile delinquency: A systematic review of the randomized experimental evidence. *The Annals of the American Academy of Political and Social Science*, 589, 41–62.

PETTIT, P. (1993). Suspended judgment: Instituting a research ethic. *Controlled Clinical Trials*, 14, 261–265.

PEWSNER, D., PATTAGLIA, M., MINDER, C., MARKS, A., BUCHER, H. C., & EGGER, M. (2004). Ruling a diagnosis in or out with "SpPIn" and "SnNOut": A note of caution. *British Medical Journal*, 329, 209–313.

PHILLIPS, D. C. (1987). *Philosophy, science, and social inquiry: Contemporary methodological controversies in social science and related applied fields of research.* New York: Pergamon Press.

PHILLIPS, D. C. (1992). *A social scientists bestiary: A guide to fabled, threats to, and defenses of, naturalistic social science.* New York: Pergamon Press.

PHILLIPS, D. C. (2005). *The social scientist's bestiary: A guide to fabled threats to, and defenses of, naturalistic social studies* (2nd Ed.). New York: Pergamon.

PINTO, R. C. & BLAIR, J. A. (1993). *Reasoning: A practical guide.* Englewood Cliffs, NJ: Prentice-Hall.

PITTLER, M. H., BROWN, E. M., & EDWARDS, E. (2007). Static magnets for reducing pain: Systematic review and meta-analysis of randomized trials. *Canadian Medical Association Journal*, 177(7), 736.

POPE, K. K. & VASQUEZ, M. J. T. (2007). *Ethics in psychotherapy and counseling* (2nd Ed.). San Francisco, CA: Jossey-Bass.

POPPER, K. R. (1959). *The logic of scientific discovery.* London: Hutchinson.

POPPER, K. R. (1970). Normal science and its dangers. In I. Lakatos & A. Musgrave (Eds.), *Criticism and the growth of knowledge.* Cambridge: Cambridge University Press.

POPPER, K. R. (1972). *Conjectures and refutations: The growth of scientific knowledge* (4th Ed.). London: Routledge and Kegan Paul.

POPPER, K. R. (1979). *Objective knowledge: An evolutionary approach* (Rev ed.). New York: Oxford.

POPPER, K. R. (1992). *In search of a better world: Lectures and essays from thirty years.* New York: Routledge.

POPPER, K. R. (1994). *The myth of the framework: In defense of science and rationality.* M. A. Notturno (Ed.), New York: Routledge.

PORTER, R. (2000). *Quacks: Fakers & charlatans in English medicine*. Charleston, SC: Tempus.

PRATKANIS, A. R. & ARONSON, E. (2001). *Age of propaganda: The everyday use and abuse of persuasion* (Rev Ed.). New York: Owl Books.

PRYOR, K. (2002). *Don't shoot the dog: The new art of teaching and training (Rev. Ed.)*. Surrey: Ringpress.

QUINSEY, V. L., HARRIS, G. T., RICE, M. E., & CORMIER, C. A. (1998). *Violent offenders: appraising and managing risks*. Washington, DC: American Psychological Association.

RACHLINSKI, J. J. (2005). Heuristics, biases, and governance. In D. J. Koehler & N. Harvey (Eds.), *The Blackwell handbook of judgment and decision making* (pp. 567–584). Oxford, England: Blackwell Pub.

RAMPTON, S. & STAUBER, J. (2002). *Trust us. We're experts: How industry manipulates science and gambles with your future*. Torcher/Penguin.

RANK, H. (1982). *The pitch*. Park Forest, IL: Counter-Propaganda Press.

REID, W. J. (2002). Knowledge for direct social work practice: An analysis of trends. *Social Service Review*, 76, 6–33.

REID, J. B., PATTERSON, G. R., & SNYDER, J. (Eds.) (2002). *Antisocial behavior in children and adolescents: A developmental analysis and model for intervention*. Washington, DC: American Psychological Association.

RISING, K., BACCHETTI, P., & PERO, L. (2008). Reporting bias in drug trials submitted to the Food and Drug Administration: Review of publication and presentation. *PLoS Medicine*, November 2008, 11, e217.

ROSA, L, ROSA, E., SARNER, L., & BARRETT, S. (1998). A close look at therapeutic touch. *JAMA*, 279, 1005–1010.

ROSE, S., BISSON, J., & WESSELY, S. (2004). Psychological debriefing for preventing post traumatic stress disorder (PTSD). In *Cochrane Library*, Issue 3. Chichester: Wiley.

ROSEN, A. & PROCTOR, E. K. (2002). Standards for evidence-based social work practice. In A. R. Roberts & G. J. Greene (Eds.), *The social workers' desk reference* (pp. 743–747). New York: Oxford.

RUBIN, A. & PARRISH, D. (2007). Problematic phrases in the conclusions of published outcome studies: Implications for evidence-based practice. *Research on Social Work Practice*, 17(3), 334–347.

RUNCO, M. A. (2006). *Creativity: Theories and themes: Research, development, and practice*. New York: Elsevier.

SA, W. C., KELLEY, C. N., HO, C., & STANOVICH, K. E. (2005). Thinking about personal theories: Individual differences in the coordination of theory and evidence. *Personality and Individual Differences, 38,* 1149–1161.

SACKETT, D. L., RICHARDSON, W. S., ROSENBERG, W., & HAYNES, R. B. (1997). *Evidence-based medicine: How to practice and teach EBM.* New York: Churchill Livingstone.

SACKETT, D. L., STRAUS, S. E., RICHARDSON, W. S., ROSENBERG, W., & HAYNES, R. B. (2000). *Evidence-based medicine: How to practice and teach EBM* (2nd Ed.). New York: Churchill Livingstone.

SAGAN, C. (1987). The burden of skepticism. *Skeptical Inquirer, 12,* 38–74.

SAGAN, C. (1990). Why we need to understand science. *Skeptical Inquirer, 14,* 263–269.

SARNOFF, S. K. (2001). *Sanctified snake oil: The effects of junk science and public policy.* Westport, CT: Praeger.

SCHATTNER, A., BRONSTEIN, A., & JELLIN, N. (2006). Information and shared decision-making are top patients' priorities. *BMC Health Services Research.* 6:21.

SCHILPP, P. A. (Ed.) (1974). *The philosophy of Karl Popper, Vol. 2.* LaSalle, IL: Open Court.

SCHNEIDER, D. J. (2004). *The psychology of stereotyping.* New York: Guilford.

SCHWARTZ, I. M. (1989). *(In)justice for juveniles: Rethinking the best interests of the child.* Lexington, MA: Heath.

SCULL, A. (2005). *Madhouse: A tragic tale of megalomania and modern medicine.* New Haven, CT: Yale University Press.

SEECH, Z. (1993). *Open minds and everyday reasoning.* Belmont, CA: Wadsworth.

SHARPE, V. A. & FADEN, A. I. (1998). *Medical harm: Historical, conceptual, and ethical dimensions of iatrogenic illness.* New York: Cambridge University Press.

SHEA, B., MOHER, D., GRAHAM, I., PHAM, B., & TUGWELL, P. (2002). *Evaluation & the Health Professions,* 25(1), 116–129.

SHERMER, M. (1997). *Why people believe weird things: Pseudoscience, superstition, and other confusions of our time.* New York: W.H. Freeman.

SHIN, J. H., HAYNES, R. B. & JOHNSON, M. E. (1993). Effect of problem based, self-directed Undergraduate education on life-long learning. *Canadian Medical Association Medical Journal, 148,* 969–976.

SHLONSKY, A. & SAINI, M. (2007) EBP within an Interdisciplinary/ Multidisciplinary Team Context: An analysis of peer-reviewed publications. Presented at the Society for Social Work Research. San Francisco, CA.

SILVERMAN, W. A. (1980). *Retrolental fibroplasia: A modern parable.* New York: Grune & Stratton.

SILVERMAN, W. A. (1993). Doing more good than harm. In K. S. Warren & F. Mosteller (Eds.), *Doing more good than harm: The evaluation of health care interventions* (pp. 5–11). New York: New York Academy of Sciences.

SILVERMAN, W. A. (1998). *Where's the evidence?: Debates in modern medicine.* New York: Oxford.

Skepdic.com

SKOLBEKKEN, J. A. (1998). Communicating the risk reduction achieved by cholesterol reducing drugs. *British Medical Journal*, 316, 1956–1958.

SKRABANEK, P. & MC CORMICK, J. (1998). *Follies and fallacies in medicine* (3rd Ed.). Chippenham, England: Tarragon Press.

SLOVIC, P., FINUCANE, M., PETERS, E., & MAC GREGOR, D. G. (2002). The affect heuristic. In T. Gilovich & D. Griffin (Eds.), *Heuristics and biases: The psychology of intuitive judgment* (pp. 397–420). New York: Cambridge University Press.

SNYDER, M. & WHITE, P. (1981). Testing hypotheses about other people: Strategies of verification and falsification. *Personality and Social Psychology Bulletin*, 7(1), 39–43.

SPROULE, J. M. (1994). *Channels of propaganda.* ERIK Clearinghouse.

STACEY, D., SAMANT, R., & BENNETT, C. (2008). Decision making in oncology: A review of patient decision aids to support patient participation. *CA: A Cancer Journal for Clinicians*, 58, 293–304.

STANGE, K. C. (2007). Time to ban direct-to-consumer prescription drug marketing. *Annals of Family Medicine*, 5, 101–104.

STRAUS, S. E., RICHARDSON, W. S., GLASZIOU, P., & HAYNES, R. B. (2005). *Evidence-based medicine: How to practice and teach EBM.* Edinburgh: Elsevier, Churchill Livingstone.

STROHMAN, R. C. (2003). Genetic determination as a failing paradigm in biology and medicine: Implications for health and wellness. *Journal of Social Work Education*, 39(2), 2169–191.

STROUP, D. F., BERLIN, J. A., MORTON, S. C., OLKIN, I., WILLIAMSON, G. D., RENNIE, D., et al. (2000). Meta-analysis of observational studies in epidemiology: A proposal for reporting. Meta-analysis of observational studies in epidemiology

(MOOSE) group. *Journal of the American medical Association,* 283, 2008–2012.

SWARTZ, R. J. & PERKINS, D. N. (1990). *Teaching thinking: Issues and approaches.* Pacific Grove, CA: Critical Thinking Press & Software.

SWEENEY, H. M. Twenty-five ways to suppress the truth: The rules of disinformation. http://www.proparanoid.com

SZASZ, T. (1994). *Cruel compassion: Psychiatric control of society's unwanted.* New York: Wiley.

SZASZ, T. S. (2003). *Liberation by oppression: A comparative study of slavery and psychiatry.* New Brunswick, NJ: Transaction Press.

TALLENT, N. (1988). *Psychological report writing* (3rd Ed.). Englewood Cliffs, NJ: Prentice Hall. (See also 4th Ed. 1993).

TAVRIS, C. (1994). The illusion of science in psychiatry. *Skeptic,* 2(3), 78–85.

TAVRIS, S. C. & ARONSON, E. (2007). *Mistakes were made (but not by me): Why we justify foolish beliefs, bad decisions and hurtful acts.* New York: Harcourt.

TETLOCK, P. E. (2003). Correspondence and coherence: Indicators of good judgment in world politics. In D. Hardman & L. Macchi (Eds.), *Thinking: Psychological perspectives on reasoning, judgment and decision making* (pp. 233–250). New York: Wiley.

THOULESS, R. H. (1974). *Straight and crooked thinking: Thirty-eight dishonest tricks of debate.* London: Pan.

TINDALE, C. W. (2007). *Fallacies and argument appraisal.* New York: Cambridge University Press.

TUCHMAN, B. W. (1984). *The march of folly: From Troy to Vietnam.* New York: Ballantine.

TUFTE, E. (2007). *Beautiful evidence.* Cheshire, CT: Graphics Press.

TURNER, M. E. & PRATKANIS, A. R. (1998). Twenty-five years of groupthink theory and research: Lessons from the evaluation of a theory. *Organizational Behavior and Human Decision Processes,* 73 (2/3), 105–115.

TURNER, E. H. & ROSENTHAL, R. (2008). Efficacy of antidepressants. Editorial. *British Medical Journal,* 336, 516–517.

TVERSKY, A. & KAHNEMAN, Q. (1973). Availability: A heuristic for judging frequency and probability. *Cognitive Psychology,* 5, 207–232.

TVERSKY, A. & KAHNEMAN, D. (1982). Judgment under uncertainty: Heuristics and biases. In D. Kahneman, P. Slovic, & A. Tversky (Eds.), *Judgment under uncertainty: Heuristics and biases.* Cambridge: Cambridge University Press.

UTTAL, W. R. (2001). *The new phrenology: The limits of localizing cognitive processes in the brain.* Cambridge, MA: MIT Press.

VALENSTEIN, E. S. (1986). *Great and desperate curse: The rise and decline of psychosurgery and other radical treatments for mental illness.* New York: Perseus Books.

Van Der Weyden, M. B., Armstrong, R. M., & Greggory, A. T. (2005). The 2005 Nobel Prize in physiology or medicine. *Medical Journal of Australia,* 183(11–12):612–614.

WABER, R. L., SHIV, B., CARMON, Z., & ARIELY, D. (2008). Commercial features of placebo and therapeutic efficacy [Research letter]. *Journal of the American Medical Association,* 299, 1016–1017.

WALTON, D. (1991). *Begging the question: Circular reasoning as a tactic of argumentation.* New York: Greenwood.

WALTON, D. (1992a). *The place of emotion in argument.* University Park, PA: Pennsylvania State University Press.

WALTON, D. (1992b). *Slippery slope arguments.* New York: Oxford University Press.

WALTON, D. (1995). *A pragmatic theory of fallacy.* Tuscaloosa, AL: The University of Alabama Press.

WALTON, D. (1996). *Arguments from ignorance.* University Park, PA: The Pennsylvania State University Press.

WALTON, D. (1997). *Appeal to expert opinion: Arguments from authority.* University Park, PA: The Pennsylvania State University

WALTON, D. (1999). *Appeal to popular opinion.* University Park, PA: Pennsylvania State University Press.

WATSON, D. L. & THARP, R. G. (2007). *Self-directed behavior: Self-modification for personal adjustment* (9th Ed.). Belmont, CA: Thompson/Wadsworth.

WEBSTER, R. (2002). Shieldfield: How did it happen? *The Cleveland Inquiry.* Downloaded 9/24/08.

WELCH, H. G. (2004). *Should I be tested for cancer? Maybe not and here's why.* Berkeley, CA: University of California Press.

WELLBUTRIN (1992). WELLBUTRIN (bupropion HCL), the non serotonergic alternative to Prozac (fluoxetine HCL) for many paden. *American Journal of Psychiatry,* 149(5), A33–A31.

WENNBERG, J. E. (2002). Unwarranted variations in healthcare delivery: Implications for academic medical centres. *British Medical Journal,* 325, 961–964.

WESTON, A. (1992). *A rulebook for arguments* (2nd Ed.). Indianapolis, IN: Hackett.

WILKES, M. S. & HOFFMAN, J. R. (2001). An innovative approach to educating medical students about pharmaceutical promotion. *Academic Medicine*, 76, 1271–1277.

WILLIAMS, L. A. (1995). Race, rat bites and unfit mothers: How media discourse informs infamous welfare legislation debate. *Fordham Urban Law Journal*, XXII, 1159–1196.

WINEMILLER, M. H., BILLOW, R. G., LASKOWKI, E. R., & SCOTT HARMSEN, W. (2003). Effect of magnetic vs sham-magnetic insoles on plantar heel pain. A randomized controlled trial. *JAMA*, 290, 1474–1478.

WILLIAMS, W. M. & CECI, S. J. (1997). How'm I doing? Problems with student ratings of instructors and courses. *Change: The Magazine of Higher Learning*, 29, 12–23.

WOFFORD, J. L. & OHL, C. A. (2005). Teaching appropriate interactions with pharmaceutical company representatives: The impact of an innovative workshop on student attitudes. *BMC Medical Education*, 5.

YOUNG, J. H. (1992). *American health quackery*. Princeton, NJ: Princeton University Press.

ZECHMEISTER, E. G. & JOHNSON, J. E. (1992). *Critical thinking: A functional approach*. Pacific Grove, CA: Brooks/Cole.

ZWARENSTEIN, M., TREWEEK, S., GAGNIER, J. J., ALTMAN, D. G., TUNIS, S., HAYNES, B., et al. (2008). Research methods and reporting: Improving the recording of pragmatic trials: An extension of the CONSORT statement. *British Medial Journal*, 337, A2390.

Index

Content validity, 255

Contingency table, 261

Correlation, 117, 254

Corroboration, 32

CONSORT guidelines, 177, 229

Courage, intellectual, 18

Creativity, critical thinking and, 4

Credibility, truth and, 28

Criterion validity, 255

Critical discussion, 19, 36, 39

Critical thinking
 characteristics of, 5
 costs and benefits of, 49–51
 definition of, 4
 ethical decision making and, 304–307
 importance of, 6–7
 integral to evidence-based practice, 19–26
 personal barriers to, 364
 related knowledge, skills, and values,
  14, 15–19
 teaching of, 347, 349–351

Critically appraised topic (CAT), 197–199,
 201–203

Critical-thinking skills, evaluating the teaching
 of, 347, 349–351

Criticism, 35–37

Culture of thoughtfulness scale, 344–347

Cynicism, 40

Databases, for practitioners, 174

Descriptors, for locating better evidence, 175

Desire stimulating, advertising and, 73

Diagnostic and Statistical Manual-IV. See DSM-IV

Diagnostic tests, evaluating, 277–281

Dispositions, critical thinking and, 17

Diversion, 127

Documentation, uncritical, acceptance of,
 115–116

Domain-specific knowledge, critical thinking
 and, 14–15

DSM-IV, 134, 283, 286

Effect size, 239–240

Either-or, 130

Emotional appeals, 41
 features of, 44–45
 harmfulness of, 43–45

Empathy, intellectual, 18

Empiricism, 23, 24

Error as process, 317–322

Ethical concerns, checklist of, 304

Ethical decision making, critical thinking and,
 303–306

Ethical dilemmas, 303

Evaluation
 of agency services, 221, 223–227
 argument, 8–9, 309–311
 of claims, 7–8, 32, 59, 333–336
 of classification systems, 283–287
 of diagnostic tests, 277–281
 form, teaching, 349–351
 of research, 289–291, 293–294
 of study quality, 231–246
 of the teaching of critical-thinking skills,
  347, 349–351
 of treatment effects, 231–244

Evidence, 49–51, 229
 and critically appraising research reviews,
  247–251
 and evaluating effective studies, 231–246

Evidence-based practice, 19–26, 169–183,
  185–193, 195–199, 201–203, 205–207,
  209–213, 215–221, 223–227, 357–359,
  361–362

Evidence-based purchasing, 197, 221

Evidence-based teams, 185–193, 195–196

Excuses, 367–368

Face validity, 255

Facts, 33

Fair-mindedness, 18

Faith in reason, 18

Fallacy (ies), 103–105

common practice, 107–119, 121–124

    gambler's, 145–146

    motivational source of, 101

    post hoc, 86, 117–118

    practice, 155–156

    recognizing, 9

    regression, 143

    spotting in professional contexts, 157, 159–160

Fallacy film festival, 87, 153–156

Fallacy of labeling, 116

Fallacy spotting, 157, 159–160

False dilemma, 130

False negative, 259–260

False positive, 260

Falsifiability, 36

Falsification, knowledge development and, 27

Field instruction, 205

Focusing on successes only, 111, 156

Framing effects, 142–143

Fraud, recognizing, 11

Fundamental attribution error, 141–142

Gambler's fallacy, 145–146

Good intentions, 50, 68, 171

Groupthink, 86, 129–130, 161–163, 165

Groupwork, 125

Hardheartedness, 110–111, 139, 213, 215–220

Harm, 6, 68–69, 83, 130, 145, 170, 179, 277, 317

    and emotional appeal, 43–45

Heuristics, 29, 139, 140

Hindsight bias, 141

Homogeneity, 254

Human-service advertisements

    features of, 73–76

    spotting form, 77–78

Humility, intellectual, 18

Illusion of knowing, 28–29, 363

Informal fallacies, recognizing, 9

Informed participants, 207, 209–212

Informed point of view, 31

Integrity, intellectual, 18

Intellectual traits, valuable, 18

Intentions, 68–70

Interdisciplinary teams, 7, 185–193, 195–196

Internal consistency, 254

Intervention, making decisions about, 53, 55–57

Intervention plans, reviewing, 297

    checklist for, 299–302

    Intuitive and analytical thinking, 29–30

Journal club, 353–356

Justification, 317–318

    knowledge development and, 27

Knowledge, 48

    beliefs about, 59, 61–63

    critical thinking and, 14–16

    developing falsification in, 27

    justification in, 27

    knowing and illusion of knowing, 28–29

    objective, 28

    personal, 28

    specialized, critical thinking and, 4

Labeling fallacy, 116

Language, thoughtful use of, 12

Law of large numbers, 144

Law of small numbers, 144

Logical positivism, 41

Manner, 128–129

Meta-analysis

    of Observational Studies (MOOSE), 177, 186

    steps in determining validity of, 251

Meta-cognitive, 16

Methodological search filters, 189, 195

MOOSE. *See* Meta-analysis of Observational Studies

Motivation, 16, 27, 171, 363, 364

Multiculturalism, 45

Natural frequencies, 268

Newness, relying on, 113–115

Nonfallacy items, 131

Number needed to treat (NNT), 261, 262

Objective knowledge, 28

Objectivity, scientific, 37, 39

Omission bias, 145

Opinions, 27

Outcome measures, face validity of, 255

Overconfidence, 143

Oversimplification, 108, 116–117

Paradigm, 43

Parsimony, scientific reasoning and, 38–39

Perseverance, intellectual, 18

Personal knowledge, 28

Persuasion, reasoning and, 31–32

Persuasion strategies, recognizing, 12–13

Pharmaceutical industry, 66, 68, 116

Point of view, informed, 31

Popularity, 23, 51, 130

Positive prediction value (PPV), 266–267

Post hoc fallacy, 86, 117–118

Posttest probability, 242

Practice fallacies/pitfalls, 155–156

Practitioner types, 112

Predictive validity, 255

Predispositions, critical thinking and, 17

Premises, 9, 15, 127, 307, 308, 309–310, 313–314

Pretest probability, 241, 242

Prevalence rate, ignoring, 144–145

Probabilities, 146

    posttest probability, 242

    pretest probability, 241, 242

    translating into frequencies, 273–274

    using, 263–264

Problem description, 170

Process, 19

    error as, 317–318, 321–322

Professional thinking form, 89, 91–102

Proof, 32

Propaganda, 65–67

Propaganda bias, 30–31

Propaganda stratagems, recognizing, 10

Pseudoscience, 44–46

    recognizing, 11

"Psychobabble," 12

Purpose, critical thinking and, 4

Quackery, 46

    recognition of, 11

Qualitative checklist, 177

Quality filters, 175

Quality of reporting of meta-analysis (QUORUM), 178, 229

Quality of study rating form (QSRF), 232–234

Questions

    COPES, 172, 195

    regarding different kinds of claims, 219–220

    hard, 213, 215–220

    PICO, 185, 186, 188, 189, 195

    posing, 171, 181–183, 185, 188, 205

    Socratic, 217–218

QSRF. *See* Quality of study rating form

QUORUM. *See* Quality of reporting of meta-analysis

Random assignment, 237

Ratcheting, 318

Rationalizing, 27

Reasoning, 27

    clinical, 139

    compared to rationalizing, 27

    persuasion and, 31–32

    scientific, 17–20

Sufficient grounds criterion, argument analysis and, 310

"Sweeping generalization," 9

Teaching evaluation form, 349–351

Templating, 317

Testimonials, relying on, 86, 108–109

Test-retest reliability, 254

Theory, 36

Theory-ladenness, 39

Thinking, 29

Thoughtfulness, encouraging a culture of, 341, 343–346

Total quality points (TQP), 239

TQP. *See* Total quality points

Tradition, relying on, 113–115

Transparent reporting of evaluations with nonrandomized designs (TREND), 178

Treatment effects, evaluating, 231–244

TREND. *See* Transparent reporting of evaluations with nonrandomized designs

Truth, 31
credibility and, 28
reasoning and, 31

Uncritical documentation
accepting, 115–116

Urgency stressing, advertising and, 73

Vagueness, 12, 107, 109–110, 253, 287, 323, 329

Validity, 254–256
concurrent, 255
construct, 255–256
content, 255
criterion, 255
face, 255
predictive, 255

Values, critical thinking and, 13, 16–19

Warrants, 9, 307, 308, 313–314